The Logic of Incarnation

The Logic of Incarnation

James K. A. Smith's Critique of Postmodern Religion

Edited by Neal DeRoo and Brian Lightbody

With contribution and response by James K. A. Smith

☙PICKWICK *Publications* • Eugene, Oregon

THE LOGIC OF INCARNATION
James K. A. Smith's Critique of Postmodern Religion

Copyright © 2009 Wipf and Stock Publishers. All rights reserved. Except for brief quotations in critical publications or reviews, no part of this book may be reproduced in any manner without prior written permission from the publisher. Write: Permissions, Wipf and Stock Publishers, 199 W. 8th Ave., Suite 3, Eugene, OR 97401.

Pickwick Publications
A Division of Wipf and Stock Publishers
199 W. 8th Ave., Suite 3
Eugene, OR 97401

www.wipfandstock.com

isbn 13: 978-1-55635-969-9

Cataloging-in-Publication data:

> The logic of incarnation : James K. A. Smith's critique of postmodern religion / edited by Neal DeRoo and Brian Lightbody.
>
> xxviii + 212 p. ; 23 cm.
>
> isbn 13: 978-1-55635-969-9
>
> 1. Postmodernism—Religious Aspects. 2. I. DeRoo, Neal. II. Lightbody, Brian. III. Smith, James K. A. IV. Title.

BR115.P74 L5 2009

Manufactured in the U.S.A.

Contents

Acknowledgments vii

About the Contributors ix

Abbreviations xiii

Introduction—Neal DeRoo xv

PART ONE: Critiquing Postmodernism

1. The Logic of Incarnation: Towards a Catholic Postmodernism —*James K. A. Smith* 3

PART TWO: Receiving the (Postmodern) Tradition

2. Determined to Reveal: Determination and Revelation in Derrida—*Neal DeRoo* 41

3. On Universality and Christian Particularism in a Postmodern Trio: James K. A. Smith, Jacques Derrida, and Søren Kierkegaard—*Leo Stan* 57

4. Undecidability and Indecidability: Does Derrida's Ethics depend on Levinas's notion of the Third?—*Brian Lightbody* 71

5. Tasting the Inscape of Haecceity with Hopkins, the Franciscan Philosophers, Nietzsche, and Derrida—*Marko Zlomislić* 84

6. Defending a Universalizable Culture of Particularities (With and Against James K. A. Smith)—*Mehdi Wolf* 99

PART THREE: Applying the Critique

7 Deconstructing Institutions: Derrida and the "Emerging Church"—*Peter Schuurman* 111

8 All (For)Giving: The Gift or Preaching (Forgiveness) Backwards—*James Vanderberg* 120

9 Saving the Whale or Dancing with Dolphins? —*Andre Basson* 128

10 Taking Derrida, Lyotard, and Foucault to Tim Horton's: Experiencing the Modern and the Post-modern in Canada —*Stan Skrzeszewski* 139

PART FOUR: Critiquing the Critique: Questions Moving Forward

11 Is James K. A. Smith Afraid of Postmodernity? —*Wendy C. Hamblet* 157

12 Who's Afraid of Theology?: A Conversation with James K. A. Smith on Dogmatics as the Grammar of Christian Particularity—*Mark Bowald* 168

13 Unlike any other Hope: The Eschatological Structure of Hope —*James H. Olthuis* 182

14 Is the Grace that Calls Whale-Riders Back to Catholicism any more Amazing for Smith than for Derrida and Caputo? —*David Goicoechea* 193

PART FIVE: Responding

15 Continuing the Conversation—*James K. A. Smith* 203

Acknowledgments

THE EDITORS OF THIS volume would like to thank Brock University, the Brock Philosophical Society, and especially Andre Basson and David Goicoechea for organizing the conference on James K. A. Smith that inspired the present work.

We would also like to thank Chris Spinks, Diane Farley, and everyone at Pickwick Publications for their hard work and patience in answering an endless number of emails and resolving all the problems that arose: truly an amazing achievement, given who they had to work with.

In addition, we would like to thank the Social Sciences and Humanities Research Council of Canada (SSHRC), which is partially responsible for the completion of this volume, and whose support is greatly appreciated.

Finally, we would like to thank James K. A. Smith, for his innovative thinking which inspired this book, his help in bringing this book to completion, and his patience with nagging editors who pestered him through what otherwise could have been a wonderful semester in Britain. Most importantly, we would like to thank Jamie for his friendship, and for the example he gives of how to be a Christian and a philosopher, and how to do both well.

About the Contributors

ANDRE BASSON is Christian Reformed Campus Minister and Adjunct Professor in the Medieval and Renaissance Program at Brock University in St. Catharines, ON, Canada. After obtaining his doctorate in Late Latin Literature from the University of Provence (Aix-Marseille I) in France, he taught Classics at various universities in South Africa and the US before arriving at Brock. He is currently working on a book on the poetry of Paulinus of Nola, a Christian Latin poet from the fifth century.

MARK BOWALD is Assistant Professor of Religion and Theology at Redeemer University, (Ancaster, ON, Canada) and Adjunct Assistant Professor of Systematic Theology at Wycliffe College in Toronto. He is the author of *Rendering the Word in Theological Hermeneutics: Mapping Divine and Human Agency* (Ashgate, 2007) as well as several related articles and reviews in various publications and journals. He also serves as Theology Editor for *Christian Scholar's Review*, and is currently working on a second book on Hermeneutics entitled *Divine Rhetoric: Reading Scripture in the Ethos of the Trinity*.

NEAL DEROO is Teaching Fellow in the Department of Philosophy at Boston College. He is the co-editor of *Phenomenology and Eschatology: Not Yet in the Now* (forthcoming from Ashgate), and has lectured worldwide on topics ranging from Husserl to psychoanalysis. He has contributed to *The Heythrop Journal*, *Essays in Philosophy*, and other journals.

DAVID GOICOECHEA is Professor Emeritus of Philosophy at Brock University. He has published widely in the areas of philosophy of love, existentialism, philosophy of religion, post-modernism and the history of philosophy. He is the coeditor of *Great Years of Zarathustra 1881–1981* (Rowman and Littlefield and University Press of America, 1983), *The Question of Humanism: Challenges and Possibilities* (Prometheus, 1996),

The Resurrection of Derrida's Glorious "Glas" (Global Publications at SUNY Binghampton, 1997), *Jen Agape Tao with Tu Wei-Ming* (Global Publications, 1999) and *Varieties of Universalism: Essays in Honour of J.R.A. Mayer* (Thought House, 2000) and is currently writing a 15-volume series on the history and philosophy of love in the West.

WENDY C. HAMBLET teaches Genocide Studies and Contemporary World Moral Problems at North Carolina A&T State University. She is the author of *The Sacred Monstrous: A Reflection on Violence in Human Communities* (Lexington, 2004) and *Savage Constructions: The Myth of African Savagery* (Lexington, 2008) and co-editor of *Psychological Interpretations of War* (New York: *Peace Review*, 2006). She has also contributed many essays to edited volumes and journals such as *Monist, Ratio, Journal of the British Society for Phenomenology, Existentia Meletai Sophias,* and the *Journal of Genocide Research*. In addition, she is a member of the faculty of the Genocide and Human Rights University Program (in collaboration with the Zoryan Institute), an active member of The Concerned Philosophers for Peace and the International Association of Genocide Scholars, and is an accredited and practicing Philosophical Counselor and Ethics Consultant.

BRIAN LIGHTBODY is Visiting Assistant Professor of Philosophy at Brock University. He is the author of *Philosophical Genealogy* as well as numerous book chapters and articles in journals such as *KRITERION, Quodlibet, Contemporary Philosophy* and others. His main areas of interest include epistemology, Foucault, and Nietzsche.

JAMES H. OLTHUIS is Emeritus Professor of Philosophical Theology at the Institute for Christian Studies in Toronto, and a Psychotherapist in private practice. Among his publications are *Facts, Values, and Ethics* (VanGorcum, 1968); *I Pledge You My Troth* (Harper Collins, 1975); *Keeping Our Troth* (Harper Collins, 1986); and *The Beautiful Risk* (Zondervan, 2001; Wipf & Stock, 2006). He has also edited *Knowing Other-wise* (Fordham University Press, 1997); *Towards an Ethics of Community* (Canadian Corp. Studies in Religion, 2000); *religion with/out religion* (Routledge, 2001); and, with James K. A. Smith, *Radical Orthodoxy and the Reformed Tradition* (Baker, 2005).

About the Contributors

PETER SCHUURMAN is Campus Ministries Coordinator for the Christian Reformed Church in North America. He is also part-time faculty, teaching World Religions in the Religion and Theology Department at Redeemer College (Ancaster, ON, Canada). He is a regular columnist in the *Christian Courier*, where he examines topics of worldview, faith, and university culture.

STAN SKRZESZEWSKI is a "Philosopher Practitioner" with a passion for organizing and facilitating Philosophers' Cafés—open philosophical discussions. He is a writer and frequent speaker on topics ranging from cosmopolitanism to the emerging job market for creative philosophers. He is the author of *The Knowledge Entrepreneur* (Scarecrow, 2005) and is currently writing a book on the meaning of wine.

JAMES K. A. SMITH is Associate Professor of Philosophy at Calvin College in Grand Rapids, Michigan. He is the author of several books, including *The Fall of Interpretation: Philosophical Foundations for a Creational Hermeneutic* (InterVarsity, 2000), *Speech and Theology: Language and the Logic of Incarnation* (Routledge, 2002), *Introducing Radical Orthodoxy: Mapping a Post-Secular Theology* (Baker Academic/Paternoster, 2004), *Jacques Derrida: Live Theory* (Continuum, 2005), and *Who's Afraid of Postmodernism? Taking Derrida, Lyotard, and Foucault to Church* (Baker Academic, 2006). He has also edited several volumes, including most recently, *After Modernity? Secularity, Globalization, and the Re-enchantment of the World* (Baylor University Press, 2008), and translated Jean-Luc Marion's *The Crossing of the Visible* (Stanford University Press, 2004). He also serves on the editorial boards of several journals, including the *Journal of the American Academy of Religion* and *Faith and Philosophy*.

LEO STAN is currently Postdoctoral Fellow at the Centre for Theory and Criticism, University of Western Ontario, Canada. His doctoral work focused on the notion of otherness in Søren Kierkegaard's authorship. He has lectured on Kierkegaard, Nietzsche, phenomenology of religion, and the theology of the Gulag.

JAMES VANDERBERG is currently the Christian Reformed campus minister at the University of Guelph, working with others to build a bridging Christian community. A graduate of the Institute for Christian Studies

(Toronto), he wrote a master's thesis entitled "Forgiveness: The Gift and Its Counterfeit." He speaks regularly, both in and outside of the church, on the points of intersection between postmodern philosophy and Christian faith.

Mehdi Wolf is a member of the Bahá'í Community of Canada.

Marko Zlomislić is professor of philosophy at Conestoga College, Institute of Technology and Advanced Learning in Kitchener, ON, Canada, where he teaches courses in Postmodernism, Visual Cultures, and Ethics. He is the author of *Jacques Derrida's Aporetic Ethics* (Lexington, 2007), and is currently writing a critique of Slavoj Žižek's work.

Abbreviations

WORKS BY JAMES K. A. SMITH

DH   "Determined Hope: A Phenomenology of Christian Expectation," in *The Future of Hope: Essays on Christian Tradition Amid Modernity and Postmodernity*, edited by Miroslav Volf and William Katerberg, 200–27. Grand Rapids: Eerdmans, 2004.

FI   *The Fall of Interpretation: Philosophical Foundations for a Creational Hermeneutic*. Downers Grove, IL: InterVarsity, 2000.

IRO   *Introducing Radical Orthodoxy: Mapping a Post-Secular Theology*. Grand Rapids: Baker Academic, 2004.

LT   *Jacques Derrida: Live Theory*. London: Continuum, 2005.

ST   *Speech and Theology: Language and the Logic of Incarnation*. London and New York: Routledge, 2002.

WAP   *Who's Afraid of Postmodernism?: Taking Derrida, Lyotard, and Foucault to Church*. Grand Rapids: Baker Academic, 2006.

WORKS BY JACQUES DERRIDA

DMT   "Demeure: Fiction and Testimony." In Maurice Blanchot and Jacques Derrida, *The Instant of My Death: Fiction and Testimony*, translated by Elizabeth Rottenberg, 13–103. Stanford: Stanford University Press, 2000.

FK   "Faith and Knowledge: The Two Sources of 'Religion' within the Bounds of Reason Alone." In *Acts of Religion*, edited and introduction by Gil Anidjar, 40–101. New York: Routledge, 2002.

FL	"Force of Law: The 'Mystical Foundation of Authority.'" In *Acts of Religion*, edited and introduction by Gil Anidjar, 228–98. New York: Routledge, 2002.
GD	*The Gift of Death*. Translated by David Wills. Chicago: University of Chicago Press, 1996.
GT	*Given Time I: Counterfeit Money*. Translated by Peggy Kamuf. Chicago: University of Chicago Press, 1994.
Linc	*Limited Inc*. Translated by Jeffrey Mehlman and Samuel Weber. Evanston, IL: Northwestern University Press, 1988.
ON	*On the Name*. Translated by David Wood, John P. Leavey, Jr., and Ian McLeod. Stanford: Stanford University Press, 1995.
VM	"Violence and Metaphysics." In *Writing and Difference*, translated by Alan Bass, 79–153. Chicago: University of Chicago Press, 1978.

Introduction

Neal DeRoo

JAMES K. A. SMITH is fast becoming a major voice in the world of postmodern theology. One of his major strengths is his ability to show that theology matters inside and outside the world of scholarship. His wonderful new series, The Church and Postmodern Culture (from Baker Academic), challenges the picture of academia as an ivory tower, showing instead how the church and the academy need each other. By illustrating the value of theology for the contemporary church, Smith's work shows that our everyday practices are informed by our theory, and that our theory is another of our everyday practices. By showing how a lack of awareness of its own underlying philosophy has led the church down a particular path, Smith also illustrates the danger of naively assuming that theory is practiced by university professors from Monday to Friday, while Christian practice is carried out by the pious on Sunday mornings (leaving Saturday, I suppose, for sports and yard work). Nor, is it enough (though it is certainly a start) to drag the professors to church, and to send the pious out of church to "do the Lord's work until he comes." Rather, we must fundamentally re-think the interaction between theory and practice; we must come to understand that the theories of philosophers and theologians lie deep in the core of the church. These theories are not so much the bones that are subsequently fleshed out into the body of Christ, but rather the food that we ingest and the nourishment that shapes us and our movements. And we are what we eat.

Philosophy and theology, then, are not just "food for thought," but are also food for the soul. Hence, it is imperative that we understand what we think and why. It is an important and necessary part of religious life that we understand the theories that shape our worldview, and ensure that our theory and our religion are properly aligned.

THE TWO DIRECTIONS OF POSTMODERN RELIGION

The desire to align religious theory and practice is an underlying principle of James K. A. Smith's work. It leads him in two directions: first, a deep intellectual analysis of the thinking that underlies the church; second, an examination of the practices and activities of the church, in light of her most deeply cherished goals and aspirations. This two-fold movement, at once theological and pastoral, nose-in-the-book intellectual and dirt-under-the-fingernails practical, has led Smith directly to the path of postmodern religion. Postmodern religion also moves in these two directions. On the one hand, philosophers and theologians like Jacques Derrida, John D. Caputo, Richard Kearney,[1] and others are doing innovative and interesting work involving the most recent thought in postmodern philosophy and theory. On the other hand, Emergent Church movements, such as the Ikon movement led by Peter Rollins and the conversation associated with people like Brian McLaren, have tried to re-imagine contemporary Christianity and the Church in a postmodern cultural setting.[2] Smith's work engages postmodern religion in both of these facets. Academically, he has published a great deal on Derrida and Caputo.[3] For the less-academic churchgoer, he has written a great deal in more popular magazines,[4] and has been extensively involved in church-related projects.[5] Therefore,

---

1. Cf. Derrida, *Acts of Religion*; Caputo, *Prayers and Tears*, and *The Weakness of God*; Kearney, *The God Who May Be* and *Anatheism*. For more on these thinkers, cf. Sherwood and Hart, *Derrida and Religion*; Olthuis, *Religion with/out Religion*; and Manoussakis, *After God*.

2. For more on these particular manifestations of the Emergent Church movement, cf. Rollins, *How (Not) to Speak of God* and *The Fidelity of Betrayal*; brianmclaren.net; and McClaren, *Church in Emerging Culture*, and *The Last Word*.

3. Smith has written extensively on Derrida, not only in LT, and WAP, but also in FI, ST, DH, "A Principle of Incarnation," "Determined Violence," and elsewhere.

4. Cf. "Teaching a Calvinist to Dance" and "The Secret Lives of Saints," to name but the most recent. Some of his more "public" essays are to be collected in Smith, *The Devil Reads Derrida*.

5. For example, his work on the Church's role in urban neighborhoods as a fellow at the Center for Social Research at Calvin College (2006–2008), and his work concerning Christian pedagogy and curriculum with the Valparaiso Project on the Education and Formation of People in Faith (2008–2010) and the Lilly Fellows Program (2007).

Introduction

in order to accurately survey Smith's work and its influence, it is necessary to approach him from both the scholarly and the church-related angles.

That is what we have tried to do in the present work. We have asked academics, clergy, and laypeople working in church-related careers to speak to their experience with Smith's work and to its influence on their professions. This has led to a diversity of topics that reflects the diversity of contributors. This book will examine Smith's work and its effect on everything from how philosophers read the Medieval Franciscans, 19th century Danish iconoclasts, and 20th century French pseudo-atheists, to the Bahá'í faith, the Christian ministry on university campuses, and even to where we buy a cup of coffee in the morning. In addition, we also wanted to provide a place for people of these various backgrounds to raise problems and to pose questions back to Smith and his logic of incarnation, thereby allowing their various experiences to help shape Smith's work as it goes forward. In doing all this, we hope to show, not only the range of Smith's own work, but also the wide-ranging implications of the logic of incarnation that he espouses.

THE LOGIC OF INCARNATION: A CELEBRATION OF DIFFERENCE

Before we outline the contents of the book, let us take a brief moment to consider this logic of incarnation. At its heart, the logic of incarnation strives to reimagine the world by way of the Christian doctrine that God became flesh and dwelt in the world. This implies that the everyday world of particular people in particular places contains a value (if it is good enough for God, it sure ought to be good enough for us!) that challenges some traditional assumptions regarding the evil nature of this world, as compared to the eternity of the "life hereafter" in heaven. It implies, also, that both the finite world and the infinite God must be understood in such a way that they can be joined together without losing either the world's finitude or God's infinity, as the definition of Christ's nature as fully human and fully divine by the Council of Chalcedon (AD 451) makes clear.[6]

---

6. The "Chalcedonian Definition" reads as follows: "Therefore, following the holy fathers, we all with one accord teach men to acknowledge one and the same Son, our Lord Jesus Christ, at once complete in Godhead and complete in manhood, truly God and truly man, consisting also of a reasonable soul and body; of one substance with the Father as regards his Godhead, and at the same time of one substance with us as regards his manhood; like us in all respects, apart from sin; as regards his Godhead, begotten of

That the infinite entered the finite means that both the finite and the infinite, both the created world and the Creator God, must be understood in accordance with this fundamental tenet of the Christian faith. The logic of incarnation strives for precisely such an understanding.

A major implication of this is that God values particularity, what makes groups or individuals unique. By extension, this also implies, since God is good and just, that there is nothing bad or inherently unjust about expressing our particularity: there is nothing inherently violent or unjust about proclaiming my specifically *Christian* beliefs about the world and humanity's place in it. Stating, for example, that I believe Christ to have been God incarnate, does not do a disservice to Jewish or Islamic believers who think this to be wrong, perhaps even blasphemous. The logic of incarnation seems to set the stage for the possibility that God blesses and encourages differences in creation. If differences are then blessed and ordained by God, there is no reason that we need to understand difference *qua* difference, that is, difference itself, being different, as something that is to be avoided. Rather, we should enjoy and celebrate differences as part of God's plan.[7]

THE URGE TO UNITY IN POLITICS AND RELIGION

The celebration of peaceful difference would be a welcome respite in a world of dangerous, often violent, fundamentalisms. Many people seek to achieve peace by looking for what is common to the differing sides, rather than celebrating the differences. This strategy is common to both secular Liberal[8] politics and (many) inter-religious and ecumenical movements.

the Father before the ages, but yet as regards his manhood begotten, for us men and for our salvation, of Mary the Virgin, the God-bearer; one and the same Christ, Son, Lord, Only-begotten, recognized in two natures, without confusion, without change, without division, without separation; the distinction of natures being in no way annulled by the union, but rather the characteristics of each nature being preserved and coming together to form one person and subsistence, not as parted or separated into two persons, but one and the same Son and Only-begotten God the Word, Lord Jesus Christ; even as the prophets from earliest times spoke of him, and our Lord Jesus Christ himself taught us, and the creed of the fathers has handed down to us."

7. For how this differs from other postmodern accounts of religion, especially that put forward by Derrida and Caputo, see Smith's first essay in this work, "The Logic of Incarnation: Towards a Catholic Postmodernism."

8. It is important to distinguish between Liberalism, as a political doctrine espousing procedural justice, individual rights, and the separation of church and state, from liberality, which is a particular (radical or "left-leaning") way of being Liberal. In the sense of

Introduction

In secular politics, religion is seen as a divisive force that has the power to erupt into violent disagreement. Since the purpose of the state is (only) to provide a space where citizens can live and act in peace, without their individual rights being violated, religion's supposed propensity toward violence (which would violate the "inalienable" rights to life and security) makes it something that is antithetical to the goals of the (secular) state.[9] But, because a right to believe whatever one wishes to believe without coercion from the government is another "inalienable" right, religion cannot simply be outlawed. Hence, the division between beliefs, which are private, and the space of public action: religion is fine, as long as it remains in the realm of private belief and not public action. This entails that the particular beliefs of different people and religions have no place in the discourse or actions of public politics. In our secular, democratic countries, the particularities of religious beliefs must be left behind for the over-arching politics that unite us: individual rights, democratic power, and the separation of church and state.

Similarly, in many inter-religious and ecumenical movements, the ability to come together is sought only in that which is common to the different religions. Similar ethics, codes of conduct (usually something like the Golden Rule), and emotive feelings are cited as proof that all religions really, at their core, are either a) different takes on the same religion; or b) so similar that their differences pale in comparison to the overwhelming similarities. Both of these tactics seek to base the possibility of discussion between different religious groups not on what makes them unique, but on what makes them the same. The differences are to be ignored, or at least downgraded, in light of the similarities, which constitute the real ground of fruitful inter-religious dialogue.[10]

While seeking to emphasize similarity is not inherently bad, its application in politics and interreligious dialogue leads to certain problems. The first is in the formation of our self-identity. Secular politics calls us

---

Liberalism, all politicians in Western democracies are Liberals, though surely they are not all liberal in their Liberalism. I will mark this difference by using a capital "L" for the political doctrine, and a lower-case "l" for the sense of being left-leaning. For an excellent statement of Liberalism as a political doctrine, cf. Rawls, *Political Liberalism*.

9. For more on religion's place in the secular state, cf. Habermas, "Religious Tolerance," and Taylor, *The Secular Age*.

10. This cannot be said of all interreligious movements; cf., Kearney, *Anatheism*, and "The Inter-religious Imagination."

to identify ourselves based primarily on secular political beliefs rather than religious ones. In other words, we are called to identify ourselves as belonging *first* to a political entity (i.e., a nation-state) and only *secondarily* to a religious group or order. Our status as the Body of Christ, for example, is subjugated to our status as citizens of Canada or the United States.

The second, and related, problem is the practical power of our religious beliefs for everyday action. If we are to relegate our religious beliefs to the sphere of private belief, or speak to others based on what we share with them rather than on what makes us unique, then our most dearly held beliefs must necessarily fail where we need them most: in living our lives. Liberalism states that no one can stop us from believing whatever we'd like, including beliefs about how we are to act. Therefore, no one can really stop us from using our religious beliefs to determine how we are to act. But our actions themselves can be, and are, regulated and legislated. This is not tyrannical, because our laws are based, at least in part, on our own will: democracy is not just government, but self-government. However, if we cannot use our religious beliefs to help legislate our actions, then our religious beliefs cannot be used to form the laws that govern our life. This either causes us to come up with other (often disingenuous) reasons to justify our actions non-religiously, or it ceases to be *self*-government at all, as we are no longer allowed to use our entire self—that is, to truly and honestly be who we really are, in the most important, dearly-held parts of our self—to make decisions.

This inability to be our true selves also affects our ability to appreciate all that the world has to offer. When we cannot speak authentically about what makes us unique, and when others cannot do the same for themselves, we are all deprived of the ability to authentically learn from each other about the many different things in this world. It would be like a gathering of chefs who come together to learn and talk about the different world cuisines. If each chef talks only about what his cuisine has in common with the cuisine of others, we might ultimately learn that people everywhere eat vegetables and starches, but we would miss out on the wonderful diversity of international food. Imagine thinking Chinese people understood Italian cooking because they both eat starches (as if "starch" captures all the different tastes of fried rice and pasta), or that Bostonians are familiar with Indian *dal* because they too eat baked beans! Not only is something essential lost from each cuisine when we try to

Introduction

reduce it to what it has in common with other cuisines, but our overall quality of life would be minimized if we could not recognize and appreciate the differences in regional foods.

HOW CAN A LOGIC OF INCARNATION HELP?

Like chefs, we should be able to stand up, as religious people, and proudly declare what makes our religion unique and special without fear of starting a fight. We should be able to add to the religious palette of the world by holding to what we believe, rather than by emphasizing how we are like others. We are not all the same. We do not all eat the same things, and we do not all have the same theories, religious or otherwise. It is precisely because of these differences that we get the vast variety of beliefs, customs, rituals, and liturgies that color our world and make it diverse. The logic of incarnation is an attempt to come up with an underlying theory of the world that makes sense of this, and enables us to see the varieties of life as a glorious spice cabinet that seasons us all differently, rather than as a battleground for war and discord. How well is it able to do so? What does it have to offer that is unique from other theories and views? These are the kind of questions that the next fifteen chapters ask and begin to answer.

The book opens by outlining Smith's critique of contemporary postmodern religion. Tackling both the theory and the practice, James K. A. Smith himself, in "The logic of incarnation: Toward a Catholic Postmodernism," demonstrates what exactly he means by the "logic of incarnation" by showing how it differs from the "Logic of Determination" he sees in the theoretical work of Jacques Derrida and John D. Caputo, arguably the two most popular figures in postmodern religion. By "out-narrating" the violence and individualism that he sees as characteristic of the Logic of Determination, Smith is able, by the end of the piece, to show that a return to the tradition of Catholic Orthodoxy is, perhaps, the most radical postmodern hermeneutics, and he calls the reader to move past Liberal politics to embrace a more authentically communal and ecclesial view of the world, one that fully embraces postmodernism by allowing us to return to traditional Orthodoxy.

After this excellent introduction to the logic of incarnation, the second section of the book questions Smith's reception of the tradition on which he bases his argument. This questioning begins with Neal DeRoo's "Determined to Reveal: Determination and Revelation in Derrida," which raises some questions about the viability of applying Smith's Logic of Determination to the work of Derrida. After moving back and forth through Derrida's oeuvre to suggest a way of reading Derrida otherwise, the paper ends by explaining how this debate on how to read Derrida affects Smith's project of taking Derrida "to church."

The third chapter, "On Universality and Christian Particularism in a Postmodern Trio: James K. A. Smith, Jacques Derrida, and Søren Kierkegaard" by Leo Stan, uses the Danish philosopher Søren Kierkegaard to critique Derrida's deconstructive reading of ethics and justice. In revealing the way that Derrida universalizes, and therefore loses, the particularity and singularity of Abraham emphasized in *Fear and Trembling*, Stan is able to show that Kierkegaard assists Smith's project by highlighting the importance of particularity and singularity, while at the same time posing a subtle critique of Smith's appeal to communitarianism.

Brian Lightbody picks up this discussion of Derrida's account of ethics in "Undecidability and Indecidability: Does Derrida's Ethics depend on Levinas' notion of the Third?" In this chapter, Lightbody takes on the admirable task of proving to the Analytic branch of philosophy that Derrida's ethics are philosophically interesting and worthwhile. They are so, Lightbody claims, only because of their reliance on Emmanuel Levinas's notion of the "Third." By demonstrating the reliance of Derrida's ethics on Levinas's account of the Third, Lightbody implies that any critique of Derrida's account of ethics (including, one can infer, Smith's critique) must engage seriously with Levinas if it is to be philosophically convincing.

This project of tracing the philosophical influences of Derrida, and thereby filling out the "tradition" in which he stands, is continued by Marko Zlomislić in the fifth chapter, "Tasting the Inscape of Haecceity with Hopkins, the Franciscan Philosophers, Nietzsche, and Derrida." In this paper, Zlomislić reveals the poetic inheritance of Gerard Manley Hopkins and the Franciscan philosophers in Derrida's work, thereby suggesting that perhaps Derrida himself can be considered a part of the Catholic tradition to which Smith calls us back. This very conclusion, and Zlomislić's poetic way of bringing us to it, raises questions about the limits of tradition, calling into question the relationship between individuality and tradition, and suggesting that the borders of any tradition—and perhaps also those of any individual—are fluid and dynamic, and therefore difficult to pin down into any kind of "orthodoxy."

Introduction

Finally, Mehdi Wolf raises the question of tradition again in his "Defending a Universalizable Culture of Particularities (With and Against James K. A. Smith)." In this fascinating example of interreligious conversation, Wolf uses his Bahá'í faith to raise questions about what, precisely, constitutes the Catholic tradition. Suggesting that it is the universal project of divine revelation, and not any of the particular religious dispensations, that ought to be given pride of place, Wolf uses Bahá'í principles and teachings to fundamentally reorient the relationship between universality and particularity, critiquing both Caputo's "religion without religion" (for being overly universal at the expense of the particular) and Smith's call to radical orthodoxy (for being overly particular at the expense of the universal).[11] This chapter enacts the adherence to particular religious beliefs that Smith calls for in interreligious dialogue while at the same time questioning the viability of Smith's incarnational account.

If the second section of the book focuses on Smith's reception and account of tradition, including postmodern tradition, the third section shifts its focus away from the past and toward the present. Emphasizing less the scholarly foundation of Smith's project, this section seeks to understand how Smith's account of the logic of incarnation can be useful for those working on the frontlines of the Christian religious life.

Peter Schuurman begins this section of the book with a discussion of the religious movement known as the "Emergent Church." After showing four ways that the Emergent Church movement finds itself allied with the work of Jacques Derrida, Schuurman goes on to point out a fission with the Emergent Church movement between "discontinuous" Emergents, who seem to follow a more Derridean path, and "ancient-future" Emergents, who seem to be closer to the call to radical orthodoxy that Smith suggests. Schuurman ends, echoing Smith, by questioning how postmodern the Emergent Church movement is willing to be by wondering how orthodox it is willing to be. By calling into question the "Logic of the Market," Schuurman not only expertly introduces the Emergent Church movement to those previously unfamiliar with it, but he also poses serious questions to those who find themselves sympathetic to this new religious "sensibility."

James Vanderberg, in chapter seven's "All (For)Giving: the Gift; or, Preaching (Forgiveness) Backwards," tries to develop the ramifications of

---

11. I do not mean to suggest that Smith calls us to the theological movement of Radical Orthodoxy, just that he calls us to a radical form of Christian orthodoxy.

Derrida's thought, and Smith's critique of it, for the pastoral act of preaching. In "parasitic" conversation with Derrida and Smith, Vanderberg develops a new theory of preaching, what he calls "preaching (forgiveness) backwards." He ends by suggesting that this new account of preaching will change the way the church thinks (and acts) about repentance, gratitude, and God's forgiveness in salvation.

Shifting the conversation from the pulpit to the chaplain's office, Andre Basson seeks to elaborate new guidelines for campus ministry in light of the work of Smith and the Catholic dissident theologian Hans Küng, in "Saving the Whale or Dancing with Dolphins?" Drawing on his own experiences as a university chaplain, Basson uses Küng's accounts of truth and the needs of the contemporary church to suggest that, rather than the metaphor of "saving the whale" employed by Smith in WAP (drawn from the movie *Whale Rider*), a better description of campus ministry might be offered using the metaphor of "dancing with dolphins" (drawn from the movie *Dancing with Wolves*): the ideas of cross-cultural reconciliation evoked by that movie, as well as the playfulness of the metaphor, are, Basson contends, more apt for the place of Christian ministry in the narrative soup of today's multi-faith campuses than the cultural behemoth of yesteryear suggested by the whale metaphor.

Stan Skrzeszewski expands the focus of Smith's work by shifting to the new spaces of meeting and identification in our contemporary secular society: the coffee house. In the last paper of this section, "Taking Derrida, Lyotard, and Foucault to Tim Horton's: Experiencing the Modern and the Post-modern in Canada," Skrzeszewski shows that there is more to the different coffee houses then beans and pastries. Highlighting the different philosophies behind Starbucks, the independent coffee house, and Tim Horton's (Dunkin Donuts would be the closest American equivalent to this Canadian icon), Skrzeszewski expertly shows that where we buy our coffee matters, and, based on that, some of us are perhaps more postmodern than others.

The fourth section of the book begins to talk back to Smith. The authors of this section raise questions and concerns about Smith's logic of incarnation. This beginning of a dialogue, supplemented by Smith's response in the final section of the book, is intended to suggest future avenues of exploration and clarification that the logic of incarnation requires.

Introduction

The first such suggestion comes from Wendy Hamblet, in her chapter entitled "Is James K. A. Smith Afraid of Postmodernity?" Hamblet claims that the most characteristic aspect of postmodernity is its radical skepticism, that is, its call for humble self-examination and the appreciation of the limits, rather than the heights, of human wisdom. She then goes on to suggest that Smith's work calls for this type of self-reflection and self-examination, if it is to be truly postmodern (as skeptical) and also postmodern (as taking account of the fears of religious fanaticism raised by many modern thinkers). Without such postmodern skepticism, Hamblet claims, Smith risks converting postmodernism into Christianity, rather than accurately taking it to church.

On the other side of the coin, Mark Bowald wonders if there is still place in Smith's radical orthodoxy or Catholic postmodernism for theological dogmatics. In his "Who's Afraid of Theology?: A Conversation with James K. A. Smith on Dogmatics as the Grammar of Christian Particularity," Bowald explores what he sees as a shift from Smith's earlier to his more recent work in terms of his views on theology and the incarnation, wondering how this change affects the possibility of using theology as the "grammar" of the Christian community. Pointing out the subtle shifts in Smith's oeuvre opens the question of where the logic of incarnation will take us in the future, including the possibility that the logic of incarnation would be best served by abandoning the language of "Incarnation" altogether.

In counterpoint to any hesitancy regarding orthodoxy, James H. Olthuis questions just how orthodox Smith's understanding of eschatology, and especially eschatological hope, is, in light of the work of recent theologians like Moltmann. In "Unlike any other Hope: The Eschatological Structure of Hope," Olthuis argues, contra Smith, that Christian hope is not like any other hope, but rather is distinctly Christian in its eschatological orientation. This difference opens the possibility of *rapprochement* between Derrida's account of structural messianicity and Christian eschatological hope, a *rapprochement* that leaves a door open, always open, to aporias, undecidability, and faith.

Finally, David Goicoechea ends this fourth section of the book with his chapter, which asks "Is the Grace that Calls Whale-Riders Back to Catholicism any more Amazing for Smith than for Derrida and Caputo?" In asking this question, Goicoechea continues a theme found in many chapters of this fourth section that seeks to know how the postmodern church, as Smith sees it, is different from the premodern Church of Peter and Augustine (but also of Inquisitions and Crusades). Goicoechea, like Olthuis before him, again seeks to recover some of Derrida and Caputo's deconstructive religion, and the "weak God" that comes with it, in the face of Smith's critiques, and for the purposes of furthering Smith's project. It is not, then, that the grace mentioned in the title eludes Smith, but that it is found in Derrida and Caputo as well, and Goicoechea wishes to know if it is possible for Smith's radically orthodox Catholic postmodernism to accommodate the grace found in Derrida and Caputo (as well as Luther and Calvin).

After all these questions are posed to Smith, the fifth section of the book, and the final chapter, give Smith a chance to respond to these and other questions raised by the contributors in their essays, and so to continue the dialogue begun and carried out throughout this book. The dialogue moves on several levels (and sometimes many of these levels simultaneously): Smith and the postmodern religious tradition, Smith's work and the church, the contributors and the tradition, and, finally, the contributors and Smith himself.

And though Smith gets the final chapter here, in this book, do not think that this gives him the final word. Derrida's conception of the counter-signature—that every text is not only written and "signed" by the author, but is subsequently read, and therefore "counter-signed" by the reader, giving both author and reader credit in the constitution of the meaning of the text—suggests that the next word is given to you, the reader. And this next word is not itself the final word, for we can continue the conversation until the end of time. Indeed, Smith's work suggests, as spiritual and thoughtful Christians, we must never cease to discuss the Church and the theology that guides her. It is in this spirit (or should I say Spirit?) that this book is offered. May it be a helpful step in an ongoing project of shaping the Church according to genuinely Christian principles, so that the theological theory that nourishes the Church will leave her a beacon of health in a world that is too often sick.

Introduction

WORKS CITED

Caputo, John D. *The Prayers and Tears of Jacques Derrida: Religion With/out Religion*. Bloomington: Indiana University Press, 1997.

———. *The Weakness of God: A Theology of the Event*. Bloomington: Indiana University Press, 2006.

"The Definition of the Council of Chalcedon (A.D. 451)." Accessed June 12, 2008. Online: http://www.reformed.org/documents/index.html?mainframe=http://www.reformed.org/documents/chalcedon.html.

Derrida, Jacques. *Acts of Religion*. Edited by Gil Anidjar. New York: Routledge, 2001.

Habermas, Jurgen. "Religious Tolerance—The Pacemaker for Cultural Rights." In *Philosophy* 79 (2004) 5–18.

Kearney, Richard. *Anatheism: Returning to God After God*. Cambridge: Cambridge University Press, forthcoming.

———. *The God Who May Be: A Hermeneutics of Religion*. Bloomington: Indiana University Press, 2001.

Kearney, Richard, editor. "The Inter-Religious Imagination." A special issue of *Religion and the Arts* 12, nos. 1–3 (2008).

Kierkegaard, Søren. *Fear and Trembling*. Translated by Howard V. Hong and Edna H. Hong, Princeton: Princeton University Press, 1983.

Manoussakis, John Panteleimon. *After God: Richard Kearney and the Religious Turn in Continental Philosophy*. New York: Fordham University Press, 2005.

McLaren, Brian. *The Last Word and the Word After That*. San Francisco: Jossey-Bass, 2005.

Olthuis, James H., editor. *Religion With/out Religion: The Prayers and Tears of John D. Caputo*. New York: Routledge, 2001.

Rawls, John. *Political Liberalism* Expanded Edition. Cambridge: Cambridge University Press, 2005.

Rollins, Peter. *How (Not) to Speak of God*. Brewster, MA: Paraclete, 2006.

———. *The Fidelity of Betrayal: The IR/Religious Heart of Christianity*. Brewster, MA: Paraclete, 2008.

Sherwood, Yvonne, and Kevin Hart, editors. *Derrida and Religion: Other Testaments*. New York: Routledge, 2004.

Smith, James K. A. "A Principle of Incarnation in Derrida's [*Theologische?*] *Jugendschriften*." *Modern Theology* 18 (2002) 217–30.

———. "Determined Violence: Derrida's Structural Religion." *The Journal of Religion* 78.2 (1998) 197–212.

———. "Teaching a Calvinist to Dance." *Christianity Today* (May 2008), 42–45.

———. *The Devil Reads Derrida and other Essays on the University, the Church, Politics and Art*. Grand Rapids: Eerdmans, 2009.

———. "The Secret Lives of Saints." *The Banner* (2008) 42–43.

Taylor, Charles. *The Secular Age*. Cambridge, MA: Harvard University Press, 2007.

PART ONE

Critiquing Postmodernism

1

The Logic of Incarnation
Towards a Catholic Postmodernism

James K. A. Smith

INTRODUCTION: TWO CHEERS FOR POSTMODERNISM

THERE WAS A TIME when "postmodernism" was sexy and edgy, an *enfant terrible* that could both draw a crowd and elicit tirades from fathers worried about their daughters' honor (so to speak).[1] But now it seems to be a bit like punk rock: the sort of thing that white guys in their 40s and 50s are fixated upon, in a strange blend of avant garde nostalgia (or perhaps a nostalgia for what once passed as avant garde). Derrida, Foucault, and Levinas now hover somewhere between has-beens and "classics," while (relatively) fresh, new voices like Žižek and Badiou have captured the hearts and imaginations of those who inhabit that strange space between European philosophy, theology, and the church.[2]

And yet, the term "postmodernism" still seems to get something done. Nobody thinks it is a definitive "school of thought" or even a unified phenomenon.[3] But it seems to remain a useful heuristic term, a loose

---

1. Why does John Lithgow in *Footloose* keep popping into my head here? (I don't mean to thereby thus suggest that Kevin Bacon is the personification of postmodernism.)

2. We often use the shorthand "continental philosophy of religion" to name this quasi-field.

3. The exception are (mainly evangelical) critics of postmodernism who seem to think that there is some sort of "school" of postmodernism with a *madrasas* or educational bunker buried deep below UC Irvine, churning out "postmodernist" philosophers

moniker that names a certain *Zeitgeist* (or *Angst*) and functions as a big tent that gathers together a constellation of conversations and concerns that articulate a number of different critiques of modernity. (And postmodernism still seems to be the kind of thing that gets paternalistic "Dads" worried about the corrosive influence postmodernism has on "the kids.") So it seems that calls for a moratorium on the word might be a bit hasty; duly qualified, the term still has some good (though humble) work to do.

Postmodernism, for me, is a shorthand reference to a constellation of philosophical sources and sensibilities emanating largely from France that, in the light of earlier German critiques (particularly in the work of Martin Heidegger), articulate various criticisms of "modern" frameworks that first emerged in the late middle ages and gained steam in the early modern period, up through the various Enlightenments (German, French, English, and Scottish). In other words, I take the "post" to be quite humble and responsible: this is not the announcement of a new era or of any radical rupture with the past, not the in-breaking of an unprecedented epoch nor the overturning of the entire philosophical tradition, and certainly not any kind of a messianic arrival of a god who will finally save us. But it does name a sense that "something's going on," both within philosophical discussions and on the ground in lived practice.

With respect to the latter, I think it is helpful to make a further heuristic distinction between postmodern*ism* as a constellation of philosophical and theoretical discourses and postmoderni*ty* as another loose heuristic label for a plethora of cultural phenomena that are associated with late modernity: the globalization of markets and the homogenization of commercial cultures, the exponential development of technology (particularly communications technology), the ubiquity of new media, etc. (see WAP, 20n8). I take these phenomena to be the fruit and culmination of shifts effected in modernity. In the same way, while postmodern*ism* represents a critique *of* modernity, the philosophical voices of postmodernism certainly didn't accomplish any acrobatic rupture with respect to modernity: indeed, both Foucault and Derrida, for instance, would come to situate their own work as extensions of modernity, situated within the Enlightenment project (WAP, 95–99; LT, 88–91). But one has to take such claims with a grain of salt since these "new" Enlightenments

---

X, Y, and Z (as in "Jacques Derrida, a postmodernist philosopher, thinks that we all live in books…").

The Logic of Incarnation: Towards a Catholic Postmodernism

are also trenchant critiques of much of the founding *animus* of modernity. All this is just to say that things are messy: there is no neat-and-tidy school of "postmodernist" philosophers; there is no creed or manifesto of postmodernism and no party members required to heed a defined party line; postmodernism is not a radical, clean break from modernism, though it is a radical critique of modernity; and much that goes under the banner of "postmodern" is, in fact, the manifestation of the flowering of modernity (or its going to seed, depending on how you want to look at it).

My work has been concerned with discerning just what postmodernism means for theology, Christian philosophy, and the lived practice of the church's worship and discipleship. Undertaken in the spirit of "understanding the times" (1 Chronicles 12:32), I hope I have articulated a somewhat nuanced stance that boils down to something like this:

> *Insofar as* the church (and *mutatis mutandis*, Christian theology and philosophy) has bought into key assumptions of modernity;
>
> *And insofar as* these assumptions (for instance, regarding the nature of freedom, the model of the human person, the requirements for what counts as "rational" or "true," or what can be admitted to the "public" sphere of political or academic discourse) represent a rejection of biblical wisdom and the Christian theological heritage;
>
> *And insofar as* postmodernism articulates a critique of just these assumptions;
>
> *Then* the postmodern critique of modernity is something to be affirmed by Christians, not *because* it is postmodern,[4] but because the postmodern critique of modernity can be a wake-up call for Christians to see their complicity with modernity, the inconsistency of this with a more integral understanding of discipleship, and thus actually be an occasion to creatively retrieve ancient and

---

4. I have perhaps underemphasized this point, but it is an important one. In *Who's Afraid of Postmodernism?*, while I sometimes used the phrase "postmodern church," my argument emphasized postmodernism represented a catalyst and an opportunity for the church to remember who she is. So, it's decidedly not a question of the church getting "with it," getting hip, or getting "relevant" and up-to-date. I emphasize this here only because I think that amongst some other theologians and church leaders who are enthusiastic about postmodernism there is a lingering sense that this comes down to a matter of relevance—as if the shape of faithful discipleship is somehow determined by the need to "be postmodern." This is characteristic not only of literature associated with the "emerging" church, but also by theologians who are otherwise more careful.

pre-modern theological sources and liturgical practices with new eyes, as it were.

This is a kind of "two cheers" approach to postmodernism, sometimes mistaken as a "three cheers"[5] stance by critics, as if I enthusiastically and wholeheartedly embrace all that is "postmodern," without critique and without reservation. But the key term in this formulation is *insofar as*: there are no blank checks in my approach, though I grant that it would require some reading across my corpus (meager as it is) to get this picture. In particular, in books like *Jacques Derrida: Live Theory* and *Who's Afraid of Postmodernism?*, I sought to provide a charitable exposition of Derrida and deconstruction as a corrective to reactionary misrepresentations of his work by both friends and critics, particularly in the fields of literature and theology/religious studies. In addition, I believe that Derrida presents significant constructive resources for thinking through a variety of issues and problems from a distinctly Christian perspective. As a result, both of these works have a positive, even somewhat apologetic, flavor that tends to let criticism of Derrida recede into the background—to the point that some have suggested that my reading of Derrida represents a certain domestication of his thought, reducing the monstrous threat of deconstruction into the sort of thing that you can comfortably take home to your parents. But within WAP, one will also find a fairly strident critique of the "Derridean" strain of "deconstructive" theology that has dominated continental philosophy of religion (WAP, 116–127). One will also already find a critique of Derrida in *The Fall of Interpretation* (2000), extended and rearticulated in *Speech and Theology* (2002), and then focused on the issue of how to read and receive Augustine in *Introducing Radical Orthodoxy* (2004). The critique is even more incisive in scholarly articles directed to more specialist audiences,[6] though even here I continue to affirm much in Derrida's work as an important catalyst for Christian thought.[7] So my "two cheers" approach is meant to be a critical appropriation of postmod-

---

5. I'm not sure how far one could run with this metaphor, but it strikes me that Merold Westphal and James Olthuis also have a "two cheers" approach (maybe 2.5 cheers), whereas John Caputo and Pete Rollins represent a "three cheers" model.

6. See, for example, Smith, "Determined Violence"; Smith, "Re-Kanting Postmodernism?"; and DH. James Olthuis engages the latter essay extensively in his contribution below.

7. See, for example, Smith, "Is Deconstruction an Augustinian Science"; and Smith, "A Principle of Incarnation in Derrida's (*Theologische?*) *Jugendschriften*."

ernism and deconstruction that walks a long way with Derrida, but parts ways at a critical juncture—not out of a timidity or an unwillingness to "go all the way," but because of a principled critique of what I think are problems internal to Derrida's thought.[8]

The organizers of the conference which gives rise to this book generously suggested that my particular engagement with—and critique of—postmodernism (and "postmodern religion," in particular) represented a unique contribution to the terrain of stances. In particular, it was suggested that the most significant contribution is found in what I name "the logic of incarnation"—first articulated in *Speech and Theology* (but anticipated, I think, in the "creational" hermeneutic in *The Fall of Interpretation*) and then developed as an "incarnational ontology" in *Introducing Radical Orthodoxy* (IRO, 185–223) and further spelled out in *Who's Afraid of Postmodernism?* (WAP, 116–146).[9] My goal in this chapter is to provide a summary account of what I mean by the logic of incarnation, and why it is perhaps a unique position vis-à-vis postmodernism, and more specifically, in contrast to "deconstructive" theology. I will do so by trying to show how it contrasts with a more dominant paradigm, what I'll call a "logic of determination," which characterizes the work of Jacques Derrida and John D. Caputo—two figures whose work looms over my own, and who cast very long shadows over current discussions in continental philosophy of religion as well as more on-the-ground discussions of faith and postmodernism. This chapter cannot serve as a substitute for the arguments I've made elsewhere. In other words, this chapter is not the "Cliff's Notes" version of my argument. Instead, I will take this as an opportunity to crystallize what I have elsewhere described as the logic of incarnation, contrast it with the logic of determination, and then suggest why the former represents a Catholic, and more persistent, postmodernism.

---

8. More specifically, I would also emphasize that my critique of Derrida is not just a "transcendent" critique; that is, I don't think I (only) say that Derrida is wrong because he disagrees with orthodox Christian "positions"; rather, I hope my critique is also an "immanent" critique which—like any good deconstruction—points out internal tensions that threaten to implode the project, but thereby open space for a new reading to emerge. I take it that there is no better way to be faithful to Derrida than to deconstruct him (cp. FI, 126–27).

9. See also Smith, "A Principle of Incarnation."

PART ONE: Critiquing Postmodernism

COMPETING LOGICS: DETERMINATION AND INCARNATION

"Haunted" and Unapologetic Postmodernisms

One of the central features of the postmodern critique of modernity is an appreciation of our *finitude*—our situatedness in time and space, in bodies, in histories, in communities, and in traditions. We can never get (and never really had) a "God's-eye-view" of the world; rather, our perception and engagement with the world—how we "constitute" the world, phenomenologists would say—is shaped, informed, and conditioned by our situatedness: we come to our experience with particular expectations and habits of perception, particular ways of intending the world that have been handed down to us, constituting a sort of "tradition." Thus one might say that postmodernism, owning up to our finitude, entails an appreciation of particularity and the difficulty of achieving the sort of universality that was craved by Enlightenment dreams of a universal *polis*, a rational cosmopolis, populated by rational citizens who all shared the same vision of the Good dictated by "pure" Reason.[10]

Now, I want to suggest that while any postmodern critique worth its salt will be significantly committed to this emphasis on finitude and particularity, just how one *evaluates* and *responds to* this situation of finitude will be a point of demarcation between two different kinds of postmodernism. One strain—and it is a strain I find in Derrida and Caputo—rightly recognizes the inescapability of our finitude and particularity, but nonetheless seems to remain haunted by the Enlightenment dream of universality and purity. This strain, I have suggested, is a less persistent postmodernism (a "timid"[11] postmodernism?), because though it appreciates the ineluctable nature of our finitude and particularity, it

---

10. Granted, such a vision was animated by the best of intentions, *viz.*, overcoming the violent divisions of religious *particularity* that spawned the "wars of religion." For a particularly lucid rendition of this story, see Lilla, *The Stillborn God*. For an account that calls this standard story into question, see Cavanaugh, "A Fire Strong Enough." For my own critique of Lilla, see Smith, "The Last Prophet of Leviathan."

11. This label is a bit playful, since "timid" postmodernists such as Caputo and Rollins actually take themselves to be more radical precisely because they're willing to question and abandon "orthodoxy." I'm suggesting that this isn't radical at all—it's a repetition and completion of the project undertaken by Kant (see Smith, "Re-Kanting Postmodernism"). And thus, in a spirit equally playful and dead serious, I'm suggesting that vis-à-vis such a modern deracination of religion, it is a creative retrieval of orthodoxy that is more radical.

The Logic of Incarnation: Towards a Catholic Postmodernism

still seems to *evaluate* this situation as if it is regrettable, lamentable, and problematic—variously associating the conditions of finitude with violence and injustice. For instance, with respect to knowledge, such haunted (or timid) postmodernism reasons as follows: given that universal, God's-eye-view knowledge is impossible for finite beings; given that the Cartesian and Kantian dreams of pure, rational, universal knowledge are impossible, we must conclude that we *can't know*. "We can only believe," they'll add, in pious tones, with hand on their breast, looking up to heaven like Botticelli's *St. Augustine*. But wait a second: just because God's-eye-view knowledge is impossible, why should we conclude that knowledge *per se* is impossible? Doesn't such a concession actually leave the modern construal of knowledge in place, albeit it as an impossible ideal? Can you see why one might suggest that this strain of timid postmodernism seems to be persistently haunted by (modern) ghosts?[12] Thus this strain of postmodernism might just amount to modernism in despair[13]—and even reflect a kind of hyper-modernism, with a pedigree that is both Humean and Kantian.[14]

Another strain[15] of postmodernism that I have tried to sketch evaluates this situation very differently: it also recognizes the ubiquity and inescapability of our finitude and particularity. But rather than lamenting this situation, and refusing to be haunted by the ghosts of such dreams, this more "persistent" postmodernism relinquishes the very *requirements* of universality and purity as constitutive of knowledge, justice, etc. In other words, the more persistent critique of modernity will not only point out that modernity can't have what it wants; it will also point out that we should refuse to want what it wants. It is a critique not just of modernity's failures, but of modernity's desires.

---

12. This critique is articulated more fully in WAP, 116–46.

13. This formulation was suggested to me from a different context, viz., Yoshida's critique of Clifford Geertz as a "positivist in despair" in Yoshida, "Defending Scientific Study of the Social."

14. This is why the fruits of "deconstructive" theology sometimes feel remarkably similar to a very "modern" theologian such as Gordon Kaufman.

15. This is not at all to suggest that there are only two possibilities; there are certainly still other "postmodernisms," including the post-postmodernism of, say, Badiou. We might also do well to go back and re-consider Rorty's pragmatism as a sort of postmodernism that is less haunted by these modern ghosts. For a relevant discussion, see House, *Without God or His Doubles*. My thanks to John Scherer for conversations on this point.

PART ONE: Critiquing Postmodernism

What distinguishes "timid" and "persistent" postmodernisms, I suggest, are two very different "logics." By "logic," here, I mean an implicit working assumption about how things relate to one another, what follows from what, how things hang together, and the rules that govern such relationships. And very importantly, the sorts of "logics" I'm referring to here actually operate at the *pre*-theoretical level; they are akin to what Pierre Bourdieu describes as "pre-logical logic"[16] or what Thomas Kuhn describes as "paradigms" (see FI, 154–157). These "logics" are not so much conclusions to rational deduction, but the assumptions and presuppositions that precede, inform, and govern rational analysis. As such, they are contingent and contestable, and pretty much amount to something like "faith commitments"—even if they sometimes parade themselves as simply recognizing this is supposedly "the way things are." They amount to a *take* on the world. Or, to adopt the terminology employed by John Milbank, each constitutes a *mythos*.[17] In particular, I have suggested that "haunted" postmodernism amounts to a modernism in despair because it assumes a logic inherited from modernity, what I've called a "logic of determination." In contrast, what I'm calling "persistent" postmodernism works with a different logic, a logic of incarnation which represents a kind of "genius" given to thought by the Incarnation.[18] The genius of this logic

---

16. I can't do justice to Bourdieu's nuanced account here, which is also deployed for quite different reasons. But when he describes as "pre-logical logic of practice" that is distinct from "logical logic," he is hinting at the sort of "logics" I'm naming as the logic of determination and the logic of incarnation. See Bourdieu, *The Logic of Practice*, 19. Thus he emphasizes that "[p]ractice has a logic which is not that of the logician" (p. 86). It seems that for Bourdieu, this is the difference between a *sens* and a *logique*. In that case, one might say I'm describing a *sens* of determination and a *sens* of incarnation.

17. Milbank does so in the context of emphasizing that there can be very different "takes" on difference: one he describes as a "differential ontology" which conceives all difference as ultimately oppositional, and a second he describes as an "ontology of peace" which conceives difference differently, as analogical relations of harmony (for discussion, see IRO, 195–197). One cannot adjudicate between these by means of "logical logic" because they represent two different, competing "pre-logical" logics, two very different *mythoi*. Thus a critique must proceed by means of out-narrating the other. It is just this account of conceptions of difference as *mythoi* that, I think, makes my project analogous to Milbank's.

18. Here I just mean to invoke Kierkegaard's claim that the idea of the god condescending to leap over the abyss is not an idea that *we* could have come up with (*Philosophical Fragments*). I've discussed this in more detail in ST, ch. 5. In an analogous fashion, Milbank argues that the ontology of peace is uniquely generated by biblical wisdom and the Christian doctrine of the Trinity.

The Logic of Incarnation: Towards a Catholic Postmodernism

is that it makes it possible to conceive difference differently, and thereby to understand finitude and particularity differently as well. Let me unpack each of these in a bit more detail.

The Logic of Determination: The Violence of Finitude

Like the religious wars that spawned Kant's vision of a peaceable kingdom, the resurgence of religious fundamentalisms—Christian, Islamic, Zionist—has given birth to a new critique of "religious violence." The contemporary critique, however, signals a new intensification of Enlightenment criticisms: whereas early modern philosophers tended to criticize violence as *inconsistent with* authentic religious faith, the contemporary (or "postmodern") critique suggests that determinate[19] religious faith *necessarily entails* violence. In other words, earlier critics of religious violence tended to view religious wars as an aberration and indication of the inauthenticity of a particular form of faith; but contemporary critics contend that the very particularity of religious confession is intrinsically violent and thus, not surprisingly, produces "real" political violence. However, Kant already planted the seeds for the postmodern critique during the Enlightenment. As I discussed in my essay "Re-Kanting Postmodernism," Kant seeks to denude determinate religion of its historical particularity and thus disclose a "pure" religion of reason. In the contemporary context, such a project is taken up and intensified in the work of Jacques Derrida, whose account of "religious violence" has been influential for scholars in both philosophy and religious studies (for instance, in the work of Caputo and Hent de Vries).[20] For Derrida, religious violence stems from the *determination* or specification of religious belief by a particular content, linked to a particular historical tradition that appeals to a determinate revelation. According to this account, the particularity of religious confession will lead only to tribalism, and ultimately violence.[21]

But what is the link between religion and violence? What is it about the nature of religion that would suggest this link to violence? For Derrida, unlike some "new atheist" screeds, it is not that religion is a unique poison; rather, religion's violence stems from its commitment to instantiating a *particular* vision of justice, the good life, etc. Thus Derrida's

---

19. That is, specified, particular religious confessions.
20. See Caputo, *On Religion*; and de Vries, *Religion and Violence*.
21. For further discussion see Smith, "Determined Violence."

analysis would equally criticize "secular" visions like Marxism for exhibiting the same particularism. So what is it about particularity and determination, then, that is said to entail violence? In both his early and later work, Derrida persistently links the "determinate"—that is, particular or specified—nature of institutions to an inherent and inevitable violence. In his specific considerations of religion, Derrida argues that any and every particular, determinate, historical religion—i.e., any "institutional" religion—must be *de facto* violent and thus produce violence.[22] The same is true, he argues, of any particular determinate hope for political liberation or justice, criticizing Christian, Marxist, and even liberal "hopes" as the basis for undertaking political violence. Because of their determination or specification of a particular vision of justice, Derrida argues that these social hopes would be (and have been) the basis for legitimating the worst injustices against those who would not submit to the vision. Because these social hopes are determinate, they must be exclusionary, and are thus necessarily implicated in violence. This necessitates Derrida's attempted disclosure of an *in*determinate, unspecified "messianic" religion (as opposed to concrete, determinate messian*isms*), which is the basis for hope for a justice that is always "to come."

At work in and behind this conflation of finitude with violence is a "logic of determination." According to this logic, determination itself is violent and leads to violence; therefore, in order to avoid violence we must have, for instance, a social hope which is *in*determinate and hopes for a justice which is unspecified. The result, I would argue, can be a political rhetoric with grand claims regarding justice but which is systematically unable to articulate concrete policies—indeed, which must immediately judge all concrete policies as *un*just (though it will also want to evaluate some policies as *less* unjust than others).[23] As such, Derrida's thesis is, ironically, symptomatic of (and could be a contributor to) a couple of diverse social trends in the United States: (1) generally conservative political strategies that point to the impossibility of the ideal as the reason to cease pursuing it, and rather "settle" for certain inevitable injustices; and (2) a commonly accepted, generally liberal "secularity" thesis which, in varying terms, attempts the construction of a public, civil "religion" devoid of any particularity, both of which share a version of Derrida's

22. See Derrida, *Specters of Marx*, 49–75 and FK.
23. Such evaluation gets a little tricky, particularly because Derrida persistently emphasizes that he is not offering a "regulative ideal."

The Logic of Incarnation: Towards a Catholic Postmodernism

"logic of determination." In other words, much secularist rubric repeats similar claims because they assume a similar logic.[24] Hence, the critique of a logic of determination is not simply a question internal to scholarship on Derrida.

Derrida's premise, which equates determination with violence, can and must be called into question. However, a critique of the logic of determination cannot simply appeal to some sort of neutral, universal criteria in order to demonstrate the problems with the logic of determination. Such "logics" are part of our most fundamental ways of seeing and understanding the world—they are just the sorts of assumptions that are pre-rational. As such, they constitute fundamental, albeit implicit, narrations of the world. In short, they have the same epistemic status as faith claims. One does not adopt the logic of determination because it is "rational," or because it is demonstrated by a syllogism; rather, such a logic is assumed as the very condition for our reasonings. At the level of such logics, we're beyond the ken of proofs—of tidy syllogisms that could point out the fallacious failures of such a logic. However, that does not mean that we are beyond critique, resigned to some sort of sophomoric relativism that resigns itself to "anything goes." The way to contest this logic is two-fold: first, it needs to be unveiled as a contingent construal of the world; and as contingent, it could be otherwise. Second, it needs to be out-narrated; that is, one must offer an alternative description that can be "tried on" as an account of the world that pushes back on us through experience.

What, then, drives the logic of determination? What would make *that* logic plausible as a fundamental assumption? As I already suggested in *The Fall of Interpretation*, it seems to me that the determinate and finite would be construed as violent and exclusionary only if one assumes that finitude is somehow a "failure"—implying that we are somehow called to be Infinite. This is clearly seen in Derrida's work on ethics (FL; GD), where he argues that we are always already guilty because we—as finite creatures—cannot attend to the obligations of *all*. As he quaintly puts it, when I feed my own cat, I am guilty for *not* feeding every other cat. But of course, as finite, it is simply impossible for me to feed every cat; therefore, I am guilty simply for being finite.

---

24. Thus I think there is some tension both within Derrida and in how Derrida has been appropriated. On the one hand, his work seems to feed into a critique of secularism and counsel "post-secularity;" on the other hand, one will find him still extolling secularism at times (see LT, 115–16).

PART ONE: Critiquing Postmodernism

I would argue that not all finite decisions produce injustice. More specifically, it seems to me that one would conclude that finitude or particularity is inherently violent only if one operates with a notion of "infinite" responsibility which "faults" humanity for being finite. In short, I think in order to accept Derrida's premise that all determination or finitude constitutes violence, one would have to adopt some version of a gnostic ontology that construes finitude as a kind of "fall," an original violation. Across his corpus, Derrida links this critique of determinacy or particularity to a valorization of "purity" in the sense of a pure "regulative ideal"; that is, the erection of an ideal standard which is at the same time impossible to attain. Though he protests the label, it seems to me that Derrida constantly appeals to "regulative ideals" of purity in his later discussions of ethics, politics, and religion, such as a "pure hospitality" as the ideal for immigration, a "pure democracy" which is always future,[25] a "pure gift" as an impossible but necessary structure of experience (GT), or a "religion without religion," which is pure insofar as it has been purged of any determinant, historical content.

Indeed, it is interesting to track the logic of determination as a logic of contamination. In almost every case this is indicated by a thematics of "purity"—the "pure gift," "pure hospitality," or the other as "purely other"—which is both the criterion by which existing structures are judged unjust, but also a purity that can never be achieved. As such, we are always already unjust and implicated in an "essential violence." The result is that Derrida is, if we follow Moltmann's categories, a "utopian" thinker. Let me try to unpack this claim a bit.

In matters of justice and emancipation, formulated in terms of a Levinasian ethic of "alterity," Derrida points to a number of quasi-absolutes which function as the criterion for justice. These are structures that point to a "pure" ideal—an ideal of which we always fall short (hence the inescapability of *in*justice). We can see this in several sites (I follow a regressive procedure and expand upon only a couple of examples here):

1. "Pure forgiveness": In a context that includes discussions of South Africa and Bosnia, Derrida argues that "forgiveness forgives only the unforgivable."[26] If forgiveness is undertaken for the achievement of some end or *telos* (redemption, reconciliation, re-establishment of an normal-

---

25. Derrida, *The Politics of Friendship*.

26. Derrida, *On Cosmopolitanism and Forgiveness*, 32. Subsequent parenthetical references in this paragraph are to the same work.

The Logic of Incarnation: Towards a Catholic Postmodernism

ity), "then the 'forgiveness' is *not pure*" (32, cp. 42, 44–45). Forgiveness, in order to be "pure," must be "*unconditional*, gracious, infinite, aneconomic, forgiveness granted *to the guilty as guilty*, without counterpart, even to those who do not repent or ask for forgiveness" (34, cp. 32, 36, 40, 45). And only this ideal of "absolute forgiveness" could be the 'ground' for any ethics (35–36). We should keep in mind, however, that "pure forgiveness" is impossible, and so even our best shots at forgiveness remain unjust.

2. "Pure hospitality": In a context which includes discussions of immigration and human rights, Derrida argues that justice demands an "absolute or unconditional hospitality" which is incommensurate with "hospitality in the ordinary sense."[27] "Just hospitality" breaks with ordinary hospitality because "absolute hospitality requires that I open up my home and that I give not only to the foreigner [. . .] but to the absolute, unknown, anonymous other, and that I *give place* to them" (25). Pure hospitality begins from an "unquestioning welcome" (29). However, the impossibility of this unconditional hospitality is tied to *finitude*: "since there is also no hospitality without finitude, sovereignty can only be exercised by filtering, choosing, and thus by excluding and *doing violence*. Injustice, a certain injustice [. . .] begins right away" (55, cp. 65).

One could repeat an exposition of a similar formula as it emerges in Derrida's consideration of the gift (in GT), friendship (in *The Politics of Friendship*), religion (particularly in GD and *Specters of Marx*), justice (in FL), and the Other (in early work such as *Of Grammatology* and VM): a "pure" phenomenon is distilled as an ostensible motivator for undertaking strategies that will never reach it.[28] But this structure of an "impossible" or "pure" justice, I would contend, is the product of a repressed metaphysics

---

27. Derrida, *Of Hospitality*, 25. Subsequent parenthetical references in this paragraph are to the same work.

28. This "never" is different than Christian eschatology. In the Christian account, admittedly, there is a deep sense that "we" will never achieve a perfectly just society, etc.; but this is not the same as saying that such will never arrive. Rather, the claim is meant to signal the importance of grace. Derrida's account, however, seems to indicate a more absolutely impossibility. This is why I have always found myself puzzled that some folks find his account of justice somehow inspiring. While the Christian account is justly humble about what can be expected, work for a just here and now (in our "not yet") will be taken up and fulfilled in the advent of justice and shalom in the new heavens and new earth. So there remains a continuity between little in-breakings of justice here and now and the justice that is to come and we hope ("expect") will arrive. But Derrida's anti-eschatology contends that day is never coming. Am I the only one who then thinks, "Then why bother?"

rooted in what I've been describing as Derrida's logic of determination which, rather than inspiring revolution, provides comfort to the status quo. Derrida's premise, which equates determination with violence, can and must be called into question.

Before sketching an alternative *mythos* or "take" on finitude—the logic of incarnation—permit me to articulate a couple of reservations with Derrida's project: First, it seems to me that when he opposes "pure justice" to "ordinary justice," or offers the notion of "preethical violence" (VM 128) [and so with all of the structures above], Derrida is repeating a disturbing Heideggerian gesture, justly criticized by Caputo as Heidegger's "essentialization," closely tied to "purity" and the desire to "avoid contamination."[29] Does not Derrida offer here a similar move? Do we not find in Derrida the valorization of a certain "decontamination"— an *inoculation* against finitude, even if impossible? Second, concerning the heterogeneity and incommensurability between the "pure" ideal and the "ordinary," finite institution: if it's impossible to reach this purity, then I'm never getting any closer to it, and therefore any particular action or policy which I undertake is neither more or less just than the other—in which case, it can feed the most conservative protections of the status quo which capitalize on just such impossibility as the reason to "accept" evil and injustice as "the way things are."

Instead of adopting a logic of determination which construes finitude or particularity as a violence, I offer a logic of incarnation which honors finitude and particularity as a good.[30] The logic of incarnation rejects the premise that evaluates determination as exclusionary and hence violent; to adopt this logic is to construe embodiment itself as the basis for guilt. If one begins, instead, with an affirmation of embodiment as good, then the fact of finitude—e.g., that I can only feed so many cats—is not construed as injustice, because with the rejection of Derrida's logic of determination one must also reject infinite responsibility as a regulative

---

29. Caputo, *Demythologizing Heidegger*, 119. It's hard for me to emphasize how important this book was in my own philosophical formation.

30. Even here, it is not simply a matter of rejecting Derrida; indeed elsewhere I have suggested that there are hints of just such an incarnational logic in the early Derrida. See Smith, "A Principle of Incarnation."

The Logic of Incarnation: Towards a Catholic Postmodernism

ideal.[31] One sees just such an affirmation of embodiment in the Christian theological motifs of creation, incarnation, and resurrection.

The Nature of the Gothic and the Logic of Incarnation

Despite suggestions that Derrida's account is "realistic," that it faces up to the "facts" of our finitude, in fact this is a *mythos*, a take on the world, a faith-informed construal of finitude that represents a pre-logical commitment. But its epistemic status as a *mythos* means one could reject this premise that grounds Derrida's logic of determination and offer a counter-narrative, an alternative *mythos* that would operate on the basis of a different logic.

So what would be different according to a logic of incarnation? First, it is informed by a narrative wherein the transcendent, infinite Other condescends to finite immanence *without loss* and *without remainder*. The logic of incarnation is not just informed by a proto-Marxist Jesus of the sort one finds in Dominic Crossan or Caputo (though I'm happy to say that Jesus has more in common with Marx than Adam Smith, I think). In other words, this is not a logic that just draws upon a "prophetic" Jesus; it is a logic that is informed by the richness of Chalcedonian Christology which suggests that in Christ, we have *both* the fullness of God and humanity; not half-and-half; not one swapped for other; but rather the paradoxical (yea, mad) affirmation that in the gritty, material person of Jesus we are also encountering the fullness of the Creator ("*pleased* as man with men to dwell," as the old Christmas hymn puts it).[32]

Second, and crucial to this Chalcedonian logic, is its refusal of binary either/ors—the sort that both liberalism and fundamentalism are prone to fall into—and just the sort that I think the logic of determination replays. Notable here is the moment of evaluation that is implied in this: while the transcendent God condescends to inhabit immanence, this is not thereby a concession, and certainly not a lamentable or regrettable "necessary evil." It follows from a logic of creation that does not see the specification and particularity of finitude as an evil; rather the conditions of finitude

---

31. A similar point is articulated in Milbank's critique of Levinas and Derrida in "Can Morality be Christian?" in *The Word Made Strange*, 219–32 and "Grace: The Midwinter Sacrifice," in *Being Reconciled*, 138–60.

32. Recall the central argument of Kierkegaard's *Philosophical Fragments*, which I draw upon in ST, ch. 5.

(particularity, specification, this-ness, if you will) are affirmed as a good.[33] Indeed the Incarnation can only be properly understood in the light of the Ascension, which emphasizes that the Son's humanity is taken up and inhabited for eternity. This is why the logic of incarnation, which flows from and re-affirms the goodness of creation, finds its completion in the doctrine of the resurrection and an eschatology of the new heavens and the new earth—which is not any kind of escape from finitude as if finite particularity were inherently evil; rather, it is the hope of well-ordered particularity.

Third, as I tried to emphasize in the final chapter of *Who's Afraid of Postmodernism?*, the logic of incarnation also entails an affirmation of the contingency of history. Rather than lamenting and criticizing the Christian community for drawing boundaries, demarcating doctrine (as the "grammar" of the community), and specifying its confession, the logic of incarnation sees such procedures as inherent to what it means to be a finite community. And perhaps most scandalously, it is informed by a fundamental trust that the Spirit is at work in just such contingent, historical formulations (though this does not forestall internal critique). By affirming the contingencies of community development, the logic of incarnation rejects both the primitivism of Protestant fundamentalism (which wants to leap back over what it sees as the contaminating and regrettable influence of the Church to the purity of Jesus and "New Testament Christianity") as well as the more sophisticated primitivism of the deconstructive Jesus (who, if you look closely, pretty much want to do the same thing—it's just that *their* Jesus and New Testament look quite different).

All this is just to say that the logic of incarnation is not haunted by "purity," which always comes off as a bit un-worldly, even a bit gnostic. Indeed, if I could be permitted an analogy that stretches the conversation a bit, I would suggest that what John Ruskin describe as "the nature of the Gothic" is a pretty good translation of the logic of incarnation. Ruskin's widely influential essay of the same title, embedded in the second volume of *The Stones of Venice*, contrasts the Greek and classical aesthetic ideals of pristine perfection with the Gothic and Christian ideals which celebrate a certain un-uniformity, even a kind of valued ugliness. In the

---

33. This was the core argument of *The Fall of Interpretation*, though there I described it as a "creational hermeneutic;" now, in contrast to Derrida and Caputo, I tend to name the same construal of finitude as a "logic of incarnation."

The Logic of Incarnation: Towards a Catholic Postmodernism

Greek temple each column is perfect, symmetrical, and identical to the others—they look like they've been created by machines. In the Gothic cathedral, by contrast, one will find all sorts of differences and peculiarities, even blemishes and strange anomalies (think gargoyles). Behind this, Ruskin argues, is not just an "aesthetic," but an entire construal of human flourishing, including assumptions about the nature of human persons and the ideal human community. This is why, for Ruskin, the Gothic is not just a style—it is a vision of society, and of work in particular. For why was it that those Greek temples were characterized by machine-like precision, yea, "purity?" Because they were built by slaves. Ruskin emphasized that what distinguished Gothic architecture from earlier classical architecture, as well as later "industrial" building, was the *freedom of the craftsman*. Greek temples were built by slaves. The laborers were not properly craftsmen but rather human tools and machines. Thus classical architecture has a kind of pristine perfection about it that is artificial and mechanistic; it shows no stamp of individual artists, no mark of their particularity or specificity. And, this desire for a pristine perfection and uniformity is, in fact, a suppression of nature and individuality.

For Ruskin, the "modern" laborer was not qualitatively different. While not a "slave" in the traditional sense, he was still reduced to an unthinking machine. He put it this way:

> It is verily this degradation of the operative into a machine, which, more than any other evil of the times, is leading the mass of the national everywhere into vain, incoherent, destructive struggling for a freedom of which they cannot explain the nature themselves. Their universal outcry against wealth, against nobility, is not forced from them either by the pressure of famine, or the sting of mortified pride. These do much, and have done much in all ages; but the foundations of society were never yet shaken as they are at this day. It is not that mean are ill fed, but that they have no pleasure in the work by which they make their bread, and therefore look to wealth as the only means of pleasure. It is not that mean are pained by the scorn of the upper classes, but they cannot endure their own; for they feel that the kind of labour to which they are condemned is verily a degrading one, and makes them less than men. Never had the upper classes so much sympathy with the lower, or charity for them, as they have at this day, and yet never were they so much hated by them: for, of old, the separation between the noble and

the poor was merely a wall built by law; now it is a veritable difference in level of standing, a precipice between upper and lower grounds in the field of humanity, and there is pestilential air at the bottom of it.[34]

So the "modern" pre-occupation for pristine perfection and exquisite finish is bought with a price: the effective enslavement of the "divided" laborer. But the Gothic—which is a distinctly Christian architectural grammar—rejects such slavery:

> But in the mediaeval, or especially Christian, system of ornament, this slavery is done away with altogether; Christianity having recognized, in small things as well as great, the individual value of every soul. But it not only recognizes its value; it confesses its imperfection, in only bestowing dignity upon the acknowledgment of unworthiness. [...] Therefore, to every spirit which Christianity summons to her serve, her exhortation is: Do what you can, and confess frankly what you are unable to do; neither let your effort be shortened for fear of failure, nor your confession silenced for fear of shame. And it is, perhaps, the principal admirableness of the Gothic schools or architecture, that they thus receive the results of the labour of inferior minds; and out of fragments full of imperfection, and betraying that imperfection in every touch, indulgently raise up a stately and unaccusable whole.[35]

So to the so-called perfection of classical and modern architecture, Ruskin contrasts the beautiful *im*perfection of the Gothic:

> And on the other hand, go forth again to gaze upon the old cathedral front, where you have smiled so often at the fantastic ignorance of the old sculptors: examine once more those ugly goblins, and formless monsters, and stern statues, anatomiless and rigid; but do not mock at them, for they are signs of the life and liberty of every workman who struck the stone; a freedom of thought, and rank in the scale of being, such as no laws, no charters, no charities can secure; but which it must be first aim of all Europe at this day to regain for her children.[36]

The logic of incarnation, I want to suggest, is characterized by this Gothic affirmation of imperfection as nonetheless good, even beautiful,

---

34. Ruskin, "The Nature of the Gothic," 116.
35. Ibid., 157–58.
36. Ibid., 160–161.

whereas the logic of determination, I'm suggesting, is haunted by notions of (impossible) perfection and (impossible) purity, ends up constructing such gritty particularity as a contamination and a fall. This is just to say that when we begin from a logic of incarnation, we refuse to be haunted by modern ghosts. One might say it begins with an exorcism.

NIETZSCHE'S FAITH: OR, WHY WE NEED AN EVEN MORE RADICAL HERMENEUTICS

It is important to emphasize that the logic of determination and the logic of incarnation are two different stories about difference and particularity, two different construals of finitude, both of which have the epistemic status of faith commitments. On the one hand, then, I'm trying to point out that the construal of particularity and finitude as violent is just that: a construal, a "take" on things, a story that can be outnarrated. On the other hand, and this has been the burden of my work, I hope to make some start at "out-narrating" this story by articulating the logic of incarnation.

To clarify this point, it might be helpful to return to some key issues of hermeneutics, and to return to the figure of Nietzsche who had somewhat fallen off the radar of continental philosophy of religion (after an enthusiastic phase following the work of Mark C. Taylor). But that is changing.[37] More specifically, revisiting Nietzsche allows me to revisit an older version of the debate between Caputo's "religion without religion" and what I'm now calling a "Catholic postmodernism."

In a way, my work from the beginning to the present is very much concerned with hermeneutics. This is why Caputo's *Radical Hermeneutics*[38] was for me—like so many others—a revolutionary entrée into the field of contemporary Continental philosophy. To draw a Heideggerian analogy, in RH Caputo was my Husserl: he "opened my eyes."[39] Here I want to pursue a theme in Caputo's work to which I have been drawn from the very beginning: the thematics of undecidability and its correlation with the place of Nietzsche in Caputo's thought. Indeed, my very first publication (well, after a little piece on "theological preaching" that will never make

---

37. See Westphal, *Suspicion and Faith*, 219–82; Benson, *Graven Ideologies* and *Pious Nietzsche*; Williams *The Shadow of the Antichrist*; and Hovey, *Nietzsche and Theology*. Also relevant in this context are the writings of David Goicoechea, such as *Zarathustra's Love Beyond Wisdom*.

38. Henceforth abbreviated as RH.

39. Heidegger, *Ontologie*, 5.

it into my *Ouvres complètes*) focused on the question of undecidability in Caputo.[40] Here, I want to pick up that line of analysis by considering in particular how Caputo construes the undecidability that inhabits the space between what he earlier described as "the religious" in Kierkegaard and "the tragic" in Nietzsche (RH 272). By tracing this theme from RH, through *Against Ethics* and *The Prayers and Tears of Jacques Derrida*, up to *More Radical Hermeneutics* and *On Religion*,[41] I will suggest that an interesting shift has taken place between RH and OR regarding the place and status accorded to "the tragic" in general, and Nietzsche in particular, in the project of Caputo's "radical hermeneutics." My conclusion will include a brief recommendation for how this shift might be continued, or how a Catholic postmodernism represents an even more radical hermeneutics.

Undecidability, Faith, and the Limits of Knowledge

Undecidability, Caputo has repeatedly protested, is *not* a matter of *indecision*, but rather the condition of possibility of any decision which demands that one decide.[42] As he later summarizes, "[u]ndecidability does not mean the apathy of indecision but the passion of faith, the urgency of forging ahead where one does not see, where in principle one cannot see" (PT 338). This Derridean theme has been central and persistent throughout Caputo's corpus.

The first crystallization of undecidability—the first advent of its acute challenge—is located in the final chapter of RH (prototypical of the works to follow) where Caputo unfolds two ways of understanding suffering, two different takes on the face of the suffering other which are, strictly speaking, undecidable: the "religious" embodied in Kierkegaard (RH 278–82) and the "tragic" response of Nietzsche (RH 282–88). It is at this juncture that the haunting specter of Nietzsche makes its entrance onto the stage of radical hermeneutics, playing a major role from RH to AE.

---

40. Smith, "Between Athens and Jerusalem."

41. Caputo, *Against Ethics*; *The Prayers and Tears of Jacques Derrida*; *More Radical Hermeneutics*; *On Religion*. Henceforth abbreviated as AE, PT, MRH, and OR, respectively.

42. This was first helpfully clarified in the early exchange between Caputo and Olthuis. See Olthuis, "A Cold and Comfortless Hermeneutic"; Caputo, "Hermeneutics and Faith"; and Olthuis, "Undecidability and the Impossibility of Faith."

The Logic of Incarnation: Towards a Catholic Postmodernism

What I have always found curious about this role for Nietzsche, however, is the way in which he in fact plays a privileged part that seems to escape undecidability. In RH, the truth is cold (RH 273), which is to say, the truth is Nietzschean. It's almost as if Nietzsche has some kind of privileged "realistic" access to the way things "really are"—they're not good!—while Kierkegaard can just offer us a "construal," a therapeutic take on things which helps us "cope" with this cold reality via an "accommodation" with the chill of the "flux" (RH 271, 281).[43] The religious response of faith is simply "a certain facility to construe the darkness, to grope in the dark" (RH 279). "Faith makes its way in the dark," he concludes, "seeing through a glass darkly, and it is genuine only to the extent that it acknowledges the abyss in which we are all situated" (RH 281).

Hence, early Caputo (is it late enough to say that now?) is "transfixed by Nietzsche's tragic vision, kept up at night by his account of the disaster" (AE 54). This Nietzschean movement of radical hermeneutics seems to reach its crescendo in AE, where Caputo is also most concerned with Deleuze.[44] What in RH was the undecidability of the "tragic" and the "religious," is now the undecidable distinction between Dionysius and the Rabbi, between "heteromorphism" and "heteronomism," between the configurations of Nietzsche/Deleuze and Levinas/Derrida (AE 42–68). In AE, it is still Nietzsche who delivers "the cold truth" and has the courage to tell us "the cold fact that becoming makes no dialectical progress, that it does not recoup its losses, that the flux is the endless destruction of whatever it produces" (AE 51). This is why in AE, the religious remains a mere coping mechanism, a way of construing the way things "really" are.

> Faith is a matter of a radical hermeneutic, an art of construing shadows, in the midst of what is happening. Faith is neither magic nor an infused knowledge that lifts one above the flux or the limits of our mortality. Faith, on my view, is above all the *hermeneia* that Someone looks back at us from the abyss, that the spell of anonymity is broken by a Someone who stands with those who suffer, which is why the Exodus and the Crucifixion are central religious

---

43. Indeed, it seems that the difference between a "radical hermeneutics" which keeps things difficult and a "hermeneutics of ease" is not qualitative, but quantitative: a hermeneutics of ease is a little too accommodating, or not accommodating enough, since it is "especially adept at repressing and excluding the flux and trying to arrest its play" (RH 271).

44. It seems that this confrontation with the Deleuzian strain in French thought drops out of later Caputo.

> symbols. *Faith does not, however, extinguish the abyss but constitutes a certain reading of the abyss, a hermeneutics of the abyss.* (AE 245, emphasis added)

In this sense, faith sounds like deluding ourselves, acting "as if" the abyss were something else. This, of course, is a definition of faith that plays right into the hands of the masters of suspicion such as Freud or Marx (if anyone believed them anymore). While in AE Caputo seems to waver with some just plain indecision,[45] there is at the same time this nagging sense that things have been decided with respect to the abyss (what are we naming here?); so the question is whether we'll be able to develop a coping mechanism that prevents us from going mad with the 'reality' of the abyss. In a very Freudian way, Caputo suggests that it is precisely the mad who see the abyss for what it is: "I do not think people who are driven to the edge are getting things all wrong," he argues, "so much as that they are unreasonably right, right to an excess. [. . .] They pay too close attention to life. They are scrupulously, infinitely attentive to life and—to their misfortune—*see through* its masks, the very structures that have been put in place for our own protection. They do not know how to ignore, forget, forgive, *repress*, move on" (AE 239–40, emphasis added). So it seems those gone mad are precisely those ones who do *not* see through a glass darkly, but just plain see through things to the way the abyss 'really' is. The result of forcing "the abyss out of hiding" is too often self-destruction, "a function of overexposing oneself to something from which most of us have the prudence to take shelter" (AE 240). The rest of us—especially the religious—are more mature egos who have developed coping mechanisms which help us repress the "cold reality" of the abyss. This is why faith cannot "extinguish" the abyss, only construe it "differently," "as if" Someone were looking back (AE 245).[46] But in the end, "[w]e can never build a shelter against the winds of the flux" (RH 282).

---

45. So, too, in RH: "I do not think that anyone ever really succeeds in getting to one side or the other of this undecidable rift, that one really 'is' or 'is not' religious, wholly Augustinian or wholly Nietzschean. [. . .] I do not think that we know whether we believe in God or not, not if we face the cold truth" (RH 287–88).

46. Elsewhere I have analyzed these themes with respect to Caputo's understanding of the relationship between "faith" and "philosophy," arguing that throughout his corpus—perhaps with the exception of OR—Caputo maintains a certain quasi-Kantian affirmation of the autonomy of philosophical reason vis-à-vis faith, even when, with Derrida, he insists on a formal *credo ut intelligam* structure. See Smith, "Is Deconstruction an Augustinian Science?"

The Logic of Incarnation: Towards a Catholic Postmodernism

Despite Caputo's claim that he rejects "all forms of privileged positions above the flux and binary oppositional schemes" (RH 279), it seems to me that the very categories of the "flux" and the "abyss" are themselves accorded just that: a privileged, quite decidable status (which is quite clear if you are mad). We are told that the flux is "cold" and "dark," and hence the religious "construal" of the flux otherwise always comes second. Which means that somehow Nietzsche is always on the scene first; the flux seems to be always already inscribed by a Nietzschean stylus, as though things were "really" that bad. The flux is always already an "abyss." In what seems a curious revival of Heideggerian *a-letheia*, Caputo concludes that "[f]rom time to time the abyss shows through, the anonymous void by which we are inhabited breaks out and we are swallowed up, or very nearly. [. . .] The abyss bleeds through the cracks and crevices of ordinary existence; the void peers out from behind the minimalia of everyday life" (AE 239). So "[t]he abyss is just another name for what happens" (AE 239); but that name, of course, is not neutral, but already an evaluation, a perspective, a construal, a "take" on things which is loaded with value. The project of a radical hermeneutics is to point out the radical contingency of our perspectives (a Nietzschean 'truth' to be sure), but despite thematizing the distinction between the "religious" and the "tragic" responses to the abyss, it seems to me that Caputo fails to recognize that they very description of this "reality" as a cold, dark abyss is itself just another perspective, another "take" on things, itself a "construal." Because this undecidability does not go all the way down, in these early works I don't think radical hermeneutics is radical enough.

Contra Nietzschean Positivism

In light of its haunting dominance in the earlier works, it is interesting to note how few lines this specter of Nietzsche has in the later works such as PT and OR. Or to put it otherwise: in the later works, Jack seems to be getting more sleep. Not that the difficulty of life doesn't keep him up late, but Zarathustra's laughter seems to have abated. Why is that? Why the diminished role for this Nietzschean specter in the later work?

I would suggest that this is due to the further radicalization of radical hermeneutics.[47] By this I mean that the vestiges of a kind of "Nietzschean

---

47. Which, ironically, one might also understand as a further Nietzscheanization of radical hermeneutics, if, at the "heart" of Nietzsche (if he has one) is located his *perspectivalism*.

positivism" in RH and AE (in the description of the "abyss" and "flux") tend to drop out due to a more radical understanding of the relationship between faith and reason. In other words, it seems to me that RH and AE operated with a more classically Kantian understanding of the relationship between faith and reason, whereas the later works operate with a more Augustinian understanding of this relationship. This is due in no small part, of course, to the unveiling of such Augustinian structures in Derrida's own work, particularly *Of Spirit* and *Memoirs of the Blind*. So unlike in RH, where deconstruction seemed to inhabit a space between faith and "reason" (in Nietzschean guise), in PT Caputo opens by arguing that "[d]econstruction proceeds not by knowledge but by faith" (xxvi). This, of course, does not mark the elimination of undecidability, or a way of averting undecidability, but precisely the radicalization of undecidability that was missing from RH and AE—an omission that prevented undecidability from going "all the way down." With this more radical conception of the relationship between faith and reason, undecidability is inscribed "at the origin," so to speak. This would mean that even the descriptions of the "abyss" as "cold" and "dark"—indeed, the very *naming* of the abyss—is always already called into question, thus displacing the priority of Nietzschean construals. So the religious is not simply a construal which papers over the way things "really" are—as though we were always warding off Nietzsche; instead, one can begin with a radically different construal of that "space."[48] To put this in terms of a different context, I think RH and AE accorded a primordiality to what John Milbank describes as an "ontology of violence," whereas the later works recognize the contingency of such, opening the space for a construal of original peace.[49]

While this shift begins in PT (I don't think Zarathustra ever gets to laugh at Abraham there), we see this shift culminate in OR, where it is equally emphasized that Nietzsche's "terrifying vision of the world" is also a construal, a myth, a "fiction" (OR 54). What this points to is "the *pre*-metaphysical situation of faith. That puts Nietzsche and St. Paul on the same page, at least on this point [. . .]. Nietzsche had argued for the historical contingency of our constructions, the revisability and reform-

---

48. As suggested, for instance, in James Olthuis' understanding of this space as a "womb," or the "wild-spaces of love." John Milbank's project regarding an "ontology of peace" would be another example.

49. See Milbank, *Theology and Social Theory*, 278ff.

The Logic of Incarnation: Towards a Catholic Postmodernism

ability of our beliefs and practices, all of which, as he said, are 'perspectives' that we take on the world and that have emerged in order to meet the needs of life" (OR 58). In RH and AE, Nietzsche was not exposed to his own perspectivalism;[50] but in OR it is finally admitted that what went under the supposedly neutral rubric of the "flux" and "abyss" is always already a perspective: "Nietzsche's argument boomeranged in a way that nobody saw coming," Caputo observes. "What the contemporary post-Nietzschean lovers of God, religion and religious faith took away from Nietzsche was that psychoanalysis (Freud), the unyielding laws of dialectical materialism (Marx), and the will to power itself (Nietzsche) are *also* perspectives, *also* constructions, or fictions of grammar" (OR 59). The result is a redefinition of "reason" itself "as a historically contingent 'take' we have on things—which makes it look a lot more like 'faith'" (OR 64).

A Final Frontier for Catholic Postmodernism: Revelation

This radicalization of perspectivalism means a more radical hermeneutics must call into question the vestiges of realism at work in RH and AE. But I would like to suggest that in Caputo's more radical hermeneutics there remains two other related vestiges of a kind of Enlightenment realism found in one last pocket of "secularity" which prevents perspectivalism from going "all the way down." The first—the notion of a formal or structural "religion without religion"— I have addressed extensively elsewhere, so I won't tackle that here.[51] Instead, I will briefly consider a closely related topic: Caputo's dismissal of *revelation*.

Despite his powerful *apologia* for faith and religion (even, at times, institutional religion—even, God forbid, Pentecostalism!),[52] Caputo repeatedly refuses any notion of "revelation": "We have not, to my knowledge, been visited by some Super-revelation, some Apocalyptic Unveiling, that settles all our questions" (OR 20). "The skies do not open up and drop The Truth into our laps," he continues (OR 21). Instead, "we find ourselves forced constantly to traffic in 'interpretations,' the inescapability of which is a good way to define 'hermeneutics'" (OR 21). Thus Caputo constructs a dichotomous opposition between the inescapability of interpretation on

---

50. Perhaps we could say that RH and AE remain "secular" in this regard, while PT and OR are "post-secular" (see OR 56–59).

51. See Smith, "Determined Violence" and "Re-Kanting Postmodernism?".

52. OR 94–95.

PART ONE: Critiquing Postmodernism

the one hand, and any notion of "revelation" on the other.[53] For Caputo, any notion of revelation must entail a rejection of the ubiquity of interpretation; a notion of revelation must be linked to claims of immediacy which bypass the structure of interpretation or, in other words, claims to "bail us out and lift us above the flux of undecidability" (MRH 193). "What else does 'revelation' mean if not that The Secret has been 'revealed' to us, has been handed over to us courtesy of a 'Special Delivery'" (MRH 193)? Hence Caputo's critique: "A revelation is an interpretation that the believers believe is a revelation, which means it is one more competing entry in the conflict of interpretations" (OR 22).

In an attempt to further radicalize this radical hermeneutics, I would offer two criticisms at this juncture. First, I think Caputo has been reading too much Jean-Luc Marion (MRH 201–7),[54] or has at least fallen prey to an overgeneralization which assumes that any claims regarding revelation must also be claims to immediacy and hence denials of the ubiquity of hermeneutics.[55] But not everyone operates with such theories of revelation; my alternative exemplar of choice would be Kierkegaard's incarnational understanding of revelation, which begins from an affirmation of the inescapability of finitude (entertained by Caputo himself, it seems [MRH 201–2; 209]).[56] So it is *not* self-evident that "[t]he Divine Word is a word *outside* the text, if ever there was one!" (MRH 197). A faith-affirmation of the reality of revelation does not necessarily entail either an anti-hermeneutic claim to immediacy nor triumphalism since it remains, on this radical hermeneutic, a claim rooted in faith, which is always a claim made only through and in the face of undecidability.[57] Thus I think Caputo's critique of claims to revelation only holds for those who

---

53. It also seems that Caputo confines "revelation" to the "Word of God" understood *textually*, distinguishing between the Incarnation and revelation (MRH 286n28). Such a distinction stands in need of a Barthian—or better, biblical—understanding of the Incarnation itself as the primary site of God's revelation, the Word become flesh (John 1:14). Though God has spoken at various times and in various ways, he has now spoken *in Son* (Heb. 1:1–2). The text of the Scriptures is a (second-order) testimony to this primordial revelation of God in Christ.

54. See Marion, *God Without Being*, 139–58.

55. For my criticism of just such notions of revelation, see FI, 17–60.

56. For further articulation of this critique of Marion, see ST, 157–63.

57. Any believer worth her salt would be happy to concede with Caputo that "[u]ndecidability is the condition, the quasi-transcendental condition, of faith, the thing that makes faith (im)possible, *the* impossible" (MRH 220–21).

The Logic of Incarnation: Towards a Catholic Postmodernism

think they *know* they have a revelation in a positivist sort of way: those whose faith is not faith at all, but a kind of apodictic certainty constituted by full presence and characterized by the Husserlian dream of apodicticity (which is just plain impossible). For those who understand faith as a decision made on the basis of undecidability, and who appreciate the epistemic humility that must attend creaturely finitude, trust in revelation is not attended by such (dangerous) "knowledge."

Second, Caputo seeks to critique the believer's claim to revelation by unveiling the fact that such is only an *interpretation*. For example, the believer's confession that God was in Christ—that in Jesus of Nazareth the "Word became flesh" (John 1:14)—is only one interpretation of such an event. But the believer—unless he or she is a rationalist (i.e., a fundamentalist)—would happily concede such a point: yes, the claim that God was in Christ is an interpretation made within a horizon of faith. *But*—and here's the rub—so too is the claim that Jesus is *not* God incarnate, or the interpretation of revelation that says there is no revelation. Every rejection of the possibility of revelation would also operate on the basis of a particular faith, a particular interpretation—which means that not only should believers be less triumphalistic, but that those who reject the possibility of revelation should also pull back the troops. In other words, if undecidability really goes all the way down—if we really mean to have a more radical hermeneutics—it seems to me that the question of revelation should remain more open than Caputo treats it. Such an opening would produce an even more radical hermeneutics.

As I've emphasized above, a Catholic postmodernism embraces the scandalous contingency and particularity of God's revelation in Christ, without apology, but also without Inquisitions. It's not so much a matter of staking a claim to "a revelation" as being claimed by a Revelation which then calls us to be a peculiar people marked by our suffering *for* the world, not our triumph over it.[58]

---

58. While I'm critical of Jean-Luc Marion's account of revelation as overwhelming the conditions of interpretation, I'm here nonetheless drawing on his phenomenology of revelation in *Being Given*, 234–45.

PART ONE: Critiquing Postmodernism

WHO'S AFRAID OF ORTHODOXY?: THE INCARNATION AS A MORE RADICAL HERMENEUTICS

I've been spending time unpacking the logic of incarnation by demarcating it from what I take to be its most winsome and influential competitor, the logic of determination articulated by John Caputo (and indebted to Jacques Derrida). It is the latter's "religion without religion" which has most captivated not only academic discussions in continental philosophy of religion but also reflections on the church, particularly in "emergent" circles.[59] These two worlds come together in Caputo's most recent book, *What Would Jesus Deconstruct?* Since I'm already clearly on record[60] as a friend and fan of John Caputo's winsome 21st-century rendition of Sheldon's *In His Steps*, in closing I would like to take an opportunity to push the conversation further, taking the spirit of Jack's book seriously enough to disagree with it. I'll do so by taking a position that is not only unpopular but will seem downright counter-intuitive to many. My claim is relatively simple: that despite all the bad press and caricatures from supposedly enlightened liberals, it is in fact *orthodoxy* that constitutes the most radical appreciation of "deconstructibility." To put it a little more stridently and provocatively, I would suggest that the Jesus of Pope Benedict XVI represents a more radical hermeneutic than the Jesus we get from Schillibeeckx, that the church of Francis Cardinal George is a more radical institution than the sort of church you'd get from Gary Wills, and that the Gospel according to Stanley Hauerwas is more radical than the Gospel according to Jim Wallis. Now, to anyone who has even skimmed *What Would Jesus Deconstruct?*, that must seem like an indefensible claim. But let me take a shot at defending it.

It seems to me that Caputo's project—which in an important sense stands within a prophetic tradition of critique—operates on the basis of a distinction taken up from Derrida: a careful (though admittedly hard-to-draw) distinction between what is "deconstructible" and what is not, between what can be deconstructed and what is "undeconstructible." And it is the undeconstructible which calls out for a critique of the deconstructible. This is not simply a demolition project, but a de-*con*-struction—

---

59. See, for instance, Tony Jones's engagements with Caputo in Jones, *The New Christians*.

60. See my "Series Editor's Foreword" to Caputo, *What Would Jesus Deconstruct?*, 15–17.

The Logic of Incarnation: Towards a Catholic Postmodernism

a dismantling of harmful, oppressive and unjust structures with a view to building more peaceful, just structures that are more conducive to human flourishing. For instance, for Derrida this distinction between the deconstructible and the undeconstructible maps onto the distinction between "law" and "justice": as a contingent and historical institution of human making (that is, the fruit of *culture*), law is by its very (human) nature subject to deconstruction. Its particularity and finitude can't help but be violent, exclusionary and unjust. As something that has been constructed, it is also thereby subject to de-con-struction (with a view to *re*-building). Thus law is distinguished from *justice* which is undeconstructible precisely because it has not been constructed: it remains *to come*. It's what law and legal institutions should be after. So when we deconstruct the law and its institutions, we do so with a view to justice, haunted by justice, *called* by justice.

In *What Would Jesus Deconstruct?*, Caputo puts this distinction to work on different quarry, drawing an analogous distinction between "the church"—which is very much deconstructible and well *deserves* deconstruction—and "the kingdom"—which is undeconstructible and which calls us to the deconstruction of the church for the sake of the kingdom.[61] The church's 'man-made' traditions, laws, and rules are so much deconstructible chaff that needs to be winnowed in order to preserve the kernel of Jesus' undeconstructible kingdom message of faith, hope, love, and peace. With Nietzschean echoes (and very much in the spirit of Nietzsche's friend, the theologian Franz Overbeck), Caputo also suggests that such a deconstruction of the church for the sake of the kingdom comes down to the task of sorting out the "human all too human" from the "divine": later (Pauline) accretions regarding sexual ethics or the institution of an episcopacy are "human" elements that deserve deconstruction, while Jesus' call to nonviolence and to tend to the poor are taken to be "divine" undeconstructibles. Deconstruction is "good news" for the church insofar as it helps us sort out the two.

I'd like to push back on this thesis a bit. First, very briefly, this is a particularly odd sort of distinction to invoke in the name of deconstruction which, from its earliest days, campaigned against unstable binaries.[62]

---

61. At times the distinction also feels like it plays out as a distinction between Jesus (undeconstructible) and Paul (very much deconstructible), echoing folks like John Dominic Crossan. Or a distinction between the Jesus' Gospel and "the Bible."

62. Granted, I think this is a problem internal to the Derridean corpus. While on the one hand I have argued for a fundamental continuity between the "early" and "later"

PART ONE: CRITIQUING POSTMODERNISM

To what extent does such a vision of the kingdom function as an "original supplement?" How or why is this kingdom not akin to Rousseau's dream of an original speech (so roundly criticized by Derrida in *Of Grammatology*)? What are the prospects for articulating the supposedly impossible and undeconstructible Gospel without immediately falling back into the mire of deconstructibility? And if such a Gospel eludes articulation, then are we not back to a transcendental signified (again, the subject of sustained critique in *Of Grammatology*)? While I don't have space to do so here, it would be interesting to take Caputo's *What Would Jesus Deconstruct?*, drop it in as a replacement to Rousseau's *Origin of Language*, and then undertake the same sort of deconstructive critique to which Rousseau's *Essay* was subject in *Of Grammatology*. Indeed, it would be interesting to take Derrida's own "Force of Law" (clearly a key text for Caputo's project) and subject it to the same kind of careful critique to which Derrida subjected Rousseau in 1967. Reading early Derrida against later Derrida, noting the instabilities and internal dissension within his corpus, is a way of being faithful to Derrida's deconstruction. Subjecting Caputo's church/kingdom distinction to the same deconstructive critique might also be more faithful to *l'esprit de deconstruction* than maintaining it.

Second, while justice and the kingdom are taken to be both impossible and undeconstructible, certain folks seem to have a corner on just what the undeconstructible looks like (or at least what it's *not*). This usually turns out pretty similar to whatever the Democratic party is currently peddling such that what we get in the name of an indestructible Gospel doesn't really sound all that different from the kingdoms envisioned by John Rawls or Nancy Pelosi. Jesus, it turns out, is a good liberal. And I don't mean that just as an epithet hurled by conservatives against what they don't like or what threatens their hold on the status quo. I mean that in quite a technical, philosophical sense: Jesus's Gospel turns out to be a version of liberalism insofar as it is characterized by just the kind of *laissez faire* individualism which makes religion a (still) largely private, individual affair (was anyone more liberal than Kierkegaard?). Apart from a stated predilection for higher taxes (at least in theory[63]), it seems

---

Derrida, against claims of some sort of Heidegger-like *Kehre* in his thought (see LT), I have also argued that there are important ways that the early Derrida deconstructs just these sorts of distinctions evoked by Derrida in the 1990s. See, for example, Smith, "A Principle of Incarnation."

63. Rarely do I hear deconstructive calls for taxation on the order of, say, Canada's graduated taxation scheme. And even more rarely does this deconstructive Gospel

The Logic of Incarnation: Towards a Catholic Postmodernism

generally concerned to guard the individual from any interference from either the state *or* the church. The deconstructed church turns out to be a church that desperately wants you to *voluntarily* care for the widow, the orphan and the stranger, but promises not to interfere with your body or to press you about your voluntary almsgiving. In short, this vision of the so-called kingdom sure feels a lot like Locke or Rousseau, beginning from a (still) atomistic conception of community where the basic unit is the individual; the church (or any other community) is at best a collection of consenting adults.[64] That sounds like a solidly *modern* gospel to me. (Indeed, just where does this deconstructive gospel ever disagree with the Declaration of Independence?) What's never entertained here is the possibility that Jesus' Gospel actually articulates a fundamentally communitarian and anti-liberal conception of persons and community, where the "body" (1 Cor 12) precedes and takes precedence over the individual, and where the community specifies the shape of the good life rather than leaving it up to the whims of individual pursuits of life, liberty, and happiness. Wouldn't *that* be a more radical critique of modernity? So as Stanley Hauerwas sometimes quips, the Gospel-driven church might be just the place that requires you to bring your 1040 tax return to the deacons rather than leaving your giving up to your own private, voluntary discretion. The Gospel of Jesus and the kingdom he announces looks more like rigors (and economics) of a Cistercian abbey (which ain't liberal!) rather than the gathering of some do-gooder "voluntary" society like MoveOn.org, where everybody pulls up in their Saabs demanding "justice now!," slices off a donation from their six-figure salary, then retreats in self-congratulatory glee to their Marin County mansions to sip Bordeaux and congratulate themselves on not being Republicans.

---

actually entertain the sort of socialism and abandonment of private property that was the practice of the early church (Acts 2:44–45, 4:32—5:11). In this respect, downright Victorian voices like John Ruskin and F.D. Maurice are more radical than much that traffics under the banner of "postmodern" religion.

64. Here I would commend Charles Taylor's account of the shift effected by Locke, Grotius and Hobbes which bequeathed to us the "modern social imaginary" (in *A Secular Age*, Part I). Methinks the "deconstructive gospel" can remain very comfortable within the modern social imaginary, whereas I'm suggesting that Jesus' Gospel, taken up by the Catholic tradition, runs counter to the modern social imaginary not only in the particulars of what it envisions as "the good life," but in how it conceives the very nature of freedom and community.

Finally, and most importantly, I want to suggest that Catholic orthodoxy actually makes a more radical affirmation of deconstructibility than Caputo's Derridean Jesus. Let me put it this way: Catholic orthodoxy affirms not only the desconstructibility of the church, it even affirms the deconstructibility of *the kingdom*! According to orthodox eschatology not only is the church contingent, particular, and constructed, so too is the coming kingdom.[65] "Kingdom come" is characterized by the same contingency, particularity and finitude. The deconstruction of injustice, including the reform of the church, is not driven by some dream of an impossible, undeconstructible kingdom, but in the light of a particular and still-deconstructible vision of justice.

And here's the crucial difference: the Trinitarian God of Catholic faith is not scared off by contingency, particularity or deconstructibility. Unlike the Wholly Other of the Derridean Gospel, the Incarnate God exhibits no allergy to the deconstructible. Indeed, this is the very distinctive logic of incarnation: God does not call for the deconstruction and dismantling of the deconstructible on the basis of or with a view to some undeconstructible and impossible kingdom; rather, God condescends *to inhabit the deconstructible*. If we want to ask ourselves what Jesus would do, we might consider what Jesus *did*. The Incarnation is the mad story of the undeconstructible[66] God who did not consider undeconstructibility as something to be grasped, nor did he despise deconstructibility, but rather taking the "human, all too human form" of a servant, he humbled himself to the point of inhabiting the very deconstructible structures of human law and culture—even to the point of suffering death at the hands of these institutions. But he did so *not* with a view to eviscerating the deconstructible, but rather to rightly ordering[67] it such that the contingent, particularity of this deconstructible creation might reach its proper *telos* (a loose paraphrase of Philippians 2:5–11). It's not "deconstructibility"

---

65. The other crucial difference between a Derridean gospel and the Catholic tradition is precisely the Catholic affirmation of eschatology as such (viz., that a particular instantiation of the kingdom is coming *and will arrive*) whereas the Derridean kingdom is always and only *to come* and will never arrive. Indeed, for Derrida, any arrival would only be the arrival of a new regime of injustice. But I can't address this difference here.

66. I take this to be a rough and acceptable translation of Anselm.

67. I mean to allude here to Augustine's notion of the "right order of love," particularly as articulated in *City of God* where the discussion is most germane to our context here.

The Logic of Incarnation: Towards a Catholic Postmodernism

that's the problem; it is the particular, wrongly-ordered configurations of the deconstructible that are at issue.

The scandal of Catholic ecclesiology is that this logic of incarnation then extends to an *institution*, the church Catholic, which is now configured as the body of which Christ is the head. The same Spirit that inhabited and empowered the incarnate Jesus (e.g., Luke 4:1, 14, 18) is given to the ecclesial community (Acts 1:8). This continues the logic of incarnation: the undeconstructible God continues to condescend and inhabit the very deconstructible institution that is the Church. Far from being infallible or perfect, nonetheless the institution is an extension of this logic and bears within it all the resources it needs to make sense of its own failures. Indeed, two of its most significant seasons (Advent and Lent) are seasons of penitence; it gathers as a community weekly to confess its failures (when was the last time the Democrats got together to do that?!). But in contrast to the logic of purity that seems to motivate the Derridean critique of deconstructibility as itself a problem, the logic of incarnation testifies to a God who inhabits, affirms, and takes up all the messiness of a deconstructible institution. The Catholic affirmation of the institutional church is rooted in this logic of incarnation which is a continuing testimony of what Jesus *did*. This logic—that embraces the scandal of particularity and contingency—is, I'm suggesting, a more persistent postmodernism, indeed a *Catholic* postmodernism.

WORKS CITED

Benson, Bruce Ellis. *Graven Ideologies: Nietzsche, Derrida, and Marion on Modern Idolatry*. Downers Grove, IL: InterVarsity, 2002.

———. *Pious Nietzsche: Decadence and Dionysian Faith*. Bloomington, IN: Indiana University Press, 2007.

Bourdieu, Pierre. *The Logic of Practice*. Translated by Richard Nice. Stanford: Stanford University Press, 1990.

Caputo, John D. *Against Ethics*. Bloomington: Indiana University Press, 1993.

———. *Demythologizing Heidegger*. Bloomington: Indiana University Press, 1993.

———. "Hermeneutics and Faith: A Response to Professor Olthuis," *Christian Scholars' Review* 20 (1991) 164–70.

———. *More Radical Hermeneutics*. Bloomington: Indiana University Press, 2000.

———. *On Religion*. New York: Routledge, 2001.

———. *Radical Hermeneutics*. Bloomington: Indiana University Press, 1987.

———. *The Prayers and Tears of Jacques Derrida*. Bloomington: Indiana University Press, 1997.

———. *What Would Jesus Deconstruct?: The Good News of Postmodernism for the Church*. Church and Postmodern Culture Series. Grand Rapids: Baker Academic, 2007.

PART ONE: Critiquing Postmodernism

Cavanaugh, William. "A Fire Strong Enough to Consume the House: The Wars of Religion and the Rise of the State," *Modern Theology* 11 (1995) 397–420.
Derrida, Jacques. *Of Hospitality*. Translated by Rachel Bowlby. Stanford: Stanford University Press, 2000.
———. *On Cosmopolitanism and Forgiveness*. London: Routledge, 2001.
———. *Specters of Marx: The State of the Debt, the Work of Mourning, and the New International*. Translated by Peggy Kamuf. New York: Routledge, 1994.
———. *The Politics of Friendship*. Translated by George Collins. London: Verso, 1997.
de Vries, Hent. *Religion and Violence: Philosophical Perspectives from Kant to Derrida*. Baltimore: Johns Hopkins University Press, 2002.
Goicoechea, David. *Zarathustra's Love Beyond Wisdom*. Binghamton, NY: Global Academic, 2002.
Heidegger, Martin. *Ontologie (Hermeneutik der Faktizität)*. Gesamtausgabe 63. Edited by Käte Bröcker-Oltmanns. Frankfurt: Klostermann, 1988.
House, Vaden. *Without God or His Doubles: Realism, Relativism, and Rorty*. Leiden: Brill, 1994.
Hovey, Craig. *Nietzsche and Theology*. Philosophy and Theology. London: T. & T. Clark, 2008.
Jones, Tony. *The New Christians: Dispatches from the Emergent Frontier*. San Francisco: Jossey-Bass, 2008.
Kierkegaard, Søren. *Philosophical Fragments*. Translated by Howard V. Hong and Edna H. Hong. Princeton, NJ: Princeton University Press, 1985.
Lilla, Mark. *The Stillborn God: Religion, Politics, and the Modern West*. New York: Knopf, 2008.
Marion, Jean-Luc. *Being Given: Toward a Phenomenology of Givenness*. Translated by Jeffrey Kosky. Stanford: Stanford University Press, 2002.
———. *God Without Being: Hors-Texte*. Translated by Thomas A. Carlson. Chicago: University of Chicago Press, 1991.
Milbank, John. *Being Reconciled: Ontology and Pardon*. London: Routledge, 2003.
———. *The Word Made Strange: Theology, Language, Culture*. Oxford: Blackwell, 1997.
———. *Theology and Social Theory: Beyond Secular Reason*. Oxford: Blackwell, 1990.
Olthuis, James H. "A Cold and Comfortless Hermeneutic or a Warm and Trembling Hermeneutic?: A Conversation with John D. Caputo." *Christian Scholars' Review* 19 (1990) 345–62.
———. "Undecidability and the Impossibility of Faith: Continuing the Conversation with Professor Caputo." *Christian Scholars' Review* 20 (1991) 171–73.
Olthuis, James H., editor. *Religion With/out Religion: The Prayers and Tears of John D. Caputo*. London: Routledge, 2001.
Ruskin, John. "The Nature of the Gothic." In *The Stones of Venice*, edited by J.G. Links, 157–190. New York: Farrar, Straus & Giroux, 1960. Fist published 1898 by George Allen.
Smith, James K. A. "A Principle of Incarnation in Derrida's (*Theologische?*) *Jugendschriften*," *Modern Theology* 18 (2002) 217–30.
———. "Between Athens and Jerusalem, Freiburg and Rome: John Caputo as Christian Philosopher," *Paradigms* 10 (1995) 19–23.
———. "Determined Violence: Derrida's Structural Religion," *The Journal of Religion* 78.2 (April 1998) 197–212.

The Logic of Incarnation: Towards a Catholic Postmodernism

———. "Is Deconstruction an Augustinian Science?: Augustine, Derrida, and Caputo on the Commitments of Philosophy." In *Religion With/out Religion: The Prayers and Tears of John D. Caputo*, edited by James H. Olthuis, 50–61. London: Routledge, 2001.

———. "Re-Kanting Postmodernism?: Derrida's Religion Within the Limits of Reason Alone," *Faith and Philosophy* 17 (2000) 558–71.

———. "The Last Prophet of Leviathan," *Perspectives* (April 2008).

Taylor, Charles. *A Secular Age*. Cambridge, MA: Harvard University Press, 2007.

Westphal, Merold. *Suspicion and Faith: The Religious Uses of Modern Atheism*. Grand Rapids: Eerdmans, 1993.

Williams, Stephen N. *The Shadow of the Antichrist: Nietzsche's Critique of Christianity*. Grand Rapids: Baker Academic, 2006.

Yoshida, Kei. "Defending Scientific Study of the Social: Against Clifford Geertz (and His Critics)." *Philosophy of the Social Sciences* 37 (2007) 290–300.

PART TWO

Receiving the (Postmodern) Tradition

2

Determined to Reveal

Determination and Revelation in Derrida

Neal DeRoo

I**N** *JACQUES DERRIDA: LIVE Theory*, James K. A. Smith gives a particular account of Derrida, one that uses the theme of alterity (the Other) to show a fundamental continuity between the work of "early" Derrida and that of the "late" Derrida. What we get as a result of this (perhaps not universally popular[1]) focus is a picture of a Derrida who is, from the beginning, determined to reveal the otherness inherent in philosophy and in philosophical texts.

This focus on alterity yields a Derrida who is fundamentally ethical, and leads Derrida to a compliance, perhaps even a fascination, with religion (LT, 66). This fascination, in turn, yields a rich tapestry of Derridean texts on religion, and a burgeoning field of commentators on those texts. Smith's voice, somewhat muted in *Live Theory*, but with a bit more volume in *Who's Afraid of Postmodernism?*,[2] is among the chorus of those who criticize Derrida's views on religion, and specifically his notion of a "religion without religion," or a "messianicity without messianism."[3] The

---

1. To be introduced to a counterpoint, see Haddad, review of *Jacques Derrida: Live Theory*.

2. While the 2nd chapter details Derrida's positive contributions to religion, and specifically to a renewed notion of (a postmodern) Christianity, the last chapter reveals more of Smith's critique (cf. especially pp. 116–27).

3. Other members of this "chorus" include (cf. LT, 148n231): Terry Eagleton, Graham Ward, and John Milbank. Smith discusses this objection further in IRO, 240–43.

critique, at its heart, claims that, on Derrida's view, religion, thought of as "messianicity" (more on this in a moment), is only an empty concept, all real meaning and worth having been taken out of it in the name of some kind of "universalism."[4] The argument goes something like this: Derrida, afraid of excluding any Other, prescribes that any non-violent religious confession must be so abstract, so universal (so no one gets left out!), that it denies the possibility of a peaceful and determinate religious confession. In other words, by wanting to make sure that no one gets left out, there is nothing special left for anyone who is "in"—Derrida's religion without religion is too indeterminate to be meaningful.

In this paper, I would like to question this critique on two grounds: first, that of Derrida's determination to reveal the Other; and second, on the possibility that Derrida's "indeterminate" messianicity might have more to say, might mean more, than one would think. To do this, I will begin by briefly outlining Derrida's position on this and highlighting Smith's critique. Next, I will seek to pose my question(s) to this critique, and see whether the critique has the capacity to answer these questions. In doing so, I will put forward a few hypotheses that suggest an alternate way of understanding Derrida's "religion without religion." Finally, I will end by spelling out exactly what is at stake in this debate—why we should care, and how it might affect our taking Derrida to church.

RELIGION WITHOUT RELIGION, MESSIANICITY WITHOUT MESSIANISM?

Derrida's paradoxical phrase, "religion without religion," has been the source of much controversy over the years. Its meaning proves to be as elusive as the logic that undergirds it. The easiest way, perhaps, to get a glimpse at what it might mean is to look at the related notions of messianicity and messianism, as "religion without religion" is often thought to be synonymous with "messianicity without messianism."

The notion of the messianic plays a central role in the later work of Derrida (though Smith has done an excellent job in *Live Theory* of showing its importance in the earlier work as well). The messianic is Derrida's word for the idea of the *à-venir*, the to-come. It is, in other words, a sort

---

4. Cf. WAP, 121n13: "It must be noted that Derrida and Caputo rule out a priori any possibility of a particular, determinate revelation . . . The religion-without-religion paradigm seems to deny the very *possibility* of revelation."

Determined to Reveal: Determination and Revelation in Derrida

of catchphrase (though I'm sure he would not like to hear it called that) for the anticipation of the coming of something else, something Other. Derrida sees this idea of waiting for something to come epitomized in the Jewish theme of waiting for the Messiah. In its structural element, that is, as a "pure" waiting for the to-come (of I know not what), Derrida characterizes this as "messianicity." In its more narrowly defined moments, that is, when concretized or particularized in a particular way—when I know *what* I am waiting for—I have set the structure of messianicity into a particular mold, a (concrete) messianism.[5] It is precisely the rigidity and hardness of some of this "concrete" that Derrida is wary of.

The question of a "religion without religion," then, seems to come quite quickly to a question of determination: how determinate can/ought religions be, while still remaining peaceful religions? It is around this question, largely, that Smith levels his critique of Derrida on religion. The critique is nuanced, and has many different levels, not all of which I will be adequately able to deal with here. Instead, I will focus on two levels of the critique. On one level, the critique sees in Derrida's "religion without religion" a challenge to determination (context, boundedness) *qua* determination. On this level, Derrida's religion without religion is seen as a challenge to finitude as such, and hence to creatureliness, because, if being determinate is problematic, the ideal or model must be that which is not determinate, that is, that which has no boundaries, no limits, no context; in other words, the infinite. If the infinite is the model, though, then being a creature, and hence, by necessity, being finite, would seem to be a problem (indeed, this level of the critique reads Derrida's problems with determinacy as being just this problem with finitude).[6] This facet of the critique suggests that Derrida's problem with the messianisms is that they are violent, but this really just means that they are finite, violence and finitude being equal for Derrida.[7]

The critique of Derrida's views on religion also functions at another level, however. At this level, rather than being a critique of finitude, Derrida's religion without religion takes on the question of determination more narrowly defined: here, a concrete messianism, a determinate and

---

5. Cf. Caputo, *The Prayers and Tears of Jacques Derrida*, §§ 9–11.

6. This level of the critique is given a much more in-depth reading in FI and in Smith's earlier contribution to this book.

7. This seems to be the position of John Milbank in *Theology and Social Theory: Beyond Secular Reason*.

definite religious tradition, is construed as violent because it necessarily creates an inside and an outside group, and this is, in itself, violent. The argument seems to go something like this: leaving people out of a group is violent; being determinate necessarily leaves people out (by creating an inside and an outside); hence, being determinate is necessarily violent. This level of the critique, related to the one outlined above, but with slightly more modest claims, seems to suggest that every community, by the mere fact of being a community, is violent, and therefore bad.[8] Here, determination, giving boundaries, is construed as necessarily repressive, and this repression is what Derrida objects too.

Religion without religion, then, seems, according to certain critics, to be at odds with any idea of determination, of setting boundaries, rules, or limits. Messianicity seems at odds with any and all messianisms.

QUESTIONING THE CRITIQUE

As stated earlier, I would now like to question this critique on two different grounds. First, I would like to discuss the critique in light of some of Derrida's other, less explicitly religious, writings, keeping in mind the focus on alterity suggested by Smith; then, I would like to question the nature of the "indeterminacy" of religion without religion, and ask whether its being indeterminate really must mean that it is empty.

Questions from other Derridean texts

We have noted at least two different levels of the critique of religion without religion. I would like to question each of these levels by juxtapos-

---

8. It strikes me as implausible, if not impossible, to argue that Derrida finds violence to be not particularly bad or troubling. Derrida seems quite clearly, time and again, to come down on the side of reducing violence; of eliminating it, where possible, and reducing it, where elimination is not an option. Indeed, his focus on alterity and the Other, much esteemed by Smith in LT, would not seem to make sense if Derrida felt that the violence being done to the other was ethically neutral: neither good nor bad. While Derrida does, at times, seem to speak this way of violence (for example, in certain parts of VM), the contexts of these passages must be noted to prevent confusion and misperceptions: the violence that necessarily occurs between the self and the other is, in Derrida's words, a "preethical violence" that is also, and equally, "nonviolent" (VM, 128–29). The notion of "violence" that is at work in this context, then, is one that is not the same as the ethical violence related to the exclusion of the Other. Without these "proof texts," I think it becomes very difficult, if not impossible, to plausibly argue that Derrida is not opposed to violence.

Determined to Reveal: Determination and Revelation in Derrida

ing them to other statements of Derrida. What I hope to get out of this initial questioning is the possibility of reading religion without religion otherwise, in a way one that, perhaps, does not evidence the allergy to the determinate that the critique of Smith et al. finds there. As such, this is more of a questioning of the critique, a tentative feel, than it is an outright objection.

The first aspect or level of the critique outlined above treats religion without religion as a critique of finitude qua finitude. But why we should equate finitude with violence, as the critique seems to, is not immediately clear to me. Does not Derrida give statements and arguments in favor of finitude, embodiment, etc., against the notions of the Ideal, the Abstract, etc.? For example, Smith notes that the Other, for Derrida, is not some abstract notion, but only takes place in concrete, that is, determinate situations, such as "choosing our vacations" (GD, 69) or "feeding our cats " (GD, 71; LT, 84). Similarly, justice and hospitality do not remain abstract issues, but are translated (as best as possible) into particular instances of ethical action, for example, in the cities of refuge (LT, 70). These passages seem, at least, to suggest that accusing Derrida of being against determination or particularization per se is a difficult notion, in light of some of Derrida's other texts.

Now, it is some of these very passages that I am now citing that Smith, and others who share his critique of religion without religion, use in favor of their own position. Rather than affirming the goodness of particularization and determination, they argue, these passages show that Derrida thinks that making things particular in a concrete situation is a *loss*, a denigration, compared to the empty universality of abstract notions of Justice, of Ethics, etc. Indeed, there is something to be said for this reading of the passages in question, as Derrida seems to claim, for example, that feeding our own cat is never enough—we remain responsible for all the hungry cats in the world (GD, 71). But Derrida also says, immediately following this, that "we also do our duty by behaving thus" (GD, 71), that is, by choosing particular cats to feed, at the expense of others. He also claims that others are represented by singularities (GD, 71), not by abstract ideas of Otherness. One could suggest, then, that Derrida does not have a problem with particularization, but merely with attempts to justify how we particularize.[9] Given that all people are equally human, equally

---

9. This leads inevitably to hermeneutic questions, and whether hermeneutics is operative in Derrida, or whether hermeneutics is even possible for Derrida. When prop-

PART TWO: Receiving the (Postmodern) Tradition

Other, and therefore equally deserving of my ethical respect, how can we possibly justify the fact that we save some and not others? Derrida seems to claim that we cannot fully justify this decision, though we must make it (and not just out of *necessity*, because we are finite, but out of *responsibility*, because we are ethical; cf. GD, 70–71). The issue here seems to be not determination (or lack thereof) but decidability (or lack thereof): it is not fully decided (for us) whom we must help—there is no computer program or set of rules that can justify our helping one person and not another—so the decision of who we help is up to us. This is not indetermination, but undecidability. Could there be some deeper link between these two concepts, for Derrida? Could such a deeper link, perhaps, provide us a window into his religion without religion? We will return to this question in a moment.

The second level of the critique outlined above is less ambitious than the first. Rather than reading religion without religion as a critique of finitude, it reads it only as a critique of forming communities, or of setting boundaries (this is, of course, not entirely separable from the issue of finitude). On this reading, forming boundaries or establishing communities is inherently repressive. But again, I must raise some questions. Is Derrida not adamant that determination is *not* always repressive? As Smith points out, Derrida is quick to reject any naive association between determining rules and laws, on the one hand, and being repressive, on the other (LT, 63; Linc, 131–32). Indeed, the police, those who enforce the rules, are explicitly identified as not always repressive (Linc, 132). Derrida states that

---

erly understood, Derrida on hermeneutics might help to support a positive notion of determination: he seems to suggest (e.g., in FL), that we have a certain hermeneutical responsibility, that we must always be analyzing why we make the particular choices we make. Indeed, the work of deconstruction seems to be precisely hermeneutic, in this sense, but a hermeneutics that is always a response to, and animated by, a primordial call (of the Other, of Justice, etc.). That Derrida does not give us a hermeneutic rule book is not because he is not interested in hermeneutics, but because every situation, every *event*, requires its own particular hermeneutic: hermeneutics is essentially contextual, and, hence, essentially particular. To provide a hermeneutic rulebook, an universalizable or abstractable set of propositions that would help us know what to do in every situation, would defeat the purpose of hermeneutics, for two reasons: 1) because it would fail to recognize the unique particularity of each event—such a rulebook would compromise particularlity, and hence otherness; 2) even if one had such a rulebook, one would have to know how to apply it to particular situations—decide which situations called for which rule, choose to apply that rule to that situation, etc. In fact, the work of deconstruction seems to be always analyzing these "rulebooks" to make them more just (cf. Derrida's discussion of law as opposed to Justice in FL).

Determined to Reveal: Determination and Revelation in Derrida

the police, or something analogous to them, are not only not repressive, but are necessary to reading (LT, 64; Linc, 135), in that they help to fix the context in which any reading can possibly make sense. Given that there is nothing outside of context,[10] fixing or determining context is necessary to any use and understanding of language. Wouldn't this suggest, therefore, that far from being repressive and violent, some type of determination— some type of fixing of boundaries, of rules, of context—is a necessary part of any and all use of language?

Of course, its being necessary does not preclude its also being violent. Some will suggest that this thinking—that violence itself is necessary—is what makes Derrida an "ontologist of violence."[11] But why shouldn't we read Derrida's insistence that determinations of context are not repressive or politically suspect as suggesting, not that he is okay with violence, but that, perhaps, determining context, setting boundaries, is not, in and of itself, violent? Now, that it *can* be violent is possible, and that, I think, no one would deny. But again, there seems to be as much, or more, in Derrida's corpus, and in Smith's presentation of it, to suggest that he does not think fixing or determining boundaries (even of communities—cf. LT, 62–64) is inherently violent as there is to suggest that he thinks that it is inherently violent. Given this counter-balancing, why should we think that religion without religion preaches the violence and repressiveness of determination, of forming communities? Is there not another theory that could help us reconcile these two, seemingly competing, claims?

Indeterminacy and the "Emptiness" of Messianicity

The two claims under discussion both seem to arise from Derrida's corpus. On the one hand, religion without religion seems to suggest that Derrida is at odds with, or perhaps even opposed to, any notion of determination whatsoever: determination is a repression of the other and, given Derrida's focus on alterity, he cannot possibly support that. On the other hand, Derrida's discussions of language and ethics, specifically his notions of determining context for reading, and the importance attributed to such seemingly banal, everyday, determinate things as choosing a vacation or

---

10. Smith gives an excellent account of what the infamous Derridean phrase, "there is nothing outside the text" [*il n' y a pas d'hors-texte*] does (and does not) mean, in WAP, 31–42.

11. Cf. Milbank, *Theology and Social Theory*.

feeding the cat, seem to suggest that determination—setting boundaries, establishing contexts, etc.—has a very positive role to play in his philosophy. The best place, it would seem, to begin resolving this tension would be to look at what is meant by determination, and by extension, what is meant by indetermination or indeterminacy. What if Derrida's "indeterminate" religion without religion is not, in fact, necessarily at odds with determination?

We now come to the portion of the essay where I want to provide a few hypotheses regarding religion without religion.[12] I will do my best to justify them, or to at least make them plausible, though by no means do I hope to fully argue my case for them.

The first of my hypotheses, then, is that there is some connection between determination, as Derrida conceives of it, and decidability. When Derrida speaks against determination,[13] he seems to have in mind some kind of hard and rigid determinism in which *all things* are accounted for, and there is no room left for choice or decision.[14] This would be akin to what he elsewhere characterizes as the decidable, which is like a computer program that, with enough information, would provide what we must do in any and every given situation, free of charge, without any ethical fear and trembling required.[15] Derrida's critique of the determinacy of the concrete messianisms, then, would be nothing more than a critique of attempts to downgrade religion from a living, breathing, af-

12. I should note, too, that I do not mean to take "religion without religion" as an existing messianism, that is, as a proposed system for religious belief. Rather, as I hope to make clear, I think it points out only a *structure* of human existence. As a structure, it can be determined in varying ways, but these determinations are never the same thing as the structure qua structure.

13. And especially when Caputo speaks of it (cf. *Prayers and Tears*, *On Religion*, and *The Weakness of God*). Indeed, I often worry that when Milbank and Ward, especially, critique Derrida, the person they have in mind is actually Caputo, and they take the two as but two names for one (nihilistic) line of thought ("same nihilism, different pile," to paraphrase a popular phrase). I'm not sure that this is fair to Derrida. While I'm also not sure that they accurately represent Caputo, that is a project that must be taken up elsewhere.

14. Cf. discussion of the under-determination of contexts in Linc and *Margins of Philosophy*, and Smith's discussion of these in LT, 63.

15. It is this question of decidability v. undecidability that is at stake in Derrida's encounter with Geoffrey Bennington in *Jacques Derrida*, where Bennington tries to make of Derrida's thought a program ("Derridabase" being a take on the old computer programming code, "D-base"), while Derrida tries to keep this attempted programization open to something different, to a secret.

Determined to Reveal: Determination and Revelation in Derrida

fective spirituality into a lifeless set of rules and programs.[16] Given his praise of determination, of providing limits and boundaries to and for contexts, elsewhere, this could provide a possible, and, I think plausible, interpretation of his wariness of the concrete messianisms: it is not, e.g., Christianity, that he has the problem with, but a Christianity that has forgotten its ethical and eschatological core, and is happy to be little more than a wing of the Republican or Conservative party. If he finds this version of Christianity to be particularly ubiquitous, we should ask whether the fault there is his—or is ours, as Christians. Maybe, as Smith suggests in *Who's Afraid of Postmodernism?*, Christianity needs a bit of Derrida for the good of Christianity. Maybe it is time for the concrete messianisms to heed deconstruction's "prophetic" call.[17] At root, then, this hypothesis asks whether Derrida's word on the concrete religions ought to be the final or only word we hear from him on the question of determination and finitude.

If I have moved a bit quickly through the first of my hypotheses, it is because I would like to spend more time on the second. Here, I put forward the hypothesis that perhaps Derrida's indeterminate religion without religion, his messianicity, is not, in fact, empty and devoid of all particular content. By so doing, I seek to question whether Derrida doesn't, in fact, embrace community, rather than condemn it: does Derrida offer us something, with his religion without religion, that could provide the ground for a deeper ecclesiology, a more fundamental sense of who and what the church is?

At issue here is the question of how religion without religion relates to the concrete religions. Smith and Derrida discuss two possible ways of connection (LT, 112): one Levinasian, one Heideggerean. Levinas offers us the idea that a concrete, historical revelation, a concrete "religion," is a necessary precursor to anything like the messianic: without the concrete messianisms, we cannot understand the structure of messianicity. Heidegger, on the other hand, seems to take the opposite approach: we need some deep and primordial structure of messianicity or revealability as the condition of possibility for messianisms or concrete revelations.

---

16. Here, he would seem to be following Kierkegaard, who claimed to be doing something similar in his own work.

17. Derrida describes the work of deconstruction as "prophetic" in an interview entitled "Deconstruction and its Other," in Kearney, *States of Mind*, 156–76. For more on the idea of deconstruction as a prophetic call, cf. DeRoo, "Confluent Confessions."

PART TWO: RECEIVING THE (POSTMODERN) TRADITION

Each of these two suggestions has its inherent problems. On the one hand, to focus primarily on the messianisms, that is, on concrete revelations, is to beg the question of how we are able to receive that revelation: what in us makes us able to contact or connect with the Other as it reveals itself to us?[18] How am I able to understand the infinite other? Kierkegaard rightly notes that, if I have within myself the ability to recognize that other, than it is not really other, and I remain only within myself.[19] The ability to receive revelation, then, must be something I receive from elsewhere. While it suggests the importance of revelation to us, Levinas' view does not, in my opinion, do enough to emphasize the radicality of our nature as "gifted and called,"[20] it does not do enough to show that our very ability to *receive* revelation is itself a gift given from elsewhere.[21] On the other hand, to focus primarily on the capacity of reception, on "revealability" [*Offenbarkeit*] at the expense of revelation [*offenbarung*],[22] is to suggest, as already mentioned by Kierkegaard, that our ability to receive is something that we possess as an independent subject, as a monad who must receive something from elsewhere. An exclusive focus on the structure of revealability, then, leaves us with a picture of the monadic subject, and Smith has done an excellent job of showing, throughout *Live Theory*, that this notion of a self-present subject is precisely what Derrida has spent a career arguing against.

This brief discussion of the possible ways of relating the structure of messianicity to the determinate messianisms has set the stage for my next hypothesis. The hypothesis that I would like to put forward, following Smith (LT, 112), is to suggest that, perhaps, Derrida is no longer satisfied

18. Derrida illustrates in VM why we must be able to receive the revelation of the other, or in some way connect to the other, if the Other is to have any effect on us whatsoever.

19. Cf. Kierkegaard, *Philosophical Fragments*. I am greatly surprised that this work has made little, if any, headway into the Kierkegaard-Derrida debate. While all the attention goes to *Fear and Trembling* because Derrida deals with it more explicitly in *The Gift of Death*, it strikes me that *Philosophical Fragments* might, actually, prove to be a more fruitful avenue for discussion. Smith mentions *Philosophical Fragments*, though in a manner only tangentially (at best) related to what I am discussing here, in WAP, 27n19.

20. Cf. Olthuis, "Be(com)ing."

21. There are obvious affinities between what I am suggesting here and Marion's notion of the "interlocuted" [*interloqué*] subject; cf. Marion, "The Saturated Phenomenon," and Marion, *Being Given*.

22. Derrida offers a discussion of his relationship to the Heideggerean question of *offenbarkeit* v. *offenbarung* in FK, 46–47.

with this dilemma, with this alternative. Where Levinas seeks to find a primordial revelation, and Heidegger seeks a primordial condition of possibility of revelation, what I am suggesting here is that, perhaps, Derrida gives us something of a synthesis—or, better formulated, a co-reading, an inter-reading—of the two, with the idea that what is given in the primordial revelation is not some content, narrowly defined, but is, instead, a process, a structure, a capacity: revealability (in Heideggerean terms). What is primarily given is not something, or perhaps even someone, but what is primarily given is precisely the ability to receive (revelation).

If this hypothesis is true, then we can better understand why Derrida insists on a certain primacy of messianicity vis-à-vis the messianisms. Derrida seeks to promote this primal "messianicity," to hold out for it before or beyond the messianisms, not because he privileges the universal or the empty over the finite and the determined, but because he wants to emphasize our fundamental inter-relatedness with the Other (both God and other people, for *every other is wholly other*).[23] Messianicity, then, is not just religious, but also ethical—which is good, given that the "ethical is the religious"[24]—and this not because he conceives of religion as some type of universal respect for the dignity of humanity, but precisely because anything that would want to speak of receiving something from an infinite Other must first realize how this reception is possible, if one is to remain true to that Other. If religion without religion means something like the possibility of hospitality *before* a determinate historical revelation (of the Torah, or perhaps even of the Face of the Other), as Smith suggests (LT, 78), then this must be because Derrida thinks that this hospitality, this being "held hostage" by the other, means something like being structured by an alterity that is always already within me,[25] and that this is a constitutive part of every person, and hence is a condition of possibility for the reception of revelation. Without being structured or conditioned by the Other to be able to receive revelation, I would not be able to receive revelation. For this reason, religion, conceived of as relation with an infinite other, must be before religion, conceived of as the reception of a concrete historical revelation. But it is also true, simultaneously, that religion,

---

23. Cf. LT, 52, 80–84; and GD, 100–101, 109.

24. On the relationship between the ethical and the religious, see LT, 65–91 and GD.

25. For more on our fundamental inter-relatedness, see Derrida, *A Taste for the Secret*, 84: "The other is in me before me:... there is no 'I' that ethically makes room for the other, but rather an 'I' that is structured by the alterity within it"; cited at LT, 37.

PART TWO: RECEIVING THE (POSTMODERN) TRADITION

conceived of as relation with an infinite other, is possible only because of religion, conceived of as the reception of a revelation. Religion without religion cuts both ways: there must be a relation with an other that makes possible the reception of revelation, and hence must be conceivable without that reception, and there must be a reception of "revelation," albeit a revelation, not of a content but of a structure, that makes possible the relation to the other.

This reading, I think, can be supported by Derrida, and is even suggested by Smith's own reading of Derrida in LT and WAP. For example, as I already mentioned above, Derrida is nothing if not adamant about the fact that we are not self-present monads, fully enclosed within ourselves, but are always already (one of Smith's favorite phrases, at least as a teacher) open to the other, as Smith shows consistently throughout LT (e.g., in Derrida's readings of Husserl, Plato, and Rousseau). Alterity is not (only) exterior to us, but in some way makes us who we are as well. Also, the community's role in determining contexts (here, of reading texts, but could it not also apply to wider contexts, to the contexts which frame our lives?) is clearly explicated in LT (section 2.3.2). My hypothesis of messianicity as the revelation of revealability is little more, I think, than the radical application of the community's role in determining context.

THE IMPLICATIONS OF RELIGION WITHOUT RELIGION

I would like to end by briefly discussing the implications of this debate: why it matters and how it affects our taking Derrida "to church." This will not be a naive attempt to give "practical" weight to a largely "theoretical" endeavor (a distinction with which Derrida would no doubt disagree—LT, 114–15). Rather, I will be trying to draw out why, exactly, I found it important to disagree with Smith on this issue, when I agree with him on so much else in his presentation of Derrida, in both LT and WAP.

At some level, such discussions always have an air of fairness or charity to them: I object because I do not think Smith is being entirely fair to Derrida in his depiction of Derrida's work. But this is not all there is to it. At its core, I think, the important implications of this debate, as has already been suggested above, have to do with questions of ecclesiology, of theories of the church (*ekklesia*). Smith's reading of religion without religion misses, I think, an important aspect in which Derrida can be seen to agree with Smith's view of the postmodern church. By emphasizing the communal "giving" of my very capacity for receiving revelation, Derrida

Determined to Reveal: Determination and Revelation in Derrida

provides a theory, more explicitly outlined elsewhere,[26] of the fundamental way in which each of us is shaped by the community in which we are raised and in which we live. Realizing how fundamentally important the community is to all aspects of a person's character, including even their ability to receive revelation, should impact how the church sees itself, vis-à-vis its members. The church is not (only) a body made up of individual members, but is, more fundamentally, a body that helps to constitute its members, helps to make its members who they are. The church is not something that we can choose to join, but is a community in which we always already find ourselves committed (in multiple senses of the word).[27] As such, the church must be aware of its responsibilities as a "maker" of people.

Beyond this, though, or perhaps as an extension of this, the notion of religion without religion also has connotations for inter-religious dialogue. What is at issue in this debate, then, is the nature of how we can participate in this dialogue. If the critique of Smith and others is true, then religion without religion is little more than a radicalization of the relegation of religious beliefs to the private sphere.[28] If Smith et al. are right, religion without religion suggests that we can all agree that humanity has some "religious" structure inherent to it, but please leave the particular beliefs at home. This is a rather impoverished view of religion, in my opinion, and one that leaves us unable to use our most deeply held religious beliefs at the time when they are needed the most, i.e., when in discussion with other religious people. If religion without religion is, indeed, an empty concept, then it does little to help us preserve distinctive, determinate ways of being in the world, ways that are particular to each different religion (and to different sects within each religion, and different groups within each sect, etc.).

However, if my hypotheses prove correct, then I think religion without religion can become a powerful ally of precisely the kind of tra-

---

26. For example, in Derrida, *Adieu to Emmanuel Levinas*; see also DeRoo, "Confluent Confessions."

27. That is: 1) resolved to remain in a long-term relationship with; 2) placed somewhere for safekeeping or permanent preservation (i.e., committed to a hospital, or to prison); 3) something carried out or performed (e.g., a crime). Cf. *Oxford Advanced Learner's Dictionary*.

28. Derrida challenges the public/private distinction at several places (e.g., in *Glas* as Smith himself notes [LT, 58], and in FK).

PART TWO: RECEIVING THE (POSTMODERN) TRADITION

dition-rooted confessional living that Smith proposes in *Who's Afraid of Postmodernism?* (cf. WAP, 76–9, and 109–46), and can do so without giving up on a certain "universal" (Enlightenment?—cf. LT, 88–91) dream of peaceful inter-religious dialogue. Religion without religion, so conceived, suggests that our capacity to receive revelation is determined by the (determinate) community in which we live. This, in turn, suggests the possibility that God, understood as the ultimate Other, could provide different revelations to different people, depending on their capacity to receive that revelation. In other words, religion without religion, I think, offers the possibility of something like a universalism, without needing to sacrifice the particularity of the determinate revelations: in Derrida's words, a "universalizable culture of singularities" (FK, 56; cf. also LT, 90). My reception of God's revelation in the person of Jesus Christ is not called into question, is not radically relativized, by the fact that I was determined (conditioned) to receive revelation in a certain way. That I must be Christian to receive God's revelation is, perhaps, a fact of my particular determination, the particular boundaries and context I am in. This is a fact that I cannot change, anymore than I can change how and where I was raised. Nor is it something I must give up in order to understand a higher, more true, abstract revelation: there is no revelation outside of (con)text. There is no pure revelation, behind the particular revelations that we receive. That we receive them differently, due to context, is not a radically new idea. But if our very capacity to receive revelation is itself the first revelation, the first gift from God, then could we not wonder whether multiple revelations are part of God's plan?

That we must meet people where they are at is nothing new in the world of evangelism. Missionaries often adapt the Christian message to fit with certain already present aspects of the culture in which they minister. The notion that different religions might be God's attempt to do the same thing on a larger scale has often led to the idea that there is one true a-contextual revelation that is understood differently due to differing contexts, differing capacities to receive that revelation.[29] However, if these different capacities are themselves the first revelation of God, then could this not suggest that difference, even on this score, could be part of God's plan? We need not all be the same; in fact, God does not seem to want us

---

29. This leads to such patronizing notions as Rahner's "anonymous Christians," the idea that all good people in the world are really Christians, they just might not know it yet.

to be, or God would not have given us different capacities of revelation in the first place. Understanding our ability to receive revelation as itself a gift, a revelation, allows us to remain proud of, and in, our particular religious traditions, without having to de-value other religions thereby.[30] At least, it might. This is the last hypothesis that I will put forward.

CONCLUSION

In this essay, I have sought to re-examine the notion of religion without religion. In so doing, I have questioned the critique that reads religion without religion as devoid of content, instead suggesting that it supports the notion that the first (particular, determined) revelation is of a non-content: the ability to receive revelation. I have tried to suggest what implications this might have, on ecclesiology, on inter-religious dialogue, and perhaps even on evangelism. In so doing, I have sought to take seriously the picture of Derrida put forward by Smith in LT, a Derrida that is absolute determined (persistent) to reveal the Other. By taking this determined (persistent, but also particularized, that is, particularly Smith's view) Derrida seriously, I have questioned whether or not we could read Derrida as suggesting that the Other, too, is determined: determined (persistent) to reveal herself, the Other ensures that we are determined (given boundaries, context) in such a way as to receive her revelation. Because the Other is determined to reveal, we are determined, that we might be able to receive that revelation.[31]

---

30. It also begins to address a problem that would affect Smith's account of a radically orthodox Catholic postmodernism. If the Logic of Incarnation gives us a new way of acting in inter-religious dialogue, as the editors' introduction suggests, Smith's radical orthodoxy does not give us a *reason* for having inter-religious dialogue in the first place: as a Christian, why should I talk with Muslims, Hindus, and members of other religions? Do I speak with them to convert them? Do I use them to help me understand my own tradition? Both of these suggestions can be read as a failure to respect the difference and particularity of the other religious traditions, an attempt to reduce them to my own tradition. So why speak at all? What I have suggested above I believe begins to answer that question by suggesting that God provided a plethora of revelations, and hence there is something of God to be understood in each revelation. This neither devalues other revelations nor reduces them to my own

31. Research for this paper was done in large part due to support provided by the Social Sciences and Humanities Research Council of Canada (SSHRC), whose support is hereby gratefully acknowledged.

PART TWO: Receiving the (Postmodern) Tradition

WORKS CITED

Caputo, John D. *On Religion*. New York: Routledge, 2001.

———. *The Prayers and Tears of Jacques Derrida: Religion without Religion*. Bloomington, IN: Indiana University Press, 1997.

———. *The Weakness of God*. Bloomington, IN: Indiana University Press, 2006.

DeRoo, Neal. "Confluent Confessions: Deconstruction and/as Religious Confession." MA Thesis, Institute for Christian Studies, 2005.

Derrida, Jacques. *Adieu to Emmanuel Levinas*. Translated by Pascale-Anne Brault and Michael Naas. Stanford, CA: Stanford University Press, 1999.

———. *Glas*. Translated by John P. Leavey and R. Rand. Lincoln: University of Nebraska Press, 1986.

———. *Margins of Philosophy*. Translated by Alan Bass. Chicago: University of Chicago Press, 1985.

Derrida, Jacques and Geoffrey Bennington. *Jacques Derrida*. Translated by Geoffrey Bennington. Chicago: University of Chicago, 1993.

Derrida, Jacques and Maurizio Ferraris, *A Taste for the Secret*. Translated by Giocomo Donis. Cambridge: Polity, 2001.

Eagleton, Terry. *After Theory*. Cambridge, MA: MIT Press, 2003.

Haddad, Samir. Review of *Jacques Derrida: Live Theory*, by James K.A. Smith. *Notre Dame Press Review* (August 2006). Online: http://ndpr.nd.edu/review.cfm?id=7283.

Kearney, Richard. *States of Mind: Dialogues with Contemporary Thinkers*. New York: NYU Press, 1995.

Kierkegaard, Søren. *Fear and Trembling*. Kierkegaard's Writing 6. Translated by Edna H. Hong and Howard V. Hong. Princeton: Princeton University Press, 1983.

———. *Philosophical Fragments*. Kierkegaard's Writings 7. Translated by Edna H. Hong and Howard V. Hong. Princeton: Princeton University Press, 1985.

Janicaud, Dominique, Jean-François Courtine, Paul Ricoeur, Jean-Louis Chrétien, Jean-Luc Marion, and Michel Henry. *Phenomenology and the "Theological Turn."* New York: Fordham University Press, 2000.

Marion, Jean-Luc. *Being Given: Toward a Phenomenology of Givenness*. Translated by Jeffrey L. Kosky. Stanford, CA: Stanford University Press, 2002.

———. "The Saturated Phenomenon," translated by Thomas A. Carlson, in Dominique Janicaud et al., *Phenomenology and the "Theological Turn"*, 176–216. New York: Fordham University Press, 2000.

Milbank, John. *Theology and Social Theory: Beyond Secular Reason*. Oxford: Blackwell, 1990.

Olthuis, James H. "Be(com)ing: Humankind as Gift and Call." *Philosophia Reformata* 58 (1993) 153–72.

Ward, Graham. *True Religion*. Oxford: Blackwell, 2003.

3

On Universality and Christian Particularism in a Postmodern Trio

James K. A. Smith, Jacques Derrida, and Søren Kierkegaard

Leo Stan

How relevant is the Christian Church today, in an epoch conveniently labeled postmodern, but intrinsically torn apart by religious agnosticism, fierce fundamentalism, inflexible nationalistic traditionalisms, and politically correct cultural suspicions? James K. A. Smith attempts to answer this question audaciously and without resentment, anxiety, or reluctance. He does so by resisting the apocalyptic tone theologians or religious thinkers adopt when referring to the vicissitudes of Christianity's relation to modernity, secular politics, and epistemological relativism. Smith's ideas are both heedful of the other and emphatically shaped by Christian spirituality. Smith is also innovative enough to take Jacques Derrida, Michel Foucault, and Jean-François Lyotard to church, and persuades us that this is not such a bad idea, after all. In response, I plan to elaborate in a critical, though constructive, manner the way in which Derrida could interact with the Christian *ecclesia*. My analysis will be guided by the thought of Søren Kierkegaard, who inspired Derrida at some point, and whom Smith himself should find more significant for the spiritual regeneration he envisions.

Smith's *Live Theory* and *Who's Afraid of Postmodernism?* are traversed by a definite tension between catholicity (openness, generosity, otherness) and particularity (the revelation of Christ, communitarian identity, the beneficial reverence for marked socio-religious traditions and doctrines). The author pays equal attention to both, indeed within the confines of Christianity. The Derridean deconstructive apparatus becomes meaningful for Smith in his attempt to attain a well-rounded understanding of universality. Søren Kierkegaard and the biblical narrative of Abraham's sacrifice of Isaac enter the picture through Smith's genealogical discussion of Derrida's philosophical discussion of ethics and justice from *The Gift of Death*. Before approaching Smith's hermeneutical verdicts, I shall briefly thematize Derrida's idiosyncratic reading of Kierkegaard's *Fear and Trembling*. What I aim is to bring forward not the ineptitude of deconstruction, but rather its discrete *distortions* and arguable value for Smith's overall project of combining religious catholicity with Christian particularity. My thesis is that Derrida sacrifices Abraham's exceptional individuality on Kierkegaard's account by generalizing it in the interest of ethics and justice. In addition, I shall also hint at the ways in which Smith may discover in Kierkegaard an ancillary supporter, not only as a "proto-deconstructionist," but as a Christian (premodern) thinker, as well.

DERRIDA'S KIERKEGAARD

What primarily strikes us when studying the relationship between Derrida and Kierkegaard is how the former completely disregards the latter's explicitly Christian account of alterity. To begin, in *The Gift of Death* Derrida selects solely one book from Kierkegaard's enormous, complex, and Protean corpus. Second, while probably putting deconstruction to work, he completely brackets the context of *Fear and Trembling*[1] by means

---

1. For instance, we hear absolutely nothing about Kierkegaard's wish to undermine the rationalist Hegelianism that degraded the true spirit of religiosity. Moreover, no word is said about the pseudonymous author of *Fear and Trembling*, Johannes de Silentio, whose name explicitly resonates with the religious ineffable or secrecy that Derrida himself develops for his own goals. Third, in *The Gift of Death* we look in vain for anything related to Kierkegaard's reflections on aesthetics and visibility, which occupy almost one third of the book. Finally and most importantly, Derrida ignores the fact that *Fear and Trembling* is not Kierkegaard's last word on ethico-religious matters. In the *Postscript*, Kierkegaard has the pseudonymous author, Johannes Climacus, criticize what he calls the ethical ideality put forth in *Fear and Trembling*, while taking note of the absence of sinfulness from Silentio's meditations. Climacus argues here that Abraham is an *idealized* figure, the religious excellence of whom pales when considered from the vantage point of religiousness—or Christianity (Kierkegaard, *Concluding Unscientific Postscript*, 257–59, 261–62, 266–68, 500–501, 555–61).

of what I would term *amalgamation of planes*.² Whereas Derrida, who follows Levinas literally, considers ethics or responsibility the ultimate way to grant the other his or her singularity (LT, 71, 76–80), Kierkegaard assigns this function to religion only, which he equates with Christianity. Besides bypassing the threefold structure of existence, elaborated by Kierkegaard in such a pedantic and serpentine fashion, Derridean deconstruction is interested only in unearthing the ethics and justice hidden within the Kierkegaardian religiosity. Suggestively enough, this "archeological" endeavor is done by obliterating the monotheistic *transcendence* Kierkegaard has been so adamant about throughout his entire authorship. Moreover, deconstruction mixes the quite dissimilar meanings of the ethical itself put forward by Kierkegaard in *Either/Or* II (1843), *Concept of Anxiety* (1844), and especially, *Works of Love* (1847). To complicate things even further, we should remember that Kierkegaard operates with two categories of religiosity. These are taxonomically designated A and B, Kierkegaard's purpose being to differentiate between a creationist pantheism and the Christian soteriology, a dichotomy Derrida appears equally oblivious to.

Now, let us return to Derrida's generous student, James K. A. Smith, and see what exactly a deconstructive bracketing of *Fear and Trembling* consists of. As a "corrective to Levinas's hyperbole" (LT, 80),³ Smith's

---

2. Smith understands religion as "a non- and other-than-philosophical source of practices, habits, and thought," or as "the in-breaking of transcendence and [radical] alterity," which commands us "to consider every other wholly other" (LT, 75; comment in brackets mine). Even if Smith admits that for Derrida and Levinas, the borders between God as the wholly Other and human alterity are quite fluid, the implications of this remark are never thematized. Nevertheless, I think that, despite its affinities with this line of thinking (LT, 72), Smith's radical orthodoxy would be more congruent with Kierkegaard's Christianity than Levinas's (or Derrida's), purportedly Judaic, equation of God with "every other as every bit other." Regarding sinfulness, Smith mentions in passing Kierkegaard's *Philosophical Fragments* in tandem with the reflections of a 17th century author, John Owen. However, he does not initiate any discussion of the relevance of this doctrinal topic for a postmodern Christian church (WAP, 27n19).

3. Smith admits that Derrida's heterology is fundamentally informed by Levinas's distinctly Jewish account of alterity and that deconstruction itself has a Levinasian ring to it (LT, 76). Simultaneously, Derrida objects against the "ethical violence" issuing from the possibility that the self be fully absorbed by the obligation to the first other. Such engrossment can be interrupted by the advent of "the third" other who mediates the emergence of politics or the Levinasian notion of justice (LT, 77). Again, no mention is made by either Derrida or Smith about the category of "the third" in Kierkegaard, for whom the proper relation to human alterity is always triadic, as it vertically passes through God. See in this sense, Kierkegaard, *Works of Love*, 44–134.

PART TWO: Receiving the (Postmodern) Tradition

Kierkegaard constitutes Derrida's gateway to the incommensurability between knowledge and justice. In other words, Kierkegaard introduces Derrida to the aporia of human responsibility, namely that humans *must* decide and act against a perpetual irrevocable undecidability (LT, 80–2).[4] Why is Kierkegaard's Abraham a paragon of the core madness of responsibility, according to Derrida? Here, again, the latter brackets the authorial intention of *Fear and Trembling* and distils Abraham's response to the call of the absolute Other (God) into a *judicial anthropology*. That is to say, similarly to the august father of faith, *all* humans are subjected to an elementary, ultimately undeconstructible, justice which, in fact, goes against the normative universalism of ethics (LT, 83).[5] Smith thus realizes that "if it is the essence of responsibility to respond to the call of the Wholly Other ... then once we appreciate that *every other is wholly other* ... we can see that this Abrahamic situation of an infinite responsibility under the conditions of undecidability is, in fact, the situation of everyone. If every other is wholly other, we are all Abraham" (LT, 84; GD, 78). So, when exposed to deconstruction and a phenomenological epoché of the context, Søren helps Jacques articulate the axiom that the difference between the human and divine alterity is null (LT, 66)[6] or that "every other

---

4. In contradistinction to Levinas, Derrida finds ethics intrinsically dangerous because it proclaims justice as urgent, unavoidable, and ultimate, however, in full awareness that no one could ever gather enough information to be able to deliberate and act justly. In short, both "ethics and politics ... start with undecidability," and this renders every resolution sheer madness (LT, 82).

5. Here, Smith is not completely faithful to Derrida's linking of responsibility with both the universal and the singular. In *The Gift of Death* we are explicitly told that "responsibility ... demands on the one hand an accounting, a general answering-for-oneself with respect to the general and before the generality, hence the idea of substitution, and, on the other hand, uniqueness, absolute singularity, hence nonsubstitution, nonrepetition, silence, and secrecy" (GD, 61).

6. True enough, Derrida has astutely noted that, in prioritizing a radical type of otherness, Levinasian ethics "is no longer able to distinguish between the infinite alterity of God and that of every human" (GD, 84). However, is Derrida not liable to the same critique when stating that my neighbor and my beloved are "as inaccessible to me, as secret and transcendent as Jahweh"? (GD, 78; see also GD, 108–9). On the one hand, Derrida considers God "absolutely transcendent, hidden, and secret, not giving any reason he can share in exchange for this doubly given death [in Abraham's sacrifice], not sharing anything in this dissymmetrical alliance" (GD, 73). On the other hand, by an unjustified leap Derrida purports that God is simultaneously similar to "each of us, everyone else, each other [who] is infinitely other in its [sic] absolute singularity, inaccessible, solitary, transcendent, nonmanifest, originarily nonpresent to my *ego*" (GD, 78). cf. WAP 132; LT, 78–9.

is the Messiah" (LT, 91). Irrespective of the indisputable originality of this approach, what gets lost is the unique dialectic between particularity and universality, proposed by *Fear and Trembling*.

CRITIQUES

The first controversial element of Derrida's deconstructive reading occurs when Abraham, the embodiment of the "gift of death," is believed to be lacking all hope (GD, 72). Because he wants to use Abraham as the instantiation of a gratuitous act, Derrida states that the sacrifice of the promised son requires a total renunciation.[7] When raising the knife upon Isaac, Abraham has to lose all expectations of his son's retrieval. For, if he sacrifices with the slightest intention of receiving something in return, Abraham would reinscribe his deed into an economical exchange; this economy could then adulterate the purity of the gift he is expected to typify. In this, however, Derrida passes over (deliberately or not) the subtle teleology that Kierkegaard intended to reveal in the biblical story. Kierkegaard tirelessly repeats that during the three days of his journey, the father of faith constantly believed that he would receive his son back due to the specific promise that Yahweh's chosen people will spring from Isaac's seed. In *Fear and Trembling*, Abraham appears as entertaining the

---

7. Suggestively enough, Abraham as depicted in *The Gift of Death* has many affinities with Kierkegaard's "knight of infinite resignation"; Kierkegaard, *Fear and Trembling*, 42–52. Kierkegaard exemplifies the attitude of infinite resignation through unrequited love. He affirms that, upon becoming aware of the impossibility of being together with the beloved, the lover is in the position of making the infinite movement of resignation. When every earthly hope regarding one's love is totally given up, the individual acquires peace of mind, inner consistency, and composure. The knight of infinite resignation does not give up his love. On the contrary, he accesses the timelessness of love through recollection. But whatever happens to his beloved in the temporal-immediate sense does not interest him any longer for, by resigning himself infinitely, he severed all ties with the concrete historicity of the beloved. The dissimilarity between resignation and faith is now obvious. The knight of faith "does exactly the same as the ... knight [of infinite resignation] did: he infinitely renounces the love that is the substance of his life, he is reconciled in pain. But then the marvel happens; he makes one more movement even more wonderful than all the others, for he says: Nevertheless I have faith that I will get her ... by virtue of the fact that for God all things are possible." Kierkegaard, *Fear and Trembling*, 46. It is evident now that Abraham or any other genuine believer has a specific hope, which makes it difficult to speak here about a pure gift. On the other side, due to his affinities with the daily life of a bourgeois philistine, the knight of faith seems to support Derrida's insight that subjective identity is constituted by an inscrutable secrecy. Compare Kierkegaard, *Fear and Trembling*, 38–41 and GD, 58–61, 80.

express, though absurd, *certainty* that God will return Isaac, regardless of the result of his sacrifice.[8] As ironic as it might sound, the thorny implication is that, whereas Derrida deconstructs the Kierkegaardian version of Abraham to describe a pure or non-economical gift,[9] *Fear and Trembling* draws a quasi-economic portrait of Abraham, notwithstanding one that is replete with contradictions.[10]

Derrida "democratizes" the Abrahamic plight for the sake of establishing a hyperbolic ethics (LT, 66–72),[11] or responsibility which is "condemned a priori to paradox, scandal, and aporia" (GD, 68). However, while correctly observing that in Abraham we deal with the failure or violence of ethics in the face of justice (insofar as any responsible act or decision ultimately proves sacrificial),[12] the Parisian thinker is forced to omit Kierkegaard's original intention of situating Abraham within a par-

8. Kierkegaard, *Fear and Trembling*, 49.

9. Obviously, the Derridean hermeneutic is allergic to all possible teleology inherent to Isaac's sacrifice. The existence of any aim in Abraham's attitude decisively undermines Derrida's contention that sacrificing Isaac must be completely gratuitous. In other words, there is in Kierkegaard's reading of Isaac's binding a very subtle economy which obstructs the possibility of taking this Biblical narrative as a salient example of a gift without return. More importantly, the first major question raised by *Fear and Trembling* is whether there exists a "*teleological* suspension of the ethical" in Isaac's sacrifice, the answer being affirmative.

10. "Let us go further. We let Isaac actually be sacrificed. Abraham had faith. He did not have faith that he would be blessed in a future life, but that he would be blessed here in the world. God could give him a new Isaac, could restore to life the one sacrificed." In the same vein: "But Abraham had faith specifically for this life—faith that he would grow old in this country, be honored among the people, blessed by posterity, and unforgettable in Isaac, the most precious thing in his life, whom he embraced with a love that is inadequately described by saying he faithfully fulfilled the father's duty to love the son, which is indeed stated in the command: the son whom you love" (Kierkegaard, *Fear and Trembling*, 36, 20; see also ibid., 115).

11. Moreover, Kierkegaard himself is seen as the proponent of a "pure ethics," but with no further comment as to the conspicuous *limits* of the ethical, which the Danish thinker revealed by emphasizing the paradoxical side of Christianity (GD, 92f.).

12. Kierkegaard speaks of the failure of ethics when clashing with *religious tasks*, not justice. For him, the coordinates of the Abrahamic faith are: silence, isolation, paradoxicality. Human alterity (Abraham's spouse, Sarah, the servants, Isaac himself) appears in this context secondary and helpless. Kierkegaard goes even further and holds that, if conceived in intersubjective terms, ethics is actually *distractive*, inasmuch as the elect has to evince his loyalty to the transcendent by *murdering* the dearest one. Regarding the encounter with the divine Other in faith, the rules and codes ordering social interactions prove pointless, if not utterly dangerous. Contrast this point with GD, 61 and note 6 above.

ticularly *religious* framework wherein the Judeo-Christian absolute Other intervenes in history in ways that might defy even Derrida's messianic justice.[13] Succinctly put, Derrida must ignore Kierkegaard's dialectic of faith from *Fear and Trembling* precisely because it would deconstruct what he considers undeconstructible.[14]

We have already seen that to Derrida, Abraham is not an exceptional figure. Abraham's universality lies in his iconic status, symbolizing the unconditional duty towards the alterity of the other, an obligation which, however, we all inevitably transgress.[15] Here, the Derridean hermeneutic goes against another point from *Fear and Trembling* which renders any attempt to universalize Abraham's condition, if not inapt, at least questionable. Although religious knighthood is an ideal to which we should all

13. Puzzlingly enough, Derrida admits that Abraham's relation to God is "a relationship without relation because God is absolutely transcendent, hidden, and secret." However, a few pages later he reasons: "If God is completely other, the figure or name of the wholly other, then ever other (one) is every (bit) other" (GD, 72f, 77). Note that God is "textualized," he is a "figure or name." Nonetheless, in the monotheistic tradition God is conceived as the sovereign, personal, living, unique deity who is ontologically placed above all creation and creatures, though indiscernibly pervading them, too; cf. also WAP, 132. Compare with Smith's depiction of Derrida's dictum "Il n'y a pas de hors-texte" (WAP, 34–42).

14. Derrida practices deconstruction in the name of an *undeconstructible* justice which arguably haunts the concrete customs, institutions, and practices of the law (LT, 67). In stark contrast, Kierkegaard embraces the Pauline view that law was not only fulfilled but also overcome in Christ due to its sin-laden potentiality. For instance, in *Works of Love*, we are expressly advised to "let the judge appointed by the state ... [or] the servant of justice work at discovering guilt and crime; the rest of us are called to be neither judges nor servants of justice, but on the contrary are called by God to love, that is, with the aid of a mitigating explanation to hide [the neighbor's] multitude of sins" (Kierkegaard, *Works of Love*, 293). With respect to the Law, Kierkegaard thinks that what it "was not capable of accomplishing, as little as it could save a person—that Christ was." And he continues: "Whereas the Law with its requirement became everyone's downfall because they were not what it required and through it only learned to know sin, Christ then became the downfall of the Law; because he was what it required ... Christ came not to abolish the Law but to perfect it; therefore from this time forth, it exists in the perfect fulfillment" (Ibid., 99). For Pauline references, see especially Rom 7:5–9 and 8:2–4, but also 3:28; 4:13–16; 5:13, 20; 6:14; 10:4.

15. "As soon as I enter into a relation with the other, with the gaze, look, request, love, command, or call of the other, I know that I can respond only by sacrificing ethics, that is, by sacrificing whatever obliges me to also respond, in the same way, in the same instant, to all the others. I offer a gift of death, I betray, I don't need to raise my knife over my son on Mount Moriah for that. Day and night, at every instant, on all the Mount Moriahs of this world, I am doing that, raising my knife over what I love and must love, over those to whom I owe absolute fidelity, incommensurably" (GD, 68).

aspire, nobody, according to Kierkegaard, will ever become an existential replica of Abraham, unless his name is, of course, Jesus Christ.[16] So, if Kierkegaard's original goal is, as I hold, to confront us with Abraham's *transcendently* informed *singularity* which goes against the ethical goodness understood in intersubjective terms; if as direct inheritors of the Enlightenment project, Derrida and Levinas, on Smith's evaluation,[17] defend the idea of justice, democracy, and ethics, while dissolving all spiritual particularity and being exclusively human-other-oriented, then how are Abraham's unparalleled individuality and private relationship to transcendence on Kierkegaard's account suitable for a "messianism without the messianic"[18] or pure hospitality?[19]

Furthermore, if we accept, together with Smith's Derrida, that "the event that we await is the in-breaking of the other *as other*: the hope, beyond all 'messianisms', of a universalizable culture of singularities" (LT, 90), the question becomes to what extent is Kierkegaard's unmistakably *Christian* thought relevant within the postmodern ambiance. On my reading, if we are to go beyond the limits of *Fear and Trembling*, the philosophical friction between Copenhagen and Paris intensifies and originates in two fundamentally different heterologies.[20] As Derrida shows,

---

16. True enough, Kierkegaard faces, in this sense, a definite aporia. On the one hand, he holds that it takes *all* human powers to perform the movement of infinite resignation; on the other, Abraham is the one (probably, the single one) that performs the second movement whereby he gets back the very finite that he intended to sacrifice. The question remains: by virtue of what powers does he get it back, as long as he used all his inner resources for giving up Isaac? Commentators have suggested that Kierkegaard hints here at the need for grace in the accomplishment of faith. I would add a second possibility: Abraham is a limit-case or an ideal(istic) non-concrete paradigm meant to undermine Hegel's goal of interpreting religious faith within a rational framework. See Kierkegaard, *Fear and Trembling*, 49–53.

17. Especially, LT, 78–9, 88–91. Also WAP, 118–20, 122, 142.

18. Derrida, *Adieu*, 67; as quoted in LT, 78–9.

19. Interestingly enough, in speaking of the "Great law of Hospitality" and the "pure welcome" (LT, 70–71), Derrida (or Smith) should find support in the Christian doctrinal statement that God forgives, loves or welcomes everyone, including the basest of sinners. This concords with God's absolutely unfathomable decision to let the Son take on a human body and die on the cross for the reconciliation with humanity and the eradication of corruption. For Kierkegaard, most probably on the wake of Paul, every human, when faced with the divine, is and remains sinful. All conceivable purity belongs exclusively to the wholly and holy Other. Moreover, the salvific hospitality with which God receives those who decide to follow Him unconditionally is as unadulterated as possible.

20. The difference between the two thinkers can also be understood from a temporal standpoint. Whereas for Derrida, it is the future promise and hope that allow the

most probably with Levinas's heterology in mind, the deconstructed God represents the "phenomenological correlate," so to speak, of *every human other* summoning me indefinitely to absolute responsibility and justice.[21] By contrast, in Kierkegaard's philosophy, which is inextricably linked with Christian metaphysics, humanity is at an infinite qualitative distance from the divine.[22] By appropriating all the doctrinal premises of the Christian religion, Kierkegaard argues that sin has effected an unsurpassable hiatus between the immanent and the transcendent. On this very ground God descends in history as a human individual, the self-sacrifice of whom atones for the creature's profound corruption. In contradistinction, Derrida is interested only in the dialectic between radical justice and the extant laws or judiciary-political institutions. Thus, he focuses only on the singularity of the human other and conceives traditional transcendence just as a textual trace within intersubjectivity.

To further illustrate this pivotal dissonance, let us see how *The Gift of Death* tackles an explicitly Christian issue found in the sixth chapter of Matthew, namely Jesus's injunction that his followers dedicate their life to God's kingdom and resist all temporal wellbeing. Specifically, Christ

---

messianic fruitfully to haunt the realms of praxis, law, politics, and mores, in Kierkegaard's Christian mind frame, the present is prioritized over the other two temporal ecstases. For Kierkegaard, it is essential that the human being adopt the right stance before God, namely to bring Jesus into contemporaneity or to make Him *present*. That is why he states that "the difficulty with the essentially Christian emerges every time it is to be made present, every time it is to be said as it is and said now, at this instant, at this specific instant of actuality, and said to those, precisely to those who are living now" (Kierkegaard, *Christian Discourses*, 231). Conclusively, "in relation to the absolute, there is only one time, the present" (Kierkegaard, *Practice in Christianity*, 63). See also I Cor 15:51; Mark 5:42; Luke 8:55.

21. "God is completely other, the figure or name of the wholly other," "the name of the possibility I have of keeping a secret that is visible from the interior but not from the exterior" (GD, 77, 108). Thus, for Derrida, God is not the good Creator and everlasting Sustainer of Judaism or the Savior of Christianity. Rather, God is conceived as a) the limit-horizon of secrecy; b) a pertinent symbol of the instant of decision; c) the ultimate sense of human subjectivity in Kierkegaardian terms; d) the sublime gaze that sees without being seen, requires without self-justification, summons to abominable acts and ineffable ordeals (as in Abraham's case) (GD, passim).

22. Smith considers that "insofar as the other is absolute, infinite and unconditioned, the mode in which I am to relate to the other is one of absolute, infinite, unconditioned *welcome*" (LT, 71). However, Smith never asks how such possibility coheres with the Christian doctrine of sinfulness. No orthodoxy, irrespective of its radicality, can afford to dismiss the fundamental implications of sin in the human condition and the God-relationship.

advises us to forgive so that we will be forgiven, to hide the discomfort of our duties, such as fasting, from the face of others, and to stay disclosed only to God, "who sees in hiddenness" and compensates accordingly. Moreover, no Christian should "store up for oneself treasures on earth where moth and rust destroy and where thieves break in and steal;" rather, says Jesus, "store up treasures for yourselves in heaven" (Matt 6:19–20). This particular commandment is taken by Derrida as a peremptory example of "the infinite and dissymmetrical economy of [Christian] sacrifice" which

> always presupposes a calculation that claims to go beyond calculation, beyond the totality of the calculable as a finite totality of the same. There is an economy, but it is an economy that integrates the renunciation of a calculable remuneration, renunciation of merchandise and bargaining ... In the space opened by this economy ... there emerges a new teaching concerning giving or alms ... [which] creatures cannot calculate and must leave to the appreciation of *the father as he who sees in secret* ... [Thus] an infinite calculation supersedes the finite calculating that has been renounced. God the Father, who sees in secret, will pay back your salary, and on an infinitely greater scale. (GD, 107)

What the French thinker finds germane in the Christian human-divine interaction is, in fact, a phenomenological-deconstructionist reformulation of what Nietzsche condemned concerning the slave mentality of Christianity: worldliness with all its goods and benefactions must be abandoned and denigrated in order to gain and gather other invisible imperishable treasures in heaven. Moreover, the human rapports with the Christian deity run along the following lines: God allows the faithful to his celestial court only insofar as the faithful does what is expected from him or her (repent, be merciful, abdicate earthliness, believe in God, and fulfill His commands). It is noteworthy that, at least implicitly, Derrida appears here less hospitable with the Christian soteriology and its impenetrable foundation, to which Kierkegaard was more than generous and receptive.

The question I want to pose at this juncture is: can we extend Derrida's sublimated economy of sacrifice to Christianity as a whole? In this sense, Kierkegaard could provide both a reliable answer and a pertinent criticism of Derrida. In his books Kierkegaard spilled a lot of ink suggesting that the salvific advent of the God-man happened out of an unconditional love, i.e. out of a decision the gratuity of which escapes all understanding. In *Philosophical Fragments, Sickness unto Death*, and particularly in *Works of Love*, he argues that sinfulness can be overcome solely by the unfathomable event of God's embodiment in a concrete individual who, as the suffering truth, accepts the most ignominious death, viz. crucifixion. Christ's descent on earth, his entire life, the meaning of his salvific mission, his atrocious, albeit triumphant, end are all rooted in *agape* which is the utter subversion of any economy in Derrida's sense. Moreover, the unequivocal appropriation of human sinfulness and its spiritually nefarious denouement have compelled Kierkegaard to hold that "before God one is always in the wrong." Consequently, merit in religious matters should be renounced entirely by means of kenosis and humility. Due to the nothingness effected by sin, religious achievements are rather a sign of divine favor, the pure gift of grace. Thus conceived, Christianity resists the economical undertone that Derrida detects in Matthew 6. For Kierkegaard, there can never be a bilateral barter between God and man. The transcendent opened itself to humankind in and through love, i.e. groundlessly. Furthermore, the sole treasure expected by the transcendent "in return" is altruistic: the neighbor love in light of God's universal mercy. The Christian transcendent Other has already made an inestimable gift through the God-man. For Kierkegaard, it is solely by believing in the redemptive capacity of Jesus and by mimetically reenacting his earthly drama that a person will become a single individual who hopes, while repentant, for reconciliation in *eschaton*.

This point leads me directly to the final section of my argument. James K. A. Smith wishes to lay the ground for a "postmodern Christian Church." On his estimation, this Church should frankly accept plural interpretations of the Biblical texts; it should retrieve the traditional hermeneutic practiced in dogmatic theology and Christian Patristics; it should bring back to life those ancient practices that celebrate ecclesia as the "body of Christ"; in short, Smith recommends "a robust confessional theology and ecclesiology that unapologetically reclaims premodern practices in and for a postmodern culture" (WAP, 116). In refusing to guide itself by the ideal of universal objectivity, such radical postmodern orthodoxy embraces a hospitable perspectivism, while simultaneously proclaiming Christ's scandalous distinctiveness.[23]

23. WAP, 121n13. Because Smith's ecclesiastical community defines itself along the lines of "a logic of incarnation that honors finitude and particularity," the postmodern

PART TWO: RECEIVING THE (POSTMODERN) TRADITION

I take Smith to be saying that the catholic dimension of Christianity lies both in its hermeneutical generosity[24] and its embrace of premodern or ancient sacramental-ecclesiastical practices. This orientation—both sensible to universality and affirmative of alterity—is supplemented by an elemental affirmation of particularity: the fact that God gave himself to us in and through Jesus's birth, sufferings, crucifixion, and resurrection.[25] Briefly stated, postmodern Christianity should be a combination of "a generous orthodoxy and healthy catholicity" (WAP, 132). Most probably, Smith is deeply indebted to deconstruction for its ecumenicity and its justice to alterity. However, he approves as much of the complex, tumultuous, and rich history of the Church, together with its unique dogmatics and multifaceted liturgy.[26] As we do not get a clear image of how Christian particularity is going to relate to other religious beliefs, monotheistic or not, one might ask whether Smith's notion of catholicity represents an attempt to uncover the unity of all religious expressions or solely Christianity's peculiar and efficient response to the momentous challenges of postmodernity.[27] In any case, the overall dilemma is as follows: if Christian particularism lives by a hospitable welcoming of heterogeneous religions, it

---

church "must proceed unapologetically from the particularities of Christian confession as given in God's historical revelation in Christ and as unfolded in the history of the church's response to that revelation" (WAP, 122, 123). Here, Smith finds fault with Derrida, whose religion without religion appears impervious to religious specificity and especially, to incarnationalism. Furthermore, Radical Orthodoxy proves more postmodern than Derrida's doubt-laden, ahistorical, a-geographical, transcendental religion itself (WAP, 121–22, 126).

24. Here I coalesce Smith's positive reception of Derridean textualism and his desideratum that Christianity cultivate an ongoing generosity vis-à-vis time, history, and tradition. If the access to the latter three is mediated by texts, as Smith implies in his discussion of Derrida's deconstruction, then generosity and catholicity are primarily of a hermeneutical nature.

25. For Smith, it is Christianity's distinct belief in incarnation which makes evident "the goodness of particularity affirmed at creation [Gen. 1:31]" and "extended in and by the body of Christ, which is the church" (WAP, 122).

26. Smith speaks, in fact, of an ecumenical "community of memory" which openly and paradoxically appropriates "the scandal of particularity," granted by the Christian traditions and their distinctive eschatology (WAP, 135).

27. Smith contends that ecclesiastical catholicity must constitute a genuine weapon against both sectarianism and contemporary paganism or secularity (WAP, 133).

must either accept its relativity and face dilution, or openly acknowledge the absoluteness of its *truth*, while risking to turn anti-postmodern.[28]

At this juncture, allow me a quick confession. I come from Eastern Europe, more exactly Romania, a land full of contrasts and contradictions. Whereas politically and socially, my country continues to struggle (and hopelessly so) with issues dating back to the dawn of modernity, religiously it should boost the interest of Western theologians and scholars of religion. I, as the overwhelming majority of Romanians, am an Eastern Orthodox and from this point of view, I cannot but be enthusiastic to discover a voice (Smith's) which does not speak the dichotomal language of Western Christianity, and which does not dismiss as primitive—or even worse, as idolatrous—the ancient Christian liturgy, monastic traditions, Mariology, and cult of saints. Smith also recaptures a long-forgotten or repressed Christian understanding of materiality, corporeality, affectivity, imagination, and aesthetics. All of these and many more—e.g., the reaffirmation of sacraments, the theology of the pre- and post-ressurectional body, the iconic creativity meant to compensate for the symbolic emasculation effected by Reformation—are with us and alive in the present practice of Eastern Orthodoxy, to this day understudied, if not completely unexplored in the West.

One last comment by which I hope to increase the constructiveness of what was said throughout this paper. Again, with Kierkegaard in mind, I think that Smith's insistence on the imperative recuperation of the ecclesiastical-communitarian dimension runs the danger of collectivism, although a spirit-oriented one. Here, Kierkegaard's lesson seems invaluable because in his religious anthropology the primacy is held by subjectivity over any form of association, the ecclesiastical one included. At the same time, when generously understood, Kierkegaard's Christian individualism allows for a communitarian expression of worship. Still, what Kierkegaard feared more than anyone else was that any affirmation of the ecclesia, even the one vouched by the doctrine itself, eventually might take away the personal, strenuous, and continual commitment to-

---

28. In line with Smith's hermeneutic pluralism, it could be argued that Christianity appears as one among the many expressions of the sacred, this time without being afraid to admit to its particular doctrine, practice, rituals, and *Weltanschauung*. However, Kierkegaard would ask here whether the very absoluteness of Christianity (professed and proclaimed by its very doctrine) is thus not going to be attenuated, if not irreparably undermined.

wards the radical alterity of God and the paradoxical alterity of Christ. It is not my goal here to go into the details of the soteriology underlying Kierkegaard's thought. Suffice to say that, according to Kierkegaard, humankind's highest requirement is strictly related to salvation and consists, amongst others, of individually following the ultimate exemplar, Jesus, in his earthly sufferings and unconditional devotion to God. For more often than not, *imitatio Christi* requires solitude, despair, uncertainty, in short, a martyrdom that no human other, whether in the church or in private, can assist us in lovingly assuming.

WORKS CITED

Kierkegaard, Søren. *Christian Discourses*. Translated by Howard V. Hong and Edna H. Hong. Princeton, NJ: Princeton University Press, 1997.

———. *Concluding Unscientific Postscript to Philosophical Fragments*. Translated by Howard V. Hong and Edna H. Hong. Princeton, NJ: Princeton University Press, 1992.

———. *Fear and Trembling*. Translated by Howard V. Hong and Edna H. Hong, Princeton. NJ: Princeton University Press, 1983.

———. *Philosophical Fragments*. Translated by Howard V. Hong and Edna H. Hong. Princeton, NJ: Princeton University Press, 1985.

———. *Practice in Christianity*. Translated by Howard V. Hong and Edna H. Hong. Princeton, NJ: Princeton University Press, 1991.

———. *The Sickness unto Death*. Translated by Howard V. Hong and Edna H. Hong. Princeton, NJ: Princeton University Press, 1980.

———. *Works of Love*. Translated by Howard V. Hong and Edna H. Hong. Princeton, NJ: Princeton University Press, 1995.

4

Undecidability and Indecidability

Does Derrida's Ethics Depend on Levinas's Notion of the Third?

Brian Lightbody

JAMES K. A. SMITH in LT puts forward a rather weak claim in my view when he states that Levinas's influence on Derrida is (merely) "*present in the very ethical thrust of Derrida's early work*" (LT, 76). It is my contention that a much more forceful and interesting claim can be made. I argue that Derrida's ethical position is *dependent* in large part (though not entirely) on Levinas's ethics of hospitality. Thus, it is not only imprecise, but rather banal to suggest, as Smith does, that it is sometimes "difficult to distinguish the voices of Derrida and Levinas in these texts" (in reference to Derrida's early writings) when we can state instead and with a fair degree of certainty, that Derrida has neither an original nor philosophically interesting ethical position independently of Levinas (LT, 76).

In order to show this, it will first be necessary to argue that Derrida's philosophy is worth discussing. Perhaps no other recent "philosopher" has drawn the collective ire of scholars working in the so-called analytic philosophical tradition than the late Jacques Derrida. Indeed, many analytics would bristle at the suggestion of even describing Derrida as a philosopher. Such pervasive contempt for Derrida amongst analytics I will argue, is based on one of the three following reasons:

PART TWO: RECEIVING THE (POSTMODERN) TRADITION

1. That Derrida is just a bad philosopher and makes many claims which are clearly false;
2. Derrida's philosophy is nonsensical;
3. Derrida's philosophical insights are neither profound nor even "philosophically interesting" but are rather common, trivially true and pedestrian claims.

In the first part of the paper, I explain each of these charges and defend Derrida from the first two. I argue that the final charge does have some merit and in order to acquit Derrida from this charge further philosophical investigation into Derrida's philosophy (in the analytic style) is required. Insofar as an analytic appreciation and interpretation of Derrida is rare or in "its infancy" as James K. A. Smith notes, then it is incumbent upon analytics to scrutinize Derrida's writings, carefully and charitably in order to justify any one of the above charges.

In the second part of the paper, I examine, in an "analytic fashion," Derrida's term "undecidability": a key concept for Derrida's *aporetic* ethical position. I argue that there are two possible interpretations of "undecidability." I call the first position, "undecidability" and show that undecidability is indeed, trivially true. However, I also demonstrate that we may glean a second interpretation of 'undecidability' that rests on Levinas's notion of "the Third." I call this more robust interpretation of undecidability, "indecidability" and conclude by demonstrating that indecidability is an important, profound and philosophically interesting concept. In this way, I will prove not only that Derrida's ethical position relies on Levinas's notion of the Third, but also that this reliance ensures the viability of viewing Derrida as a interesting and profound philosopher.

PART 1: THE THREE CHARGES

> Seneca, as one of the most enlightened men of his age, should have aimed at a character which would have been above the possibility of suspicion: but we must remember that charges such as those which were brought against him were the easiest of all to make, and the most impossible to refute.[1]

---

1. Farrar, *Seekers After God*, 83.

Undecidability and Indecidability

As explained above, the first charge holds that Derrida is simply a bad philosopher; his arguments are weak, unclear, or simply nonexistent. This charge was first articulated in the analytic philosophical tradition, to my knowledge, by Barry Smith in 1992. Smith, along with some twenty other prominent philosophers of the analytic stripe, was distraught over the possibility of Derrida receiving an honorary doctorate degree in philosophy from Cambridge University. In what has now come to be known as the "Cambridge affair," Smith et al. argued that Derrida was undeserving of such an honor because:

> In the eyes of philosophers, and certainly among those working in leading departments of philosophy throughout the world, M. Derrida's work does not meet accepted standards of clarity and rigour.... Academic status based on what seems to us to be little more than semi-intelligible attacks upon the values of reason, truth, and scholarship is not, we submit, sufficient grounds for the awarding of an honorary degree in a distinguished university. (*The London Times,* Saturday May 9, 1992)

Though Smith and his cohorts originally gave Derrida "the benefit of the doubt" they later came to realize that his views were "either false or trivial." (*The London Times*, Saturday May 9, 1992).

I think the first charge (that Derrida's views are simply false), is rather easy to dismiss. For to argue that presumably *all* of Derrida's philosophical positions, arguments and insights are false is to invoke an all too easy distinction between truth and falsity in the first place. As Derrida demonstrates, such simplistic binary oppositions are anything but simplistic and are far from being binary and oppositional. Rather, truth and falsity (like sense and non-sense) entangle one another, give play to one another and in some definite sense are dependent on one another. If we really wish to study Derrida under the most charitable circumstances possible, (which I believe is one of the hallmarks of the analytic tradition), then we must take what he says seriously and we must study him carefully. The first charge, then if it is to have any real force must allow Derrideans or those sympathetic to Derrida's philosophy, to have the opportunity to defend him by using the means, methods and tools of analytic philosophy. Indeed, Derrida has already convinced me in *Limited Inc,* that he got the better of John Searle as it were, by demonstrating that he too can do analytic philosophy with the best of them (cf. Linc). The question then is if Derrida can explain his theories, positions and ideas in analytic terms then why doesn't he adopt an analytic style in all of his works? This is an intriguing question and one that requires further investigation. Thus, we should continue to "give Derrida the benefit of the doubt" rather than claiming too hastily that he is simply a bad philosopher. As James K. A. Smith notes on this score, in LT: "This [referring to an analytic interpretation of Derrida] opens a way of reading Derrida that is only in its infancy, but repays more labour" (LT, 103). I argue, accordingly, that the first charge be dropped because analytics simply have not given Derrida the benefit of the doubt at all, but rather have presumed his guilt, and what's more have not even offered Derrida an opportunity, as it were, to defend himself.

The second charge holds that Derrida's work is nonsensical. It is impossible to understand just what precisely Derrida's philosophical position is according to the philosophers in this group and, therefore, Derrida "cannot even be wrong." This position seems to be the default analytic interpretation when it comes to Derrida as evidenced by the comments of many analytic philosophers at the time of Derrida's death on October 8th of 2004. A. C. Grayling, for example, in the obituary section of *The London Guardian Times* on October 12th 2004, believes Derrida to be nothing more than a peddler of paradoxes. In the same section, Roger Scruton noted that "Derrida's work is difficult to summarize because it is nonsense." Whatever Derrida may be, according to this group, he is most certainly not a philosopher.

Taking this criticism even further, we may hold that Derrida's texts may be more important for their entertainment value than for their philosophical merit. Brian Leiter has recently reposted on his blog a game that one of his old law school friends would play with Derridean "wannabes" and acolytes. His friend writes:

> My colleague would open one of Derrida's works to a random page, pick a random sentence, write it down, and then (above or below it) write a variant in which the positive and negative were interchanged, or a word or phrase was replaced with one of opposite meaning. He would then challenge the assembled Derrida partisans to guess which was the original and which was the variant. The point was that Derrida's admirers are generally unable to distinguish his pronouncements from their opposites at better than a chance level, suggesting that the content is a sophisticated

Undecidability and Indecidability

form of white noise. On this view, Wolfgang Pauli once said of someone else, Derrida is "not even wrong."[2]

Let's play this game. Below is a statement, randomly taken from *Of Grammatology* (p. 67), along with its variant. Which is the correct one?

1. "It is not a matter of complicating the structure of time while conserving its homogeneity and its fundamental successivity."
2. "It is a matter of complicating the structure of time while conserving its heterogeneity and its accidental non-successivity."

The correct answer is #1. The upshot of this sort of criticism is to deny Derrida any place in the great pantheon of philosophers by simply not taking his work seriously—we take Derrida quite literally when he emphasizes the importance of play and differance in philosophical deconstruction and apply these methods to Derrida's own work.

I believe we can dismiss these and similar sorts of criticisms too. To argue that Derrida's work is simply the work of a charlatan, a joker, but not a philosopher, is to fail to appreciate, fully, the scope and (possible) greatness of his thought. If Derrida is truly one of the great philosophers in the Western tradition then it may very well take decades or perhaps centuries to understand the profundity and fecundity of his thought just as many of the great philosophers were not fully appreciated in their own day. If analytic philosophers pride themselves on understanding and re-constructing concepts with clarity and precision; in formulating philosophical positions; and scrutinizing arguments carefully; then it is incumbent on analytics to study Derrida's works with as much intensity, charitable understanding and mental discipline as any of the great philosophers. Since Derrida has authored some 40 plus books along with dozens and dozens of articles, it is unfair to say then that this sort of intense study has taken place. Again the same defence above applies to this charge as well: if we are to criticize Derrida we must first take what he writes and says very seriously indeed.

With the above two charges dismissed for lack of evidence, we can now move on to the final charge: triviality. This third and final charge still has some real philosophical bite behind it and we may do well to investigate in detail if it is indeed the case that Derrida's opaque and very diffi-

2. Liberman, "The Language Log."

cult texts are really nothing more than so much philosophical tartuffery. In fact, many of Derrida's acolytes only seem to lend ammunition to this third charge either by A) seriously distorting Derrida's thought for the sake of making his work a little more digestible for a mass audience (or perhaps for analytic philosophers) or B) because they too seriously misunderstand many of the reasons that Derrida provides to substantiate his claims. In order to defend Derrida from the charge of triviality and philosophical pedestrianism, I will briefly examine what Derrida refers to as both the experience and situation of "undecidability." I will begin by distinguishing first between two different interpretations of undecidability. The first interpretation of "undecidability" I leave as "undecidability." Undecidability, as I will explain, is not only an anaemic and uninteresting claim but in addition, does not follow from its premises. The second interpretation of undecidability I will call "indecidability." I will argue that indecidability seems to be predicated on Levinas's notion of the third and that, prima facie, Derrida's indecidable ethical position buttressed as it is now by Levinas's notion of the third, may allow him to escape from this final charge of philosophical triviality.

PART II: DEFENDING DERRIDA

First, it may be instructive to start with a general summary of Derrida's ethical stance as understood by someone who seems to appreciate Derrida's ethical position and yet still remains very critical of Derrida's overall ethical project. The cultural theorist Terry Eagleton, in his book *After Theory*, describes Derrida's ethical position as follows:

> Derrida says there are moral judgements, but they lack any sort of moral or rational basis. There is no longer any relation, as there was for Aristotle or Marx, between the way the world is and how we ought to act within it, or between the way we are and what we ought to do . . . These judgements are left accordingly hanging in the air. For Jacques Derrida ethics is a matter of absolute decisions—decisions which are vital and necessary but also utterly "impossible," and which fall outside all given norms, forms of knowledge and modes of conceptualisation.[3]

If Eagleton's assessment of Derrida is correct then Derrida is truly beyond ethics—at least as ethics is traditionally understood—in a non-

---

3. Eagleton, *After Theory*, 153.

Undecidability and Indecidability

trivial and philosophically interesting sense. Ethics may be defined, roughly, as the system of rules and principles that informs individuals what the 'Good' is so that they may act in accordance with the 'Good.' More importantly, ethical rules, principles or duties are normatively binding; if we know what the good is and it is possible to do the good then we ought to act accordingly. While conversely if we know that ethical action is called for, but either A) fail to act or B) act badly, then our action may be considered amoral in the first circumstance and immoral in the second. Thus, whether the ethicist is a deontologist of either an a priori or intuitionist stripe, a welfare or non-welfare consequentialist or a virtue ethicist, ethics, it seems, is predicated on knowledge. One must know what one's duties are a la the deontologist, or, if one is a consequentialist one must know how to calculate, correctly, which action will lead to the most beneficent outcome. Finally, if one is a virtue ethicist, one must understand and cultivate specific virtues that would lead to the "good life." Though each school of ethical thought may disagree in terms of how one should settle moral dilemmas, all three schools of thought are in agreement that in order for ethics to be possible, knowledge must come first.

Derridean "ethics" however, if it still makes any sense to use this term, seems to undercut our traditional understanding of the necessary and inseparable entwinement between ethics and knowledge. According to Derrida, we can never really be certain what the ethical thing to do is in any context because we neither have enough time, enough precedent, enough history, nor enough experience in order to be able to make an 'ethical' decision in the first place (FL, 20–27). That is to say, because we are human beings we are therefore fallible while any ethical "knowledge," which may be gleaned from our all too short lives, will always be incomplete. Therefore, Derrida concludes, we never really "decide" on an ethical action. Rather, ethical decision making is more like a Kierkegaardian leap of faith or a type of madness. It is this ethical madness, this undecidability, this experience and situation in which we must act and yet we can never determine what consequence our action will have, which makes ethics "dangerous" and "impossible."

On the surface, the above argument appears to be cogent and effectively seems to undermine at the very least, but not only, all consequentialist theories of ethics. The consequentialist qua consequentialist will argue that an act is moral if the consequence of this action produces the most good—whether the good here is construed as accruing to the individual as in consequentialist perfectionism or whether the good here is construed as providing the most net benefit for all pace welfare consequentialism (i.e., Utilitarianism), the end result of an action is what is ethically important. Furthermore, in order to discover just what specific action will produce the most good, one must have a way of calculating all of the potential consequences of the particular action and then weighing the sum total of these consequences. Of course, what sort of specific calculus should be used to determine which action in an ethical situation would be the most beneficent to a single subject or group of subjects is open to various interpretations as we have hedonistic, utilitarianistic and pluralistic, species of consequentialism. That being said, all consequentialists agree that the ends are more important than the means when it comes to ethical decisions.

Derrida's argument then, if taken quite literally and seriously, seems to imply that we can never evaluate all of the potential consequences of an action in order to say definitively that the action is good or ethical. Our knowledge, experience, understanding of the context, etc. are all finite—they will always pale in comparison to the ethical denseness of the infinite. Moreover, we never know how our actions will be interpreted. Our actions may be interpreted in an indefinite number of ways and may be more influential in causing more harm than good in the long run.

In order for an action to be truly ethical according to Derrida, it must be incalculable; much like a gift. This connection between ethics and gift giving is made quite forcefully and ironically in *Given Time I: Counterfeit Money* where Derrida recounts Baudelaire's story of the counterfeit coin given to a beggar in his fictional short poem "La Fausse Monnaie" (Counterfeit Money). As the narrator explains, one cannot know for certain what sort of consequences will occur by giving the beggar a counterfeit coin: "Might it not be converted into real coins? Might it not also lead him into prison? A publican or a baker might, for example, might have him arrested as a counterfeiter or as a passer of counterfeit coins. But the counterfeit coin might also just as well serve as the seed for several day's wealth, in the hands of a poor, small-scale speculator."[4] For Derrida, this poem captures the essence of ethical decision making in that we can neither fathom how our actions will be interpreted, what consequences will occur as a result of our actions nor whether we are

---

4. Baudelaire, "Counterfeit," 58.

Undecidability and Indecidability

truly doing the right thing. Ethics, Derrida writes, "start when you don't know what to do, when there is a gap between knowledge and action" (LT, 82). Yet, Derrida says, despite our lack of knowledge, in the act of gift giving as well as in ethical action, we must take responsibility for our actions and it is for these reasons that every ethical decision is 'undecidable' and hence "impossible."

We can further expand and understand what Derrida means by the term "indecidabilite" by turning to Derrida's text *Force of Law (Force de loi)*. According to Derrida, every judgment whether legal or ethical deals with singularities; each legal case is different from the one before it and likewise every Other, we interact with, is different and wholly Other from all Others. Thus, when one is confronted with a new legal case, it is as if they were confronted by a new Other, insofar as not only must a decision be made based on incomplete knowledge, but in addition, the juridical and/or ethical decision cannot be delayed. Ethics and justice are always a matter of urgency. This combination of epistemic incompleteness, responsibility and urgency means that we will forever be haunted by our decisions precisely because, "The undecidable remains caught, lodged, at least as a ghost---but an essential ghost—in every decision, in every event of decision. Its ghostliness deconstructs from within any assurance of presence, any certitude or any supposed criteriology that would assure us of the justice of a decision, in truth, of the very event of a decision" (FL, 24–25). Basing a decision on incomplete knowledge, while in a state of impending urgency, knowing that we are still responsible for this decision and simultaneously being haunted by our decision afterwards, truly is mad. And yet, in spite of this, we are still mad for ethics, justice and fairness.

However, if we now turn to analyzing Derrida's explanation for his claim that ethical decisions are really undecidable, it appears that all that has really been argued for is "undecidability." The principal claim of Derrida's is that one always acts, ethically speaking, with incomplete knowledge. Derrida is right on this score; it is impossible to predict all of the possible consequences of an action. Therefore, my knowledge of what may possibly happen as a result of my action is merely an inconsequential drop when compared to the infinite ocean of possible consequences my action may have on the Other. Thus, Derrida suggests, since we can never know all of the possible consequences of our actions, we dive head first into this infinite ocean of ethical madness when we act.

PART TWO: Receiving the (Postmodern) Tradition

If Derrida is right, then ethics, as traditionally defined, is an irrelevant study as it is impossible to determine, with any precision, the ethical rules, virtues, or principles one should follow. But does the argument follow? Two questions emerge from our investigation: 1) Has undecidability proven that there is no objective criterion of rightness? and 2) Is Derrida's insight really that insightful or is it trivial as charge three maintains? In order to answer these two questions, I will briefly examine the most popular subspecies of consequentialism, namely utilitarianism, to determine whether Derrida's arguments are justified.

Turning to the first question (as to whether Derrida is right in claiming that because we always possess incomplete knowledge our ethical actions are always undecidable) we find that there is a problem with the argument in that that there seems to be a failure, on Derrida's part, to distinguish between two different notions of consequentialism: consequentialism as a decision making process that provides human beings with normative guidelines to follow and consequentialism as a criterion of ethical rightness. If consequentialism is merely a decision making procedure, then Derrida is *partly* right: it is impossible to predict all possible consequences of an action and thus all ethical action requires an 'undecidable' leap of faith. However, if we construe consequentialism as a criterion of right ethical conduct, then it doesn't matter whether the ethical agent is able to calculate the various beneficent or maleficent possibilities of his or her actions. We can hold that maximizing the good, in the long run, for the greatest number of people, can still be *the standard* of all ethical decision making even though no individual may be able to perform a perfectly correct utilitarian calculation. In other words, Derrida has conflated two very different things: he has conflated normative ethics with meta-ethics. All Derrida has shown is that consequentialism is predicated, in part, on faith, but he has not proven that there is no ethical criteriology to be had. Though, to be sure, we may never be able to put perfectly into place such a criteriology of rightness into practice, this does not entail that there is no criterion of rightness.

Undecidability is also trivial. Many of Derrida's most fervent disciples, who argue something like the above argument for "undecidability" in order to support the impossibility of ethics, forget that this specific criticism of consequentialist ethics was raised some 200 years earlier. The above criticism of utilitarianism that Derrida seems to articulate in *Force of Law* and elsewhere (cf. GD and FL), has often been called the omniscient problem in the secondary literature and was well known by both Bentham and Mill.[5] In this regard Bentham writes in 1789 that, "It is not to be expected that an exact account of the tendency of any act will be strictly pursued before every moral judgment, or to every legislative or judicial operation. It may, however, be always kept in mind."[6] While Mill in 1861 makes much the same point in response to the many critics of utilitarianism in the 19th century by writing:

> ... it is a misapprehension of the utilitarian mode of thought, to conceive it as implying that people should fix their minds upon so wide a generality as the world, or society at large. The great majority of good actions are intended not for the benefit of the world, but for that of individuals, of which the good of the world is made up; and the thoughts of the most virtuous man need not on these occasions travel beyond the particular persons concerned, except so far as is necessary to assure himself that in benefiting them he is not violating the rights, that is, the legitimate and authorised expectations, of anyone else.[7]

Such objections, as well as solutions to the above omniscient problem, have filled tomes in the secondary literature for the past one hundred or so years. Derrida's arguments, if they were better written, further clarified and more carefully argued, would probably remain unpublished if submitted to even a third tier analytic journal of ethics.

Given the above problems with undecidability, is it possible to save indecidability from philosophical triviality? I think that we may just be able to save undecidability by supplementing Derrida's argument with Levinas's notion of the third. James Smith in LT, sums up what Levinas means by "the third" quite nicely. He writes:

> If I am infinitely responsible for the other, then I can never measure up to the call to do justice to this Other, the face that confronts me. But then to top it off, another Other is always already on the

---

5. The clearest recent expression of this problem, as it relates to act utilitarianism as both a normative and meta-ethical theory, can be found in Chappell, "Option Ranges." Derek Parfit, of course, has also examined the same problem in his "Is Common-Sense Morality Self-Defeating?" Parfit is responding to Singer, "Is Act Utilitarianism Self-Defeating?". Finally, Gandaer Williams examines this same objection to Utilitarian theories of ethics (though he does not explicitly call it "the omniscience problem") in "Insignificance of The Total of All Value."

6. Bentham, *Introduction to the Principles of Morals and Legislation* (1789), Sec. 28.

7. Mill, *Utilitarianism* 1861, section II: "What Utilitarianism Is."

> scene—the third. If I am infinitely obligated to this first other and could never measure up to that initial call to responsibility then what am I to do with another wholly other on the scene. (LT, 77)

One way to concretize just what "the third" means and to demonstrate that Derridean indecidability is largely dependent on this notion of the Third is to think of Derrida's cat example in GD.

Derrida claims that in taking care of one cat, one must also take responsibility for deciding not to care for all of the other starving and neglected cats in the world. For example, if I decide to adopt a cat from an animal rescue center, I must look into the face of every needy cat and choose to take one over the other even though each cat, for all intents and purposes, is really indistinguishable from the rest. It is an action that causes me to feel ashamed because I recognize that I did not choose "the Third," but instead, chose "my cat." For to decide to care for this singular cat, or for this singular human being, while deciding not to care for all of those Others who I am also infinitely obligated to, is a decision that I choose, that I am responsible for and one that haunts me (cf. GD). Furthermore, this "decision" truly is indecidable: I can offer no ethical reasons as to why I am caring for this cat instead of another. Yet by deciding to care for this singular cat, I am acting irresponsibly and unethically to all of the others. My decision to care for one cat, or perhaps to give to one human being rather than another, does not seem, prima facie, to be based on either a criterion of rightness in a consequentialist sense, or even as an understanding of my a priori duties a la the categorical deontologist. To choose to care for the singular Other who is indistinguishable in any significant way from another Other, does seem to be an impossible decision and one that "requires a mad leap of faith."

The above ethical insight of "the Third," which Derrida adopts from Levinas, is non-trivial and is philosophically interesting. In addition, and contra to Smith, I have shown that Derrida's ethical position seems to be dependent, in large part, on Levinas's conception of ethics. It will be up to future analytic philosophers, interested in the ethical insights of Derrida to explore in what ways "Derridean ethics" (if this term even makes sense) distinguishes itself from Levinasian ethics. My analysis of course does not preclude us from still attempting to interpret and absorb the ethical importance of Levinas's point from some well established and traditional ethical theory. It most certainly does not entail that "indecidability" will

Undecidability and Indecidability

always be beyond the pale of ethical norms and reasons. This may seem unsatisfactory to many, but it is only unsatisfactory if one were expecting an "overlord" or "continental approach" to philosophical problems, and one cannot expect such definitive answers from an analytic, Lockean, under-labourer like myself.

WORKS CITED

Baudelaire, Charles. "Counterfeit." In *Paris Spleen*, translated by Louise Varése, 58–59. New York: New Directions, 1970.

Bentham, Jeremy. *Introduction to the Principles of Morals and Legislation* (1789). Buffalo: Prometheus, 1988.

Chappell, Timothy "Option Ranges." *The Journal of Applied Philosophy* 18:2 (2001) 107–18.

Derrida, Jacques. "Force of Law: The 'Mystical Foundation of Authority'" in *Deconstruction and the Possibility of Justice*, edited by Drucilla Cornell and Michael Rosenfeld. New York: Routledge, 1992.

———. *Given Time: Counterfeit Money*. Translated by Peggy Kamuf. Chicago: University of Chicago Press, 1992.

Eagleton, Terry. *After Theory*. New York: Basic Books, 2003.

Farrar, Fredric William. *Seekers After God*. New York: Cosmio, 2005.

Liberman, Mark. "The Language Log." Accessed January 20th 2007. Online: http://itre.cis.upenn.edu/~myl/languagelog/archives/000024.

Mill, J. S. *Utilitarianism 1861*. Indianapolis: Hackett 2001.

Parfit, Derek. "Is Common- Sense Morality Self-Defeating?" *The Journal of Philosophy* 76:10 (1979) 533–45.

Singer, Peter. "Is Act Utilitarianism Self-Defeating?" *Philosophical Review* 81:1 (1972) 94–104.

Williams, Gandaer. "Insignificance of The Total of All Value." *Ethics: An International Journal of Social, Political and Legal Philosophy* 55 (1945) 216–21.

5

Tasting the Inscape of Haecceity with Hopkins, the Franciscan Philosophers, Nietzsche, and Derrida

Marko Zlomislić

"Taste and see that the Lord is good."—Psalm 34

NOAH IS THREE YEARS old. It is summer time. We are in the car returning from Victoria Park. I decide to stop in a used bookstore. Noah is looking for *Thomas the Tank Engine* Books. He has become quite an expert on Sir Topham Hatt's railroad.

Noah and I made our way to the Philosophy section of the bookstore. The regular fare was on the shelves; used copies of Plato, Aristotle, Russell, mixed in with books on how to be positive, while managing your finances and mastering the art of astral projection. Noah was getting restless; philosophy was not his thing even though I try my best to read Nietzsche's *Zarathustra* to him before we say our evening prayers.

You can imagine my surprise when I glanced at the shelf and found a book entitled *Jacques Derrida: Live Theory*. Quickly scanning the table of contents, it became evident that the author had mastered Derrida's corpus and had written an elegant and impressive book. I thought to myself, "finally, another Catholic who has really understood what Derrida is about." I now know that the author is, if I dare use the description, a postmodern Calvinist who urges a return to catholic liturgy.

Since fully covering such a topic in the short space given to me here is an impossible task, I will lay out as much as I can onto this Eucharistic table prepared for us by Neal DeRoo and Brian Lightbody to honor the fine work of James K. A. Smith, who in a certain sense is to be cannibalized.

There will be too much to taste here. I will have to return to make sense of what will be mixed together here. From the Old Testament to Derrida, taste has been a central concern that exceeds the work of the tongue and the work of knowledge. The notion of taste also engages the philosophical concept of *qualia* involving how things seem to us or how certain experiences feel a certain way. While the work of C. I. Lewis, Daniel Dennett, and others working in the philosophy of mind need to be considered, I will not undertake this important task here.

In keeping with the taste that concerns me, this paper will examine Derrida's turn to the poetry of Gerard Manley Hopkins and how such a turn may place Derrida within a catholic and Franciscan tradition.

TASTING THE RESPONSIBLE PERSON

To explore the being of the person who is responsible and says "I" Derrida turns to the poetic insights of Gerard Manley Hopkins. Derrida asks, "what taste could this *je*, this I have?" and "what does it mean for an I to feel itself"[1] By turning to Hopkins's notion of Selftaste, Derrida shows how the responsible person is affected by the scope and scape of ipseity. While Hopkins's poetry is said to deal with nature and its landscape the primary focus given Hopkins's Catholicism is on the person and how this person tastes, feels, touches and senses the various scapes and inscapes of haecceity in all things.

Derrida writes:

> In Hopkins extraordinary lexicon, what comes to effect, identify, think, proves this selfhood, in truth that by which selfhood affirms, affects itself, "selves" itself operates on its own selving as Hopkins will say is not thought, consciousness or reflection but taste.[2]

Taste from the Latin *gusto* is the faculty by which a flavor of a thing is discerned. *Gusto* relates to the Sanskrit word *jus*, which means enjoy and be pleased. Close to St. Francis, Hopkins not only tastes the landscape but all the inscapes of being human that range from joy to deep despair. Selftaste can have no final assessment because its worth is without price

---

1. Derrida, "Justices," 698.
2. Ibid., 698.

and beyond the cost of calculative accounting. This Selftaste to follow Derrida is priceless (*san prix*). "What is absolutely precious, the other in his or her own dignity, has no price . . . *every one* is worth as much as *the other*, precisely beyond all value: *priceless*."[3]

The question of taste for Derrida engages the issue of the cannibalism within mourning; how the other is incorporated, remembered, retained in the crypt of memory; bound together in what Kierkegaard in *Works of Love* calls "the kinship of death."[4] The crypt as Derrida reminds us in *Glas*, "organizes the ground to which it does not belong."[5] While it will always be possible to taste the thing, the taste of the thing never yields its Selftaste. Even when one says, "I love the way you taste," Selftaste remains elusive and cannot be caught or contained by the palate.

Related to the word flavor is the word smolder. Smolder means to burn and smoke without flame. We can taste this smolder in the fall, in the decay and excretion of things, in the spring when the freshness of flowers, trees, grass and green boils over the landscape. Hopkins will write:

> The world is charged with the grandeur of God.
> It will flame out, like shining from shook foil.[6]

While the natural world according to Hopkins, "wears man's smudge and shares man's smell," the flavor can never be exhausted for "there lives the dearest freshness deep down things."[7] In "Pied Beauty" Hopkins raises the issue of responsibility when he declares "all things counter, original, spare, strange." Spare, from the Old English *sparian*, means "to refrain from harming, to allow to go free." Strange means alien, foreign, from elsewhere, unknown and unfamiliar and unique. We are close and yet strange to ourselves. We are strangers to our own uniqueness or haecceity that flows forth in excess that cannot be contained.

The Franciscan philosophers: Bonaventure, Scotus, and Ockham became nominalists in order to safeguard each single individual from the power of totalization. Bonaventure was enthralled by the great diversity of

---

3. Derrida, "On the Priceless" in *Negotiations*, 324–25.

4. Kierkegaard, *Works of Love*, 317. Kierkegaard continues, "I know of no better way to describe true memory than by this weeping softly. . . . No, one must remember the dead; weep softly, but grieve long." (Ibid., 319).

5. Derrida, *Glas*, 166.

6. Hopkins, *Selected Poetry of Gerard Manley Hopkins*, number 7: "God's Grandeur."

7. Ibid.

creation and to the praised the unlimited possibilities that happen in the radical leap of the new. St. Francis who imitated Jesus realized that God could be found in the inner being of all flesh. Following the Franciscans, Hopkins was inspired to find a new significance to flesh. The inscape for Hopkins bears the stamp of the divine. Each mortal thing offers itself as a witness to the splendor of God.

Vigilance calls us to protect the person bound in a bond of singularities, by not harming, by guarding freedom so as not to reduce the person to a force[8] or a maker of systems.[9] To protect the uniqueness of persons Derrida will argue that we cannot be satisfied with a neutral and conceptual analysis that reduces the difficulty of our situation, which is ultimately irreducible. Such systems deal with homogenization and calculability and "close themselves off from this coming of the other."[10] If we take seriously the uniqueness of each Self, which according to Kierkegaard is "a work of the most faithful love,"[11] then we are necessarily involved in an excessive responsibility of which we cannot be absolved not even in the moment of death where according to Kierkegaard "all ways meet."[12]

The various flavors of nature are meant to provide an awakening so that the fading fire of the Self can be mended. In Hopkins's words from his poem "The Candle Indoors":

> Come you indoors, come home; your fading fire
> Mend first and vital candle in close heart's vault.[13]

Is our taste so bleared and smeared that it requires mending with the help of salt? Salt is that which gives life or pungency. The pungent is what is sharp and poignant. Death is such a point. Once we realize that it is for the Self that we mourn how do we overcome the finality that "it is the blight man was born for"?[14] In Derrida's words from a beautiful essay that analyses the works of Gadamer and Celan we read:

---

8. For example, in the work of Gilles Deleuze.
9. For example, in the work of Niklas Luhmann.
10. Derrida, "Politics and Friendship," in *Negotiations*, 182.
11. Kierkegaard, *Works of Love*, 317.
12. Ibid.
13. Hopkins, "The Candle Indoors."
14. Hopkins, *Selected Poetry of Gerard Manley Hopkins*, number 12: "Spring and Fall."

PART TWO: RECEIVING THE (POSTMODERN) TRADITION

> For every time, and every time singularly, every time irreplaceably, every time infinitely, death is nothing less than an end *of the* world. Not only one end among others, the end of someone or of something *in the world* . . . death marks every time, every time in defiance of arithmetic, the absolute end of the one and only world, of which everyone opens as one and the only world, the end of the unique world. . . . for an unique living being, be it human or not.[15]

Following Hopkins, we can ask how things in the world touch us, seize us, and take possession of us as we seek, visit, inquire and pursue what beseeches us. The Latin *tactus* relates to the word tangent. Tangent is a meeting point. It is the point at which responsibility is engaged or ignored as the Self meets/meats itself and others in a singularity and uniqueness that cannot be leveled off. In Hopkins words,

> I consider my selfbeing, my consciousness and feeling of myself, that taste of myself of I and me above and in all things is more distinctive than the taste of ale or alum, more distinctive that the smell of walnutleaf or camphor and is incommunicable by any means to another man.[16]

Though incommunicable by any means to another person, we nonetheless attempt to communicate. Though Selftaste cannot be communicated through lips, mouth and tongue, it can be witnessed.

Is this communication of what is incommunicable and yet witnessed, called the poetry of faith? Hopkins used unusual combinations of words, unusual word order and sprung rhythm in an attempt to explode out of traditional poetic confines. The poem attempts to testify Selftaste. The poem testifies but not in the order of cognitive reason. Hopkins poetry, following St. Augustine's formulation *veritatem facere*, does the truth by attempting to be a testimony of love. In Derrida's words, this love is "without jealousy that would allow the other to be" (ON, 74). The poem reveals the instress of Selftaste, which is the energy that creates and sustains the "inscape" of the person.

NAMING THE UNNAMABLE

Is Hopkins expressing a mystical principle that eludes rational and empirical analysis? Leibniz argues that "the fundamental principle of rea-

---

15. Derrida, "Uninterrupted Dialogue: Between Two Infinities, The Poem," 8.
16. Hopkins, *The Poems and Prose of Gerard Manley Hopkins*, 117.

soning is that there is nothing without a reason, or, to explain the matter more distinctly, there is no truth for which a reason does not subsist."[17] Reason cannot communicate Selftaste yet according to Hopkins Selftaste is a truth of the person's inscape. Is Selftaste the unfathomable ground of what we are?

In the *Tractatus*, Wittgenstein shows how the limits of language are the limits of my world. In Wittgenstein's world, the solipsistic circle encloses the tongue to make it mute. However, this is not what Hopkins means by incommunicable. Can a new language be invented so that the Self can speak its taste; can express the taste of the aporetic situation? Can it name that which language cannot name, can come close to naming but never quite able to do so? Samuel Beckett's words in *The Unnamable* express this aporia nicely:

> I'm shut up, the silence is outside, outside, inside, there is nothing but here.... I'll never know, in the silence you don't know, you must go on, I can't go on, I'll go on.[18]

Beckett expresses the aporia that provokes us. We must and we cannot but we must. For Hopkins, Selftaste is ultimately known by God but if two can commune in this silence, this Selftaste can be communicated otherwise than through language. Perhaps such a thing (if we can call it a thing) has been felt by us when face to face with a lover who astounds you on the staircase during a goodnight kiss or when you are holding your child in your arms or when you are holding a dying parent or stranger. Such a thing can never be contained within the limits of reason alone. If one really believes in the *haeccitas* of Scotus then the universal cannot comprehend the singular. This is what Ockham's nominalism shows us as it protects the unique name of the person and following St. Francis, protects the uniqueness of all flesh.

The Selftaste that constitutes selfhood is an auto-affection that according to Derrida "consists in touching oneself in taste of tasting oneself in Selftaste."[19] But this auto-affection can also be hetero-affection even

17. Leibniz, *Philosophical Writings*, "Metaphysical Consequences of the Principle of Reason," 172. In "Discourse on Metaphysics," Leibniz mentions the "individual notion or haeceitas," but he does not follow through with this insight. His strict rationalism prevents him from realizing the full implications of "thisness." In his *Monadology*, he writes, "Indeed, every monad must be different from every other" (Ibid., 174).

18. Beckett, *The Unnamable (Into the Silence)*, 2602–6.

19. Derrida, "Justices," 698.

as it is a homo-affection. Though incommunicable, this Selftaste can still be communicated in its unique strangeness of being-queer. Derrida re-writes Scotus's doctrine of "this-ness" into the formula, "to be is to be queer."[20] In Hopkins's words, "All things counter, original, spare, strange."[21] The inscape of such unique self and thing requires that justice be given as we witness "each mortal thing." Following Hopkins's phrase "the just man justices," Derrida will wonder how to do justice to the person, to the specter, to all the inscapes of the Self, to memory, to mourning, to friendship and to democracy-to-come that cannot be calculated according to existing models or rules or reason and which cannot be reduced by ontology or a phenomenology of presence.

In Hopkins words, "when I compare myself, my being-myself with anything else whatever, all things alike, all in the same degree, rebuff me with blank unlikeness."[22] This unlikeness is another word for Derrida's *differance*. Derrida says:

> The thinking of differance is also, therefore, a thinking of urgency, of what I can neither elude nor appropriate because it is other. The event, the singularity of the event—this is what differance is about.[23]

The scape is the scenery view of the Self that is unlike all other selves. It is impossible to get out of this cape or to gather the other into a self-identity that can be mastered. To escape the inscape, to leave a pursuer with just one's cape is an impossibility here.

A further reason that Derrida appreciates Hopkins is that he is developing an *ethos* of taste that goes beyond the aesthetics of taste developed by Hume and Kant. Though we cannot treat these rich texts here in their entirety a few remarks will suffice for what is being attempted here.

TASTE EX-HUMED AND RE-KANTED

In his *Of the Delicacy of Taste and Passion*, Hume makes a distinction between the delicacies of passion that makes us sensitive to joys, sorrows, and the delicacy of taste, which makes us sensitive to the arts. Hume ar-

---

20. Ibid., 703.
21. Hopkins, *Selected Poetry of Gerard Manley Hopkins*, number 11: "Pied Beauty."
22. Hopkins, *The Sermons and Devotional Writings of Gerard Manley Hopkins*, 123.
23. Derrida, "The Deconstruction of Actuality," in *Negotiations*, 93.

gues that the delicacy of taste improves the delicacy of passion. Passion must be remedied by taste if possible. In *Of the Standard of Taste,* Hume attempts to show how there can be a universal recognition of greatness if there is "a proper functioning of taste."

Our taste functions properly if our conclusions are consistent with the experiences of other nations and ages. The way in which taste is developed is through practice or by observing many works of art and making comparisons. Taste is perfected once it is free of prejudice. Hume further claims that "the general principles of taste are uniform in human nature" though he acknowledges the variations in how taste is applied. Given Hume's "academic" and "skeptical" philosophy, there is no room for justification of substance and of selfhood. Hume would dismiss the issues that Hopkins and Derrida deal with as unapproachable.[24]

Hume argues that a higher and more refined taste enables us form "juster" notions of life. Hopkins does not reduce taste to sentiment. Hume's insights are very different from the Fransciscan-inspired Hopkins, who affirms "the just man justices." In other word, it is not a matter of cultivating a culture of taste so that we can form "juster notions of life."[25] In this scenario, taste would be the springboard into justice. One can of course have a taste for Shakespeare and still be a serial killer or have a taste for

---

24. Here one can also mention Ayer's many texts where there is no trace of responsibility in his exclusively linguistic analysis, which constricts what it means to be human. For examples see *Language, Truth and Logic*. The issues raised by Hopkins and Derrida do exist but cannot be seen by linguistic dogmatists which a self-imposed narrow perspective. I think the best example of the self-imposed and narrow perspective can be found in Strawson, when he writes, "Up to a point the reliance upon a close examination of the actual use of words is the best, and indeed the only sure, way in philosophy" (Strawson, *Individuals: An Essay in Descriptive Metaphysics*, 9). He goes on, "some of the themes discusses here are sufficiently general, the discussion undertaken from a certain limited viewpoint and is by no means comprehensive." Reducing individuals to logical particulars is as unsatisfactory as it is absurd. Here we clearly see what is forfeited when there is no belief in persons. Perhaps Erasmus can offer an answer, in his *Praise of Folly* we read, "Pan makes everyone laugh with his hopeless efforts at singing, and the gods would rather listen to him than to the muses themselves, especially when the nectar has started to flow freely." Alternatively, from Bishop Berkeley's "Preface" to his *Principles,* which could also be taken as a reply to Derrida's critics, Berkeley writes that we are faced with "the hasty censures of a sort of men who are too apt to condemn an opinion before they rightly comprehend it" (Preface).

25. I assume Hume here means Anglo-Saxon conceptions of what constitutes a just life.

classical music and engage in "outsourced" torture while drinking Coke Zero.

In thinking of Hume's reflections of taste and its cultivation I am reminded of the *Island of Dr. Moreau* where the dog-human, the canine-man does indeed recite W. B. Yeats poem *The Second Coming* while all the while being driven by the need to-be-canine. Taste reduced to sentiment and palate can never become a witness to Selftaste.

For Kant, the judgment of taste has a number of characteristics and combinations that seem incompatible. The judgment of taste is made from a subjective basis. For example, we take pleasure in contemplating an object or a work of art. We view Warhol's portrait of Mao, Chris Ofili's "The Holy Virgin,"[26] Andres Serrano's "Piss Christ,"[27] Jean-Michel Basquiat's "Tabac" (1984),[28] and trust that others will find our taste to have a universal validity. Kant argues, "the judgment of taste is aesthetic."[29] However, this subjective judgment must have a universal validity. In other words, to call something beautiful is to demand that others find it beautiful.

Kant's problem is to explain how this combination is possible. While scholars have devoted considerable energy to dissolving this problem, I will not add to their efforts here. The problems as I see it is not a demand to take pleasure in an object or to even attend to that object. The demand is to attend to the person who cannot be placed within any kingdom of ends that would level off Selftaste into a bland and tasteless uniformity. In Kant's language when we call an object beautiful, "we believe ourselves to be speaking with a universal voice and lay claim to the concurrence of everyone."[30]

---

26. Ofili depicts a black Madonna with dung and assorted female orifices cut out and pasted all over the canvas. He was playing with the word "holy."

27. The NEA funded Andres Serrano's photograph entitled "Piss Christ." Along the same lines, the Canada Council funded Tamara Sanowar-Makham's creation, the "ultra-maxi priest," which is a vestment gown made of sanitary pads, and intended to express "the oppressive anti-female ideology of the Catholic Church."

28. Acrylic and oil crayon on canvas showing a head smoking with the words "nervous system" and "filter" written on the canvas.

29. Section 1 title in Kant, *Kants gesammelte Schriften*, 5:203.

30. Ibid., Section 6, 203.

Tasting the Inscape of Haecceity

TASTING WITH GOD'S TONGUE

The event that perhaps unifies taste while still making it unique for each person is death. In "Countersignatures," Derrida writes, "I run to/on death. In other words, I run towards death, but also I run on death like a fuel, as an engine runs on petrol. I run on death, death is what makes me run."[31] Fuel from the Old French word *feuaile* means bundle of firewood. It relates to the Latin word *focus* or hearth. The secret of Selftaste is this fire or spark within each unique selved spark that gives us fuel and focus.[32] Our Selftaste converges on Death.[33] Here I can only trace the trajectory that such a reading would take. Our tongues would taste two testaments, old and new. Psalm 119:103 declares, "How sweet are thy words to my taste! Sweeter than honey to my mouth." Luke 9:27 declares, "But I tell you of a truth, there be some standing here which shall not taste of death till they see the Kingdom of God."

What salt will bring taste back? What taste will be finally able to discern the perverse so that the verse of God can be tasted with a sweetness that surpasses honey? Is this all that is required- a simple refinement in taste; a tasting of the right words so that we shall never taste death? How do we switch our taste for his taste so that the taste of death is avoided?

The letter to the Hebrews reads, "but we see Jesus, who was made a little lower than the angels for the suffering of death crowned with glory and honor that he by the grace of God should taste death for every man" (2:9). He tastes death for every Selftaste. He consumes it, swallows it completely so that no Self has to taste it. However, doesn't this imply that we can now taste it all without fear of final death? His tasting has transformed the Selftaste of our tongue by giving the Real thing back to us without its poisonous after-taste. We can taste the fruit of the other's Selftaste without fear of bad-taste. Is this what Christ's sacrifice on the cross actually gives us? In his poem "The Wreck of the Deutschland" (1875) Hopkins writes,

---

31. Derrida, "Countersignatures," 38.

32. Focus was first used by Hobbes in *The Questions Concerning Liberty, Necessity, and Chance* (1656) and meant the center of activity or energy. Kepler used it in *Astronomiae Pars Optica* (1604) to mean a point of convergence.

33. The British poet, Ted Hughes, who was influenced by Hopkins, writes the following in his poem "God Help the Wolf after whom the Dogs Do Not Bark": "To sweeten his slow death and mix yourself in it ... to sugar the bitterness of his raging death" in Hughes, *Birthday Letters*, 26–27.

PART TWO: RECEIVING THE (POSTMODERN) TRADITION

> Let him easter in us,
> be a dayspring to the
> dimness of us, be a
> crimson-crested east.³⁴

Here Hopkins shows how Christ is the "Lord of Life" who sends rain to dry roots. In allowing Christ to "easter in us" Hopkins affirms that death is never a finality. Derrida will agree that death is never a finality but I do not see him calling on Christ to "easter in us" since it is too simple of a solution. For Derrida, we find ourselves on the trajectory of Selftaste without any final tasting. In Derrida's words from *Signsponge* (1976), his tribute to the poet Francis Ponge we read,

> Thus the thing would be the other, the other-thing which gives me an order or addresses an impossible, intransigent, insatiable demand to me, without and exchange and without a transaction, without a possible contract. Without a word, without speaking to me, it addresses itself to me, to me alone in my irreplaceable singularity, in my solitude as well.³⁵

Does not Derrida here sound like a Fransciscan philosopher of the highest order who keeps the task of responsibility open; who keeps thinking with the aporia in order to avoid dogmatism? Derrida shows us the sharpness of the aporetic necessity we must follow for the sake of the other. This Selftaste announces the messianic. Derrida explains that the messianic

> can arrive at any moment, no one can see it coming, can see how it should come, or have forewarning of it. The relation to the other is the absence of horizon, of anticipation, there where the alterity of the other is an absolute surprise. If one can be prepared for an absolute surprise, then one must be prepared for the coming of the other as an absolute surprise- that is what I understand by the messianic.³⁶

The coming of the other arrives on a non-horizon, which does not mean the absence of horizon. It is where the horizon would be punctured by the other; always open and without saturation. For Hopkins, the incarnation is the fleshing of the Word. The Messiah for Hopkins pervades all things,

---

34. Hopkins, *Selected Poetry of Gerard Manley Hopkins*, number 18: "The Wreck of the Deutschland."

35. Derrida, *Signsponge*, 14.

36. Derrida, "A Certain Impossible Possibility of Saying the Event," 454.

thoughts and feelings. Perhaps it is at this point that Derrida parts ways with Christianity.

Derrida's last words were, "always prefer life and constantly affirm survival." Here Derrida shows us his taste and courage in the face of death and disease. He shows us his taste, perhaps not for the incarnation of the God-Man but for a certain spirit of resurrection and living-on. Rather than a return to Catholic sacramental liturgy, which for some of us is no return at all, might we not follow Derrida in thinking about the other possibility; a wholly other possibility that is the faith of deconstruction? He writes:

> We should speak here of the im-possible event, an im-possible that is not merely impossible, that is not merely the opposite of possible, that is also the condition or chance of the possible. An im-possible that is the very experience of the possible. This means transforming the conception, or the experience or the saying of the experience of the possible and the impossible.[37]

For Christians the impossible has already happened. For Derrida, there can only be an event when it is not expected or predicted. He argues that "this impossibility is not simply negative. This means that the impossible must be done. The event, if there is one, consists in doing the impossible." Derrida continues to add, "This doesn't mean that events don't occur, that there are none; what it means is that I cannot say the event in theoretical terms and I cannot pre-dict it either."[38] On the other hand, it seems as if Derrida is describing the second coming. What he says about the event sounds very similar to the words of Matthew's Gospel where we read, "No one knows about that day or hour, not even the angels in heaven, nor the Son, but only the Father . . . Therefore, keep watch, because you do not know on what day your Lord will come" (Matt 24:44). Derrida would of course add, "If the event is an event, not even the Father will know."

As I rush towards a conclusion, I ask, what would it mean to be taken to church? Can there not be some trickery involved after one realizes that one was taken? Take asks the where, not only the where but what shall we do when we are there. What do we declare in the Here, where there is neither justice nor mercy, where we gather to remember beneath the

---

37. Ibid, 453.
38. Ibid, 452.

Nietzschean arches of a shattered roof, surrounded by poppies, arguing empty points to a clear blue sky.

I fear that the good news seems to have been forgotten. We live as if haunted, staggering after a supposed creator, incarnated, drooling out words and theological phrases that remain forever in dispute much like a gospel of brittle complaints.

What is that we are so afraid to speak in these huts we have assembled—that he is the son of God and because of his incarnation, death and resurrection, can announces, as Luke does in 3:6, "All flesh shall see the salvation of God" (*Et vedebit omnis caro salutare Deo*), or that there is no God to intervene and answer. What consolations can be offered other than an Unamuno novel, coffee and donuts, Jack Daniels and other elixirs of escape? Is the promise false or are we false? The news that he announced appears to be dying. Does his message seduce only the dying who are on the take, taken in and caught up? What remains to be said?

Mute from the Old High German word *mawen* means to cry out. To be mute is to be unable to speak because of shock. The mute is what is felt or experienced but not expressed. A mute is one hired to attend a funeral as a mourner. Will we not one day all become mutes? Do we not already mourn? Here we are on the verge, on the edge or border as we attempt to speak and communicate Selftaste without becoming absolutely mute. Following Hopkins, this Selftaste will always be yonder; farther removed and yet closest to us. So close that we can taste its *tang*- it's sharp and distinctive flavor, its point or sting.[39] St. Francis kissing the leper transformed his taste. The honey-poison of the bee-sting that perhaps will not make us swell but will untie our tongue (*solutio linguae*) as we are detached to deliver this gift of Selftaste to the ones who both hate and love us, much like Jesus on the cross refusing to taste sour wine and vinegar because his tongue had not only already tasted the tang of death but had always tasted the inscape of his Father and the landscape of the kingdom come flowing with milk and honey, here, now.

> Evangelists of what? . . .
> The multitudes of men
> that Kill the single man, starvations head
> One man, their bread and their remembered wine.
> (Wallace Stevens, "Extracts from Addresses to the Academy of Fine Ideas")

39. From the Old Norse word *tangi*-point and *tunga* or tongue.

Tasting the Inscape of Haecceity

For my son Noah Anthony.

WORKS CITED

Beckett, Samuel. *The Unnamable (Into the Silence)*. In *The Norton Anthology of English Literature*, edited by M. H. Abrams et. al, 2602–6. New York: Norton, 1962.

Berkeley, George Bishop. "A Treatise Concerning the Principles of Human Knowledge." No Pages. Accessed May 12, 2008. Online: http://18th.eserver.org/berkeley.html.

Derrida, Jacques. "A Certain Impossible Possibility of Saying the Event." Translated by Gila Walker. *Critical Inquiry* 33:2 (Winter 2007) 441–61.

———. "Countersignatures." Translated by Mairéad Hanrahan. *Paragraph* 27:2 (July 2004) 7–42.

———. *Glas*. Translated by John P. Leavey, Jr. and Richard Rand. Lincoln, NE: University of Nebraska Press, 1986.

———. "Justices." *Critical Inquiry* 31:3 (Spring 2005) 689–721.

———. *Negotiations: Interventions and Interviews 1971–2001*. Edited and translated by Elizabeth Rottenburg. Stanford: Stanford University Press, 2002.

———. *Signsponge*. Translated by Richard Rand. New York: Columbia University Press, 1984.

———. "Uninterrupted Dialogue: Between Two Infinities, The Poem." *Research in Phenomenology* 34:1 (2004) 3–19.

Hobbes, Thomas. *The Questions Concerning Liberty, Necessity, and Chance* (1656). In *The Work of Thomas Hobbes of Malmesbury*. Vol. 5. Edited by William Molesworth. Boston: Adamant Media, 2004.

Hopkins, Gerard Manley. *Selected Poetry of Gerard Manley Hopkins*. Edited by Ian Lancashire. Toronto: Web Development Group, Information Technology Services, University of Toronto, 2006. No Pages. Accessed May 12, 2008. Online: http://rpo.library.utoronto.ca/poet/165.html.

———. "The Candle Indoors." *Poems of Gerard Manley Hopkins*. Edited by Robert Bridges. London: Humphrey Milford, 1918. No Pages. Online: http://www.bartleby.com/122/26.html (accessed May 12, 2008).

———. *The Poems and Prose of Gerard Manley Hopkins*. Edited by W. H. Gardner. New York: Penguin, 1953.

———. *The Sermons and Devotional Writings of Gerard Manley Hopkins*. Edited by Christopher Devlin and S. J. London: Oxford University Press, 1959.

Hughes, Ted. *Birthday Letters*. London: Faber, 1998.

Hume, David. "Of the Delicacy of Taste and Passion." In *Selected Essays*, edited by Stephen Copley and Andrew Edgar, 10–12. Oxford: Oxford World Classics, 1998.

———. *Of the Standard of Taste and Other Essays*. Edited by John W. Lenz. Upper Saddle River, NJ: Prentice Hall, 1965.

Kant, Immanuel. *Kants gesammelte Schriften*. Edited by the German Academy of Sciences. New York: de Gruyter, 1983.

Kepler, Johannes. *Astronomiae Pars Optica (The Optical Part of Astronomy)* (1604). In *Optics: Paralipomena to Witelo, and Optical Part of Astronomy*. Translated by William H. Donahue. Sante Fe, NM: Green Lion, 2000.

PART TWO: RECEIVING THE (POSTMODERN) TRADITION

Kierkegaard, Søren. *Works of Love*. Translated by Howard and Edna Hong. New York: Harper, 1962.
Leibniz, G. W. *Philosophical Writings*. Edited by G. H. R. Parkinson. London: Dent, 1987.
Stevens, Wallace. "Extracts from Addresses to the Academy of Fine Ideas." In *Collected Poetry and Prose*, 227–233. New York: Library of America, 1997
Strawson, P. F. *Individuals: An Essay in Descriptive Metaphysics*. London: Methuen, 1959.
Wells, H. G. *The Island of Dr. Moreau*. New York: Penguin, 2008.

6

Defending a Universalizable Culture of Particularities (With and Against James K. A. Smith)

Mehdi Wolf[1]

INTRODUCTION

I HAVE ENTITLED THIS article "Defending a Universalizable Culture of Singularities (With and Against James K. A. Smith)" as such seems to be a good expression of the thesis that I here wish to establish. My purpose will be to set forth the Baháʼí notion that, in a fundamental sense, it is the universal that lends importance to the particular with respect to revealed religion.[2] The view being asserted here will have certain agreements with both James K. A. Smith and John Caputo, but will ultimately differ from both Radical Orthodoxy and deconstruction as "religion without religion."

SUMMARIZING THE DIVIDE: CAPUTO AND SMITH

In his book, *The Prayers and Tears of Jacques Derrida: Religion without Religion*, Caputo presents deconstruction as a religious passion for the other, for a justice to come but that can never appear, for *l'impossible*, a faith without a specific dogma or creed, a Judaism *sans* Judaism, a *oui, oui,*

---

1. This essay provides the author's own view of the Baháʼí approach to Radical Orthodoxy and James K. A. Smith, and does not in any way represent the perspective of the Faith as a whole.

2. A Baháʼí is one who follows the teachings of Baháʼuʼlláh (1817–1892), the Persian nineteenth-century Prophet-Founder. For an academic introduction to the Baháʼí faith, see Hatcher and Martin, *The Baháʼí Faith*.

PART TWO: Receiving the (Postmodern) Tradition

and an opening up of religious institutions to the *tout autre*. It is a religion that is an extension of the Enlightenment project, a religion set within the bounds of reason alone, a messianicity without a determinable Messiah, a placeless *khora* in the desert without being in which there would be infinite tolerance beyond tolerance.³ Derrida wants, through deconstruction, to forever end the warring between among mankind's religious communities, for deconstruction, according to Caputo, is peace, without confinement to the Abrahamic religions. Derrida's religion—which is always not present and ever to come—is a purely rational and universal religion, an ethics based on the call of every other as wholly other, an infinite hospitality, where reason and faith do not compete, a declaration of freedom from dogma and doctrine, from every cult, code and historical canon. He wishes to find Levinas's Torah before Sinai, or the responsibility for the other before Moshe (LT, 78).⁴ With his tearful passion, Derrida wishes to get away from determinable theologies or faiths, for these are forever dangerous, ever tinged or tainted with the possibility (or actuality) of triumphalism, violence, oppression, and fundamentalism. Faith is never based on intuitive or absolute knowledge, and thus Derrida's religion is always indeterminate. Deconstruction is the Jewish science that exposes all faith to indefinite re-contextualization, translation, and re-interpretation.⁵

On the other side of the divide, which we here present, there is the school of Radical Orthodoxy,⁶ typified by such figures and John Milbank and James K. A. Smith.⁷ The latter, in *Who's Afraid of Postmodernism?*, writes that Caputo's quest of a religion without religion is not properly postmodern, for it still rests on the Cartesian assumption that knowledge is identical with certitude. Rather than equate the two, and then assert that all particular knowledge claims with respect to God by any religious community or believer are akin to fundamentalism, Radical Orthodoxy, according to Smith, distinguishes between knowledge of God and absolute *comprehension* (WAP, 120). For Smith, the Catholic tradition from Augustine and Aquinas to the present, while allowing for knowledge in

3. Caputo, *The Prayers and Tears of Jacques Derrida*, 155–56.

4. This writer tends to prefer the Hebrew or Aramaic names for biblical figures and/or Manifestations, to wit: "Moshe" for Moses and "Yeshua" for Jesus.

5. Caputo, *On Religion*, 47–48.

6. The most in-depth study is Milbank, Pickstock, and Ward (eds.), *Radical Orthodoxy: A New Theology*.

7. See Milbank, *Theology and Social Theory* and IRO.

the case of God, would never claim full comprehension. The additional concern, and the point that drives the whole of Smith's final chapter, is that a religion without religion becomes both anti-institutional and wholly non-incarnational (WAP, 121). In the view of Smith, the adoption of a religion without religion, without doctrine and only a passion for justice to the other, voids the whole of the church, the goodness of the material world and the purposefulness of temporality as part of being in the world.

It is thus for this reason that, according to Smith, the church must follow the example of the heroine in the film *Whale Rider*. In the story, Paikea, raised in the home of a traditional Maori chief and under the influence of her tribe's sacred traditions, challenges modernity by recovering these same traditions and thus re-invigorating her people. Similarly, Smith argues, the body of Christ must recover the traditions which it surrendered over the centuries to the advancing forces of modernity and promulgate them unapologetically to the faithful. It must cease using the findings of supposedly neutral, objective sciences and philosophies in apologetic discourse, and unrepentantly promulgate its incarnational, theological meta-discourse without any hint of surrender or capitulation.

THE UNIVERSALIZABLE CULTURE OF SINGULARITIES

In the Baháʼí view, the tension between universality and particularity, which we see in the schools of Caputo and Smith, can be overcome, while at the same time giving each side of this divide its proper due. As a foundational precept, the teachings of Baháʼuʼlláh (1817–1892), the Prophet-Founder of our Faith, assert that all revealed religions are from one divine Source, which is God alone. The great Figures of religious history, such as Moshe, Avraham, Yeshua and Muhammad, are all Messengers of one Cause. Baháʼuʼlláh writes:

> It is clear and evident to thee that all the Prophets are the Temples of the Cause of God, Who have appeared clothed in diverse attire. If thou wilt observe with discriminating eyes, thou wilt behold Them all abiding in the same tabernacle, soaring in the same heaven, seated upon the same throne, uttering the same speech, and proclaiming the same Faith. Such is the unity of those Essences of Being, those Luminaries of infinite and immeasurable splendor![8]

8. Baháʼuʼlláh, *Gleanings from the Writings of Baháʼuʼlláh*, XXII, 52.

PART TWO: Receiving the (Postmodern) Tradition

As a consequence, Bahá'ís hold that true revelation cannot, in principle, conflict with itself, for God's oneness pervades all that proceeds from Him. We shall term this the Bahá'í universality principle. Yet, this precept is tempered with a second, equally operative, namely that in each religious dispensation, meaning that span of time when a particular Revelation is in assent between one Messenger and another, there are laws and teachings which are demanded according to the material or spiritual requirements of mankind at the time. Again, quoting Bahá'u'lláh:

> In this respect, each Manifestation of God hath a distinct individuality, a definitely prescribed mission, a predestined revelation, and specially designated limitations. Each one of them is known by a different name, is characterized by a special attribute, fulfils a definite mission, and is entrusted with a particular Revelation.[9]

This we shall call the Bahá'í particularity principle. Under it, Bahá'ís will speak of the Christian dispensation, or the Islamic, and accord to each teachings and laws specific to that time and place. However, neither the promulgation or the abrogation of any given laws or teachings, of whatever dispensation, in any way void the universality principle, for these laws concern the finite nature of man and his being in the world, as a temporal and evolving creature. They are specific expressions or manifestations of God's Absolute attributes and Names ordained for a particular period.[10]

Again, Bahá'u'lláh writes, "Wherefore, should one of these Manifestations of Holiness proclaim saying: 'I am the return of all the Prophets,' He, verily, speaketh the truth. In like manner, in every subsequent Revelation, the return of the former Revelation is a fact, the truth of which is firmly established...."[11] Even as particularities succeed one another in the physical realm, one dying and another replacing it, owing to the finitude of creation, the whole of each revelation and the institutions which they found are similarly restricted. These successions, however, are true resurrections; just as one flower in a particular year is the rebirth of the one before it, and the son is the reappearance of certain qualities and attributes of both the father and mother, each revelation, each Divine Messenger, each particular law, ordained institution or establishment is

---

9. Ibid.

10. For Bahá'u'lláh's own full defense of the universality and particularity principles, see the *Kitáb-i-Íqán* "The Book of Certitude".

11. Bahá'u'lláh, *Gleanings from the Writings of Bahá'u'lláh*, XXII, 52.

Defending a Universalizable Culture of Particularities

the resurrection and salvation of the corresponding code, Being or body in the previous dispensation. It is this constant resurrection, propelled by the Names and Attributes of God which precede them, that gives importance to every particularity within each dispensation; while some aspects of a given law or teaching are retained, others are left aside, and still more appear without precedent, according to need and God's unerring and undoubted wisdom. The particularities of each dispensation also attain importance through the Goal towards which each and all are ultimately directed.

Taken together, these two principles are seen as evidence of one single Plan of God, which has, as its purpose, the civilizing of mankind. The goal of this irresistible process, according to the teachings of Bahá'u'lláh, is the establishment of a world unity, a world federation, a world religion, a world language and script. Each dispensation's authentic laws and teachings, in what Bahá'ís call the Adamic Cycle, are all part of this civilizing process. The Jewish *Shema* teaches us that God is one and to Him alone we must turn; the Christian teaching of *agape* even to one's enemy asserts the standard of love to which God wills to call us; the Islamic *shahada* re-inforces the *Shema*, commanding believers to surrender their wills to the one supreme Will; the Bahá'í teaching of unity reinforces all these and envisions a world society in which all these teachings are embraced and practiced; the Revelations to come will bring yet more advances of spiritual truth to mankind, one dispensation to the next.

RESPONSES TO RELIGION WITHOUT RELIGION

As an archetype of this view, we should look at Levinas's suggestion of a Torah before Sinai. Such a Torah would be the sum and the meaning of the Torah, namely an ethics of the other that existed before revelation. For the Bahá'í, the Torah before Sinai is the Preserved Tablet, the metaphysical scroll containing the whole of God's Knowledge and Wisdom. It is known only to the Manifestations of His Cause, and from it alone have all the Revelations proceeded. And then, the Torah before Sinai is the Names and Attributes of God[12] which pervade all creation, appearing in their most concentrated form in the Kingdom of man. In that Kingdom, these Names and Attributes are Caputo's human religious element, that which

---

12. Some mention of the Names and Attributes and their importance in Bahá'í ontology can be found in McLean, "Prolegomena to a Bahá'í Theology."

makes the human being innately religious, with or without a religious commitment.¹³ To the Bahá'í these two are, in reality, one and the same. Yet the fullness of neither is open to rational penetration of the human mind alone. For the Bahá'í, a religion without religion, in Caputo's sense, while enticing to modernism, is truly *l'impossible*.

According to the Bahá'í principles we have laid out, we should not reduce the Torah to a mere responsibility to the other or a love for God; though the authentic laws and creeds of every dispensation have an ethical purpose and *telos* which all entail love, such a station does not supercede the requirement laid upon every believer to obey them while a particular dispensation is in assent. A third principle is here operative, namely the inseparability principle, as set forth in Bahá'u'lláh's *Kitáb-i-Aqdas*.¹⁴ It asserts that faith and works are inherently one and indissoluble. On this theme, Bahá'u'lláh writes in one of His Tablets: "man's knowledge of God cannot develop fully and adequately save by observing whatsoever hath been ordained by Him and is set forth in His heavenly Book."¹⁵

Yet, with Caputo, it is true that no teaching of any revealed faith can be accepted as Absolute. For the Bahá'í, Absolutes and Infinity are confined to God alone, as Yeshua confirmed in His saying that there is none Good but God (Mark 10:18; Matt 19:17; Luke 18:19). Truth claims of revealed religions are manifestations of God's Absolute Names, and are subject to amendment or alteration at the appearance of His Messengers, as indicated by our second principle. Our knowledge is imperfect relative to that of God (1 Cor 13:9), and thus our comprehension of any one religious truth will always be less than Absolute. Relative to our station,¹⁶ capacities and perfections, however, we can have certitude, and should strive to attain it.

For the Bahá'í, a religion without religion and the continuance of the many existing metanarratives is not, in any sense, a sure defense against

---

13. Caputo, *On Religion*, 109.

14. *Kitáb-i-Aqdas*, "The Most Holy Book", is the main law book of the Bahá'í Dispensation. This wholly Arabic work was revealed in Adrianople, now Edirne, around 1873. For an introduction to the book, see the anonymously authored "The *Kitáb-i-Aqdas*: Its Place in Bahá'í Literature," 103–18; for discussion of the legal and social principles of the Aqdas, see Schweitz "The Kitáb-i-Aqdas: Bahá'í Law, Legitimacy, and World Order."

15. Bahá'u'lláh, *Tablets of Bahá'u'lláh Revealed after the Kitáb-i-Aqdas*, 268.

16. A term of particular importance in Bahá'u'lláh's Writings, the term "station" has the sense of "rank," "degree," "position," "innate given capacity," as well as "function" or "role."

Defending a Universalizable Culture of Particularities

religious competition; even if all communities were to accept that every faith is equally true, but not absolutely certain, this is not an adequate basis upon which to found a world society, for no common practical or spiritual foundation with which to regenerate the world would exist. The Baháʼí universality principle asserts that there is such a foundation; it has always existed within the totality and the particulars of all revealed religion, for all are indeed true, as Caputo asserts. However, the progressive nature of the universality principle, as outlined, seems to have escaped both Caputo and Derrida.

RESPONSES TO SMITH

With Smith, the Baháʼí would assert that holding to a particular faith claim does not necessarily entail violence against the other. Again like Smith, the Baháʼí is able to know God and the Revelations that are sent down, but such knowledge is not comprehension. What entails the harm that deconstruction so fears is lack of true religious spirit, of common foundation, a failure to seek after that unity which lets distinctions and particularities exist, and the spread of the tares (Matt 13:24–30).

Against Smith, the particularity principle asserts that it is the Manifestations of God Who are the real Whale Riders. What They recover is not tradition, but the authentic doctrines of God, as revealed in the Holy Texts. Because of this, They are all primitivists; it is They alone Who have the authority to decide which laws or teachings should be retained for the new dispensation, which should be discarded, and which should be recast in new forms. It is They Who return the Faith to its spiritual foundations, Who have the power to dismiss the accumulated traditions and customs of centuries as non-authoritative, and set the religion of God onto the course which its Revealer and Sovereign, in His wisdom, has destined for it. For Yeshua, the traditions are the tares in the wheat field (Matt 13:25), the house built upon the sand (Matt 7:26), and the plants that will be rooted up at the harvest (Matt 15:13).

Radical Orthodoxy's Christocentrism, prevalent in the works of both Smith and Milbank, and all that rests upon it, presents another problem for the Baháʼí. An exaltation of one Revelation or any one Messenger over another *in station* violates Baháʼu'lláh's universality principle. This Christocentrism also presents a logical problem: how can Radical Orthodoxy be applied to other religions, given that they are all non-incarnational?[17] Would Smith grant that other religious traditions, such as the Baháʼí, can have an account for the sacredness of the world and time, to an extent equal to or even greater than his incarnational logic? Indeed, there is such a view which sacralizes the world and time through the attributes of God, and does not rely on the primacy or agency of Christ to accomplish this goal. It is a view that allows flesh as flesh and spirit as spirit, each within its own station, neither exalted and neither debased.

The Baháʼí would again assert, as a consequence of our two principles, that the purpose of the revelations and the promulgation of new codes of law has one primary focus. Baháʼuʼlláh writes:

> The purpose of religion as revealed from the heaven of God's holy Will is to establish unity and concord amongst the peoples of the world … The religion of God and His divine law are the most potent instruments and the surest of all means for the dawning of the light of unity amongst men. The progress of the world, the development of nations, the tranquility of peoples, and the peace of all who dwell on earth are among the principles and ordinances of God. Religion bestoweth upon man the most precious of all gifts, offereth the cup of prosperity, imparteth eternal life, and showereth imperishable benefits upon mankind.[18]

The purpose of this unity is to save the world and all flesh (Luke 3:6) from the results of mankind's previous rebellions and misuses. This, indeed, is the ultimate hospitality. Baháʼís view the acceptance of religion, not as an automatic bestowal of salvation granted to the undeserving few over the unnumbered multitude, but as the undertaking of a spiritual and ethical discipline, open to all, that has set requirements and established, though evolving, parameters. Just as with a discipline such as law, which is open to all who have interest, recognize its importance and have the means

---

17. To cite but two, in the Qurʼán, we read: "In blasphemy indeed are those that say that God is Christ the son of Mary. Say: 'Who then hath the least power against God, if His will were to destroy Christ the son of Mary, his mother, and all everyone that is on the earth? For to God belongeth the dominion of the heavens and the earth, and all that is between. He createth what He pleaseth. For God hath power over all things.'" And again: "Christ the son of Mary was no more than an apostle; many were the apostles that passed away before him." (Qurʼán 5:19 and 78ff, ʻAbduʼlláh Yusuf ʻAlí translation). A treatment of the Baháʼí view of the incarnation can be found in Baháʼuʼlláh, *Gleanings from the Writings of Baháʼuʼlláh*, Sections XIX (esp. 47–48) and XX. See also Abduʼl-Baháʼ, *Some Answered Questions*, 206–7.

18. Baháʼuʼlláh, *Tablets of Baháʼuʼlláh Revealed after the Kitáb-i-Aqdas*, 129–30.

available, one's powers and insights are proportional to the effort one exerts in the pursuit of that discipline. If one exerts no effort, and does not even begin the study of the discipline, such a soul cannot be expected to attain the knowledge and understanding enjoyed by a student, let alone a professional. Yet, no effort in the discipline, once entered upon, is ignored or forgotten. Also similar to the study of law, the most current texts and methods, properly identified, are the ones that should be the most intensely studied and followed. The benefits of such a study are clear and evident to one who has pursued and submitted to it, but will be misunderstood, even feared, by those who have not. The latter may even protest that those who have studied the law see themselves as greater or more knowing than themselves. The first complaint has no basis, but the second is certainly true; those who have studied law or any discipline have more knowledge and abilities in that respect than those who have not, and we would have to justly grant this.

The spiritual and religious discipline is similar, except that the training is never-ending, and ever entails humility before the Divine Educator. The powers and capacities available under the spiritual discipline are not granted to those who would misuse them, just as no undisciplined law student can expect either to understand the material, or graduate. The true student of the spiritual discipline is not the one who claims his faith is greater than every other, and that he himself is above every other, but rather the one who radiates in abundance those qualities and attributes which typify the spiritual discipline, who surrenders self to the revealed laws and ordinances and allows God to bring forth the gems latent in him to the fullest, in this life and the next. These are the benefits of religion. What makes such a discipline exclusive is the predilection for separation; this is created not by religion, but by men.

CONCLUSION

The universalizable culture of singularities in religion, as propounded here, relies on the usage of two basic principles, as enunciated by Bahá'u'lláh: first, that all Messengers and Revelations come from the same Divine Source; and, second, that each Revelation, though it is a Manifestation and expression of God's universal Names and Attributes, accomplishes this with due attention to the particular circumstances, capacities and requirements of mankind. In concert, the particulars of a given Revelation depend upon the universal Names, but the relation is not reversible, inasmuch as God is independent of all things, most especially His Own Creation. While we have here agreed with Caputo that there is a "religion without religion," a Torah before Sinai, it is an inaccessible Torah, a Hidden Torah, made known to us only through God's progressive Revelations, according to divine wisdom. Caputo, therefore, does not give adequate accommodation for the particular faith claims and laws which authentically appear in a given Revelation. However, Smith and his Radical Orthodoxy do not suffer from this lack, since this Radical Orthodoxy is founded on the particularity of the incarnation, which is opposed to modernity. We should be appreciative of Smith for such allowance, but his Christocentric incarnational logic presents a challenge against the universality and particularity principles. Neither Caputo nor Smith, in the view of this writer, consider the possibility of progressive revelation, which accepts the truth of all revealed religions, and which, in this writer's view, reconciles the tension we named at our opening.

WORKS CITED

Abdu'l-Bahá. *Some Answered Questions*. First Pocket Edition. Collected and translated by Laura Clifford Barney. Wilmette, Ill.: Bahá'í Publishing Trust, 1984.

Anonymous. "The *Kitáb-i-Aqdas*: Its Place in Bahá'í Literature." *The Bahá'í World 1992–93*. Haifa, Israel: The Baha'i World Centre, 1993.

Bahá'u'lláh. *Gleanings from the Writings of Bahá'u'lláh*. Translated by Shoghí Effendí. Wilmette, Ill.: Bahá'í Publishing Trust, 1990.

———. *Kitáb-i-Íqán* "The Book of Certitude." Revised Edition. Translated by Shoghi Effendi. Wilmette, Illinois: Bahá'í Publishing Trust, 1974.

———. *Tablets of Bahá'u'lláh Revealed after the Kitáb-i-Aqdas*, Second Edition. Translated by Habíb Taherzadeh et al. Haifa: Bahá'í World Centre, 1988.

Caputo, John D. *On Religion*. New York: Routledge, 2001.

———. *The Prayers and Tears of Jacques Derrida: Religion Without Religion*. Bloomington and Indianapolis: Indiana University Press, 1997.

Hatcher, William S., and Douglas J. Martin. *The Bahá'í Faith: The Emerging Global Religion*. Wilmette, Ill.: Bahá'í Publishing Trust, 2002.

McLean, J. A. "Prolegomena to a Bahá'í Theology." *Journal of Bahá'í Studies* 5:1 (1992) 25–67.

Milbank, John. *Theology and Social Theory: Beyond Secular Reason*. Oxford: Blackwell, 2006.

Milbank, John, Catherine Pickstock, and Graham Ward, editors. *Radical Orthodoxy: A New Theology*. London: Routledge, 1999.

Schweitz, Martha. "The Kitáb-i-Aqdas: Bahá'í Law, Legitimacy, and World Order." *Journal of Bahá'í Studies* 6:1 (1994) 35–59.

PART THREE

Applying the Critique

7

Deconstructing Institutions

Derrida and the "Emerging Church"

Peter Schuurman

James K. A. Smith makes it clear right from the beginning of LT that deconstruction is not something we "do"—it is not a method, a technique, some sort of instrumental approach to texts. It is something that happens within something, out of its own resources. Yet, it is a "double-movement of dismantling and rebuilding" (LT, 10), with regards to institutions and systems particularly, opening them up to the possibilities of new arrangements.

At heart, deconstruction is a response to alterity, or the other, a concept that Smith uses to unpack the whole of the Derridean corpus. The "other" is that difference that becomes a reference point for critique, something Smith says Derrida derives from his Jewish background, more specifically the Hebrew Scriptures' vigilance for "the widow, the orphan, and the stranger" (LT, 14).

Deconstruction is therefore justice, and justice is hospitality, which is welcoming the other. In a nutshell, Smith says deconstruction "is a *calling*, a vocation, which undertakes an intense investigation of texts, structures and institutions in order to enable them to respond to the call of the other" (LT, 15; emphasis original).

PART THREE: APPLYING THE CRITIQUE

Put differently (in Carl Raschke's words) deconstruction is "reading texts as complex and to a certain extent *'chaotic' events of flickering meaning*, not as monolithic architectures of clarified Cartesian certainty."[1]

If Derrida is a monster for some, he is more of a *rock star* for the Emerging Church. Self-described as a "conversation," the emerging church is more subtly described by Smith as a "sensibility." This sensibility he describes as postmodern—a rejection of a reduced "individualistic 'talking-head' Christianity mainly concerned with ideas and propositions, rather than practices, formation, and community." He says it is, at core, "a deep affirmation of the Incarnation" that "seeks to recover ancient embodied practices of worship and even a more robust understanding of the sacraments."[2]

My feeling is this describes what Smith wishes it would be as much as it describes what it really is. Gibbs and Bolger in *Emerging Churches* offer thefollowing definition from their social study of the movement: "Emerging churches are communities that practice the way of Jesus within postmodern cultures."[3] That seems like a broader definition, and I'll get back to this later.

LOVING DECONSTRUCTION

Deconstruction looms large in many emerging church conversations. For example, Dan Kimball, pastor of Vintage Faith Church in Santa Cruz, divides his book, *The Emerging Church: Vintage Christianity for New Generations*, into two parts: the first is called "deconstructing," and the second part "reconstructing." There is no philosophical explanation made for this structure, however, leaving the Derridean connection on the surface level of language.

More concretely, the prolific Brian McLaren of Cedar Ridge Community Church in Washington, DC names deconstruction as the flavor of his approach in *The Last Word and the Word After That*—a book in which he finds a different reading on the New Testament's references to hell. You might call it a reading *otherwise*. McLaren says his book "seeks to deconstruct our conventional concepts of hell in the sincere hope that a

---

1. Raschke "'Why is the Emerging Church drawn to deconstructive theology?' Take Two." Emphasis added.

2. Smith, "The Emerging Church: A Guide for the Perplexed," 40–41.

3. Gibbs and Bolger, *Emerging Churches*, 44.

Deconstructing Institutions: Derrida and the "Emerging Church"

better vision of the gospel of Jesus Christ will appear." He explains it this way, with a footnote to Derridean disciple Jack Caputo:

> Deconstruction is not destruction; it is hope. It arises from the belief that sometimes, our constructed laws get in the way of unseen justice, our undeconstructed words get in the way of communication, our institutions get in the way of the purposes for which they were constructed, our formulations get in the way of meaning, our curricula get in the way of learning. In those cases, one must deconstruct laws, words, institutions, formulations, or curricula in the hope that something better will appear once the constructions-become-obstructions have been taken apart. The love of what is hidden, as yet unseen, and hoped for gives one courage to deconstruct what is seen and familiar.[4]

For McLaren, deconstruction is a quest to reach the "Undeconstructible," the mystery that lies beyond our words, which is God. Although I would contend that McLaren's views of both writing and deconstruction are a misunderstanding of the radical nature of the Derridean project, he finds within it hope for a transformed faith.

One more example—and a little more sophisticated yet—of the synergy of the emerging church with deconstruction is Peter Rollins of Ikon Ministries in Ireland and his a/theistic book *How (Not) to Speak of God*. He names Derrida directly, and compares what Derrida says about the relationship between law and justice with the relationship between religion and God. As laws are never accurate readings of justice, so religion is never a fully accurate reading on God.

"Our religious tradition testifies to God and is inspired by God," says Rollins, "yet our religious traditions do not make God present." Rollins brings Derrida together with the mystic Meister Eckhart in an a/theology that claims that the ineffable God is both absent and hyperpresent, anonymous and hypernymous, saying, "that which we cannot speak of is the one thing about whom and to whom we must never stop talking."[5]

Christianity is both fidelity to a system of belief, he says, and a cutting loose or deconstruction of such systems. It is a religion without religion, a religion that is always, like the cynics of ancient Greece, questioning, hungering, desiring, and seeking without ever arriving or possessing. It

---

4. McLaren, *The Last Word and the Word After That*, xvii.
5. Rollins, *How (Not) to Speak of God*, xii.

is a haunting rather than a having. In Derrida's words, it is messianic, or always "to come."

While Rollins keeps more closely to Derrida, he may not have the robust view of the incarnation that Smith talks about in WAP and IRO. Still, the point here is that Rollins finds in Derrida resources for his own theological work.

WHY DECONSTRUCTION?

So why is the emerging church drawn to deconstruction, and Derrida as their prophet of choice? There are no doubt numerous points of connection, but what follows are four significant shared values.

Interpretation

If texts are chaotic events of flickering meaning, you can never be absolutely certain of your reading. There are always multiple readings that are possible. This challenges the idea that faith is certainty, without doubts or misreadings, and opens up room for questioning the church and theology in emergent conversations. It also resists the idea that literal, objective interpretations of Biblical texts are possible. Finally, it negates the claim of Christianity to be "The Absolute Truth" in some sort of pristine and pure way.

If we agree that everything is interpreted, and there are multiple interpretations possible, there is now freedom for emergent congregations to play and experiment with Biblical texts and theology. Doctrines like hell, the exclusivity of Christ, various legalisms, and literalism are open for re-interpretation. Then friendly relationships with other churches and denominations with "a different interpretation" are also admissible. Even relationships with other religions become more acceptable, or at least less "black and white."

Finally, the mission of the emergent church can proceed to "read" the faith for other generations and cultures, and specifically the postmodern world, in different ways, ways that are more suitable and perhaps more seductive for that people group.

Love and Justice

Deconstruction, according to Derrida, is ethics. Singular readings of things are always violent, in so far as it is always exclusive of other read-

Deconstructing Institutions: Derrida and the "Emerging Church"

ings. To find other readings, then, becomes an act of justice and love in so far as it gives room for other voices to be heard.

In this instance, a shift takes place: now it is not as important (or even possible) to "get the right reading" as it is to "read in a just and loving way"—which means allowing other readings to exist alongside our own. When this comes to institutions, this means emergent people recognize that Christendom, the American Empire, capitalism, patriotism and our own churches can be interpreted in other ways. In fact, insofar as they do not allow for the worlds of others to exist and flourish, they become violent and oppressive institutions. This concern for "the other" drives much of emergent politics and ecclesiology.

Messianism

Deconstruction holds that no reading does justice to all, and no reading ever will. The perfect interpretation, the "right reading", the truly hospitable cultural construction is always "to come"—just like the Hebrew messiah.

This sounds like the word "emergence" in other terms. There is concern in the emergent crowd to remain open, tentative, evolving, and not name themselves as "this" or "that." They are emerging—a work in process—a church that is not a church but is rather a church "to come."

Liberation from the Determinate

Deconstruction declares that every particular reading is, in a way, "false" and even violent in its exclusiveness. It seeks to live in the dynamic between the readings rather than in any determinate reading. If all interpretations and institutions are oppressive in this way, we can never rest, never think we have arrived. We are free only when we are beyond our particularities.

Although I have quibbles with some of the other connections named above, I want to elaborate a little on a subtle but I believe significant issue with regards to this similarity between deconstruction and the emerging church. Some of this critique comes via Smith's writings, specifically, WAP.

In so far as some emerging churches (lets call this the "discontinuous emergent" church) shy away from creeds and confessions, and posit a radical discontinuity between themselves and the church that has gone on before, they share with Derrida a modern, negative view of freedom. Freedom, in this sense is a freedom *from*, freedom from restraint, particularity, tradition. This is freedom as autonomy, and can come with the non- or anti-denominational label or some sort of primitivist ecclesiology. This can be viewed as quintessentially modern, in so far as Immanuel Kant heralded the modern age by calling for a break from the "tutelage" of outside authority (tradition).

I do not want to "read" too much into these trends, but these are the hard philosophical questions that we can ask. At root, this approach may assume that to be unapologetically particular (i.e., connected to the catholic tradition of the faith) in any way is to be necessarily besmirched beyond repair. An emerging church is one that has taken the courage (Kant's term) to free itself from history, from tradition, and from all the baggage that comes with it.

Smith explains in FI that this view, at a deep philosophical level, conflates creation and fall. If to be human is to be a finite and interpreting being, and all interpretive traditions are violent, then our humanness is inescapably violent. But if word can become flesh, as it did in the "logic of incarnation" seen in Christ, interpretations can be incarnate in words and institutions that are not inherently violent. In fact, they may bring life. In effect, to unabashedly claim your historic Christian faith is to name your humanity, not to oppress others. We were created as interpretative beings, and while the fall does twist them in violent ways, in Christ our traditions need not be inescapably malevolent.

I recognize there are other emerging churches that describe themselves as a return to the ancient Christian tradition (let us call these the "ancient-future" emergents). While many of these churches are engaged in a desperately necessary retrieval project, there is potential for these churches to be co-opted by the dark side of postmodern life.

Let me explain it this way. If some ancient-future emergents do not see some sort of continuity with an authentic Christian tradition nor configure their ecclesiology in accountable relationships to a broader body, but instead they selectively appropriate parts of the tradition that they find preferable, they may be assuming another kind of autonomy—one that picks and chooses "from above" as it were. This may operate as much in a consumer framework as otherwise, and as many have said, one common way to be post-modern is to be a consumer self.[6]

This is why Smith charges the emerging church with not being postmodern enough. He keeps positing a more persistent or proper postmodernism that takes us beyond the desire for autonomy and into a community of thought and practice that stretches through time and space, in other words, a particular embodied tradition and its institutions. This is, in fact, the "catholic" Christian faith of creeds and confessional Trinitarian dogma, the sacraments, and even hierarchy. This is a call beyond both a spiritual nomadic life and the spiritual fortress of fundamentalism, and towards a sojourning with the Spirit in catholic association, en route to the City of God. We might call this third kind of emergent churches the "catholic emergent churches" (small "c"). It is not just "the same old church" but "the same old church in a new context," which is genuinely ancient-future.

The more particular you are, it has been said, the more universal you become—in so far as to be human is to be particular. There are no generic, universal human beings, any more than there is generic universal reason. I would say to students on university campuses: the more you respectfully and unapologetically express your particularity rather than slide into a generic cultural code, the more you will also free others to be their deep particular self. It is permission giving. We are all much *deeper* than we reveal ourselves to be in North American cultural life. The mass cultural amnesia that Jane Jacobs talked about in her last book *Dark Age Ahead* is what threatens us the most, not the scandal of our particularities (although, of course, particularities are not sacrosanct or salvific in themselves; they are evidence of the *humus* in our humanity—recognition that we come from the earth). The fear of particularity, as Smith says, is a negation of our finiteness, and therefore a negation of our humanity, and becomes a continuation of the disenchanted dehumanizing aspects of modernity.[7]

6. Cf. Lyon, *Postmodernity*.

7. In WAP, Smith investigates George Weigel's description of growing up in a distinctly Catholic tradition in Letters to a Young Catholic and quotes a section where Weigel elaborates on our "ghettoized" nature: "The most ghettoized people of all are those who don't know they grew up in a particular time and place and culture, and who think they can get to universal truths outside particular realities and communities ... The real question is not whether you grow up in a ghetto, but whether the ideas and customs and

PART THREE: APPLYING THE CRITIQUE

Life is lived by our choice of prepositions. Freedom can be negatively understood as a freedom from, but it can also be positively understood as a freedom to and a freedom with. Freedom need not be defined as free-floating autonomy. There is also a freedom that comes when one is empowered by deep commitments and covenants, by submission to authority and mutual accountability. This kind of freedom is not historically not what first comes to mind when you think of "The American Way," but it may be the secret to its healing.

LURE OF OBSCURITY

I will end by mentioning a great little paper entitled "The Leisure of Worship and the Worship of Leisure," by Jack Miles, the author of *Biography of God*. In it he says that museums, or what he calls secular cathedrals (and I would include universities in this, too), are contending with the same forces as religion today—that is, the forces of commodification, or "The Great American Hustle," or, to parallel Smith's terms, the logic of the market. In museums, giant video screens replace text, and garish advertising campaigns fill the entire outside walls of buildings. The question ironically is asked: "Is nothing sacred?"

Insofar as the emerging church constructs itself not as an unapologetic incarnational presence of the body of Christ but as a spirituality that markets a religious identity suitable to the preferences of a postmodern consumer culture, it does little to challenge the consumerist status quo, and as much as it eschews modern conceptual idolatries, it flirts with a new one, the logic of the market.

This is what I see as the vulnerable edge of the emerging movement, but it is a weakness I name as a partner in the conversation. This is the hard question: what if the customer is not always right, and there is a greatness that commands an allegiance beyond choice and autonomy? How can we nurture a commitment and authenticity that is neither an extension of the rule of taste nor a retrenchment in embattled fundamentalist certainty?

Miles points to the community of Taizé, France, which incidentally is a community with Reformed Christian roots shaped by catholic liturgical practice. The scripture-based music, the times of silence, and the use of

---

rhythms of your particular ghetto prepare you to engage other ideas and customs and life experiences without losing touch with your roots" (WAP, 134).

icons attracts thousands of young people every year. This style, similar to some emerging Christian campus ministry groups on universities across the country that are tied to historical denominational commitments, would be a truly post-modern alternative.

Miles quotes *Wired* magazine: "There's a huge lure to obscurity. That's one of the keys—giving people something to discover, which is the antithesis of the way most advertising works." Religious institutions, he says, "even making the most active use of showbiz techniques, cannot possibly compete in that game. But mystery is there own game, and perhaps they need to return to it."[8]

The postmodern shift can be described as a shift from mastery to mystery. Mastery puts an autonomous agent in control, manipulating things towards desired ends. It is an instrumental approach to life. Mystery, on the other hand, in the Biblical tradition, is not so much a puzzle to be solved, or a great cloud of unknowing, as it is a dogma and a sacrament revealed and received within a historically continuous community of faith.

WORKS CITED

Gibbs, Eddie, and Ryan K. Bolger. *Emerging Churches: Creating Christian Community in Postmodern Cultures*. Grand Rapids: Baker Academic, 2005.

Jacobs, Jane. *Dark Age Ahead*. New York: Random House, 2004.

Kimball, Dan. *The Emerging Church: Vintage Christianity for New Generations*. Grand Rapids, MI: Zondervan, 2003.

Lyon, David. *Postmodernity*. 2nd ed. Minneapolis: University of Minnesota Press, 1999.

McLaren, Brian. *The Last Word and the Word After That*. San Francisco: Jossey-Bass, 2005.

Miles, Jack. "The Leisure of Worship and the Worship of Leisure." A paper delivered on October 10–11, 2004 at the Davidson Conference Center, University of Southern California. Online: http://www.jackmiles.com/Home/other-works/on-religion/the-leisure-of-worship-and-the-worship-of-leisure.

Raschke, Carl. "'Why is the Emerging Church drawn to deconstructive theology?' Take Two." Accessed April 5, 2008. On-line: http://churchandpomo.typepad.com/conversation/2007/03/the_difference_.html.

Rollins, Peter. *How (Not) to Speak of God*. Brewster, MA: Paraclete, 2006.

Smith, James K. A. "The Emerging Church: A Guide for the Perplexed." *Reformed Worship* 77 (2005) 15–16.

---

8. Miles, "The Leisure of Worship."

8

All (For)Giving

The Gift or *Preaching (Forgiveness) Backwards*

James Vanderberg

THE SUN'S LIGHT FAILED. It was about noon when darkness came over the land. On a hill, overlooking the city of Jerusalem, Jesus was hung on a cross, his weight carried upon sharpened steel hammered into his flesh. Those witnesses who gathered around Jesus heard his cry, "My God, my God, why have you forsaken me?" (Matt 27:46b).

Silence, abandonment, death: these are the undercurrents that create turmoil in the Eastertide. Jesus's cry on the cross haunts the celebration that follows. It is the Lenten cry of a dying seed. How can God exact punishment on his one and only Son? How does the divine abandonment of one account for the sin of many? Is atonement a doctrine that needs to be problematized or a problematized doctrine through which we live, with the dying seed giving birth to new life?

In this essay, I want to be a parasite, falling in line with Jacques Derrida's strategy of enacting philosophy. James K. A. Smith notes, "There is a way in which every one of Derrida's texts is a collaborative work" (LT, 93). Derrida reads and writes with "pious infidelity," commenting on someone else's work, adding to, and subtracting from it (LT, 93). In this paper, I will read Derrida and Smith in conversation with my own experience in the pulpit. I will follow the contours of forgiveness, encountering the impossible, speaking of testimony, praying for that which is to come—three conversations that give permission to preach (forgiveness) backwards, even though Derrida would never have done so.

All (For)Giving: The Gift or Preaching (Forgiveness) Backwards

FORGIVENESS COMES BY WAY OF THE IMPOSSIBLE

To give, to forgive, to give the gift of forgiveness: at the root of forgiveness is the verb *to give*. There are three elements that are presupposed in the event of gift-giving—the person who gives, the one who receives and the something that is given. In GT, Derrida notes that these three elements cannot be understood apart from a prior understanding of distribution, of sharing or partition, and of circulation (GT, 6). As such, the gift is always already caught up in economic terms. Put otherwise, we give expecting something in return (at the very least a sign of gratitude), and we receive only to experience a nagging sense of indebtedness.

Derrida, however, is not simply a realist or a pessimist. Without delay, Derrida goes on to note that the gift, if there is such a thing, must not be exchanged. It must not come back to the donor; it must never be exhausted or reciprocated. In his own words, "If there is a gift, the *given* of the gift "(*that which* one gives, *that which* is given, the gift as given thing or as act of donation) must not come back to the giving"(GT, 7). The gift must be *aneconomic*, foreign to the movement of circulation or exchange, beyond calculation, itself a disruption. The gift must catch us by surprise, arriving in secret.

Here, we enter the *aporetic* land of forgiveness—a land of impossibility, filled with roads that lead only to other philosophical dead ends. Forgiveness is impossible because, as a gift, it is dependent upon the very same conditions—of exchange and calculation—that the gift of forgiveness must disrupt or displace. Forgiveness must be able to forgive the unforgivable and the unspeakable.[1] As Smith reads Derrida, he remains torn between the concrete practices of giving and the idea of pure forgiveness (LT, 72).

By way of a detour, then, we find ourselves back at the foot of the cross. The impossibility of forgiveness, as a gift, amplifies the double bind of the cross and the deafening silence of Good Friday. The gift of forgiveness, even divine forgiveness, must catch us by surprise. It must disrupt the economy of repentance and exchange. God's forgiveness cannot be, it must not be, a simple exchange of Christ's life for our sins. Forgiveness is more complicated than the neat and tidy cage of atonement. Forgiveness is a suffering impossibility.

---

1. Derrida, *On Cosmopolitanism and Forgiveness*, 32.

PART THREE: Applying the Critique

AND YET, WE TESTIFY TO THE INSTANT OF OUR OWN FORGIVENESS

Woven through much of Derrida's corpus is a discussion of the *instant*. In DMT, Derrida describes the instant as something instantaneous, a blink of an eye, an "indivisible unicity" (DMT, 30). There is nothing that can divide an instant in two; it is singular, particular, personal, here for less than a second, a nanosecond, and then gone.

The instant, however, cannot be understood, accepted or spoken of apart from testimony. An instant or experience is meaningless unless it is recognized and acknowledged, unless we bear testimony to it. This, Derrida notes, carries the instant outside of itself. "The instant is instantaneously, at this very instant, divided, destroyed by what it nonetheless makes possible—testimony" (DMT, 26). Our speaking about a singular instant is a repetition that introduces the singularity to its unwedded partner of universality; and, in the process, our testimony violates the instant and commits perjury.

Someone is going to ask, "What on earth does this mean?" What we're encroaching upon is a much longer discussion of the supplement. Let me begin by explaining it this way: When we read a book, let's say *The Life of Pi*, our encounter with the text is an event or instant that is immediately understood or transcribed within a context. *The Life of Pi* cannot be understood apart from the context of language and our own experience of the world and what tigers look like. The meaning of the text is not housed entirely within the text; it's supplemented by our very engagement with that text.

It is this notion of the supplement that ties the whole of Derrida's corpus together and that gives shape to the notion of alterity that guides Smith's LT. In *Of Grammatology*, Derrida notes that the supplement is both "a surplus, a plenitude enriching another plenitude, the *fullest measure* of presence" and "an adjunct, a subaltern instance which *takes-(the)-place of*" or violates the instant.[2] In speaking about the instant, in acknowledging it, we both add meaning to it and detract from it. In bearing testimony to the instant, to our encounter with the other, we become the parasite that Derrida recognized in himself, adding to, enriching, welcoming the other, while at the same time doing the other injustice, signing its words with our own name.

2. Derrida, *Of Grammatology*, 144.

All (For)Giving: *The Gift* or *Preaching (Forgiveness) Backwards*

All those who stand at the foot of the cross are parasites, including you and me. Derrida argues that the idea of forgiveness is impossible *and* that it arrives. The gift of forgiveness cannot arrive in any other way but in an instant, on a particular Good Friday, for example, by way of the gift. The instant the gift of forgiveness is given, it is recognized, lived upon, both added to and violated. Those who stand at the foot of the cross, those who hear Jesus' cry, bear witness to the instant of forgiveness; and, in so doing, proclaim the good news *and* sentence God's grace to pace the cage of divine atonement and violent calculation. Our testimony to God's act of forgiveness necessarily enriches *and* detracts from the grace of God. Though there is no way to extract the parasite, there is a way forward, and it's mitigated by prayerful hope.

OUR TESTIMONY IS SHAPED BY THAT WHICH IS TO COME

The arrival of forgiveness is a prayer, and, over the years, Derrida has offered up a number of prayers. John D. Caputo has noted, "Again and again we reach the same conclusion in reading Derrida, that the point of his work as an author is more performative than constative, that it is religious without a theology, that it hangs on by a prayer."[3] This prayer is spoken in secret.

As it's already been noted, the gift of forgiveness must disrupt the economy of exchange. It must resist description; it cannot be accounted for, not by religion, philosophy, politics, or any other institution or system of thought. In other words, the gift must remain secret and unphenomenalized (ON, 25). Derrida is quick to point out, however, that the secret does not hide "itself forever in an indecipherable crypt or behind an absolute veil. It simply exceeds the play of veiling/unveiling" (ON, 26). The gift of forgiveness, as a secret, comes to pass under the cover of darkness. It exceeds our description of it, our attempt to speak of it, our desire to formulate it into a doctrine, because forgiveness always already announces itself as something yet to come.

Here, we take one step further into the quasi-transcendental land of forgiveness. The gift of forgiveness, as a secret that *does* arrive in the instant, is, at the same time, a gift that beckons us from beyond our experience of that instant. Forgiveness is beyond and not-beyond, both at the same time. The idea of forgiveness cannot be encapsulated within our

---

3. Caputo, *The Prayers and Tears of Jacques Derrida: Religion Without Religion*, 328.

determinative structures or our conceptual frameworks, but it cannot, at the same time, arrive in any other way than through our experience of it. And so, forgiveness is impossible; and yet, it happens.

This is the root of most of our problems, at least in terms of our ability to speak about forgiveness. Those who have bought into the Derrida myth, as outlined by Smith, protest loudly against the quasi-transendental nature of forgiveness. If the ideal—the gift—cannot be acknowledged without violation, we can never be sure if someone is giving us the gift of forgiveness or slipping us its counterfeit, which is to say that there is no such thing as forgiveness. And people want forgiveness.

Derrida's prayers, however, are not so entirely despairing in tone. Bearing testimony to the gift of forgiveness is a matter of interpretation, and there are good and bad interpretations. As Smith notes, "Derrida emphasizes that there are important, legitimate determinations of context; in particular, the context for understanding a text, thing or event is established by a community of interpreters" (WAP, 53). Our understanding of the gift of forgiveness requires a communal effort to establish its contours; and, for two thousand years, my community has been speaking about the cross.

I would like, however, to invite Derrida one step closer to the pulpit. Not only is our understanding of the instant of God's forgiveness—the resurrection—supported by a community of interpreters, it is also shaped by that which announces itself as yet to come. The church often overlooks the importance of Christ's promised return in its attempt to understand the nature of God's forgiveness. The very idea of forgiveness exceeds our understanding, announces itself as something yet to come and serves as the addressee of Derrida's prayers. That announcement of something yet to come ought to shape how we interpret its instantaneous arrival in the course of human history some two thousand years ago. We must interpret the event of forgiveness backwards, allowing the promise of something yet to come to impact the way we come to understand the past, concerning ourselves with the hermeneutical reversal of time.

All (For)Giving: The Gift or Preaching (Forgiveness) Backwards

AND SO, WE BEGIN TO PREACH (FORGIVENESS) BACKWARDS

The church is in the position of having to recover from the analytics of exegesis. For too long, we have assumed that meaning must simply arise out of the text and/or out of the event itself. It has been assumed that the Bible is a container for truth, something that can be pried open if we use the right exegetical can opener.

In the process, we have paid little attention to the fact that testimony runs all the way down and that the truth is shaped, in part, by that which is yet to come. The sermons that we hear are a testimony to the commentaries that have been written throughout the centuries. These commentaries are, themselves, a testament to the testimony housed within the gospels, and the gospels are but a collection of the disciples' testimonies. Derrida, however, would take this one step further. Even the Word of God, which in the Reformed tradition is understood to include the whole of creation, the older and new testaments and the Word of God incarnate; even the Word of God is a testimony to something more excessive, something more original, call it God's love, grace, forgiveness, something that has yet to arrive in all its fullness.

In order to understand what happened on the cross, we must proceed backwards from this promised arrival. That which is to come, that which has yet to be unveiled, shapes our communal understanding of that which has already arrived in the instant of Christ's death and resurrection. That which calls from beyond—the gift of forgiveness—shapes our understanding of the revealed Word of God in the same way that Jesus' death and resurrection now shapes the way we read the Old Testament.

This is a prophetic move, not an exegetical one, and it has implications. To preach forgiveness backwards allows the perceived sanctity of the Biblical text to be disturbed. There's no single, perfect interpretation. Instead, the guardrails for good interpretation require community and a prior understanding of, and commitment to, the idea of forgiveness. The guardrails require community and a sense of calling.

As Jesus hangs on the cross, as his Lenten cry is released, we cannot help but hear multiple voices. We hear Jesus acknowledge the abandonment he is experiencing, but is it abandonment by his own father or the abandonment he is experiencing at the hands of his own disciples, as in "(looking up) My God, my God, (looking down) why have you forsaken me?" At the foot of the cross, we encounter Jesus's suffering—a suffering that looks like divine violence, a violence that can, at the same time, never be divorced from the work of our own hands. We encounter, at the foot of the cross, the limits of the doctrine of atonement, running headlong into the powerful image of a God who loves us so much that he would give his life for us, running headlong into the problematics of such divine calculation, running headlong into a gift that is not really a gift at all.

Not all of these interpretations are valid, and some need better defined limits. In preaching (forgiveness) backwards, we are being called to the task of interpreting together through a prior understanding of the idea of forgiveness. We are being called to recognize the lens of promise through which we peer. This does not mean that we can dismiss the violence or erase the problematics of divine calculation. We can't ignore texts that we don't like. It means that we need to understand the sacrifice and violence of the cross within the context of having already made a commitment to respond to the call of forgiveness. In that sense, forgiveness chooses us. (Did I just make Derrida into a Calvinist?) Our response to its call shapes which interpretation we allow to speak into our everyday life. As such, preaching forgiveness backwards is itself a prayer and a response to a call that is issued from beyond. Give, give the gift of forgiveness; know that you are forgiven.

By way of a closing addendum, then, let me name, without comment, the issues the church would have to wrestle with if it were to preach faithfully (forgiveness) backwards:

- The church would have to wrestle with its understanding of repentance, because repentance cannot be a precondition of a gift that must arrive with no strings attached. Repentance, in this context, can only be a proper response to the gift of forgiveness always already given.

- The church would also have to wrestle with its understanding of the scope of God's forgiveness, given on the cross, without falling prey to a certain universalism. Our understanding of God's divine amnesia would also come into question.

- And last, but not least, the church would have to wrestle with the gratitude it experiences in the context of God's forgiveness. If the gift of forgiveness is oriented by that which is to come, gratitude can not simply be a response to something that has already arrived in Christ. Gratitude, and its accompanying joy, must also be an announcement of sorts, a trumpeting toward the arrival of so much more.

WORKS CITED

Caputo, John D. *The Prayers and Tears of Jacques Derrida: Religion without Religion*. Bloomington: Indiana University Press, 1997.

Derrida, Jacques. *Of Grammatology*. Translated G. Spivak. Baltimore: Johns Hopkins University Press, 1976.

———. *On Cosmopolitanism and Forgiveness*. New York: Routledge, 2001.

Martel, Yann. *Life of Pi*. New York: Harcourt, 2003.

9

Saving the Whale or Dancing with Dolphins?

Andre Basson

In FK, Derrida emphasizes that in any discussion of religion the traditional distinction between religion and reason should be discarded. In typical Derridean fashion, he then attempts to show to what extent the development of critical and techno-scientific reason, far from being the opposite of religion, actually underpins and presupposes it.[1]

A number of years earlier, Paul Feyerabend had made the astounding claim that religious explanations for the origins of life were as valid as scientific ones. This view has also been echoed by influential thinkers like François Lyotard and Richard Rorty, who argue that both religious and scientific explanations need to be judged according to their "internal coherence."[2]

The attack against the fallacy of intellectual objectivity already began much earlier with someone like the Dutch philosopher Herman Dooyeweerd, who observed that every scientific theory was based on religious presuppositions,[3] thus replacing the Cartesian *cogito ergo sum* with the Augustinian/Anselmian *credo ut intelligam*.

This revisionist view of science may have the potential of taking the sting out of much of the antagonism that has prevailed between religion and reason since the Enlightenment, and maybe even earlier—at least

---

1. Cf. also Nault, "La question de la religion [chez Derrida]," 36–38.
2. Downing, *How Postmodernism Serves (My) Faith*, 76 and 213.
3. Ibid., 138.

since Galileo was forced by Rome in 1633 to retract his heliocentric interpretation of the universe.

Much more recently, this antagonism was very much in evidence in the early years of the founding of Brock University when secular humanism, which was then the prevailing philosophy, saw no need for organized religion of any kind on campus.[4] It is an approach to university education that can perhaps best be summed up—and caricaturized—in the words of Mr. Gradgrind in Charles Dickens's *Hard Times*: "facts alone are wanted in life. Plant nothing else, root out everything else. You can only form the minds of reasoning animals upon Facts; nothing else will ever be of service to them. This is the principle on which I bring up my own children, and this is the principle on which I bring up these children. Stick to the facts, sir."[5]

By acknowledging the plurality of different truth claims, postmodernism, it seems, has put in place a basis for some degree of dialogue, not only between religion and the sciences, but also among the various religions.

The fact that I am able to address you today as one of three full-time Brock University chaplains must surely be a sign that things have changed. In this regard, it is also noteworthy that Brock Campus Ministry has a strong multi-faith dimension, evidence of which is the recent addition to our team of a part-time Muslim and a part-time Jewish chaplain, and the establishment on campus of a multi-faith room.

But let us not be too quick to celebrate. There is no reason to be optimistic that in future faith and reason will be reconciled (although one possible way of achieving this reconciliation could be by distinguishing, as Derrida does, between religion and faith; this is a topic for another paper). As the publication of Dan Brown's *The Da Vinci Code* and, more recently, James Cameron's television documentary on the supposed discovery of Jesus's tomb amply demonstrated, for good or bad, no religious belief is any longer beyond the prying eyes of science or pseudo-science posturing as science.

---

4. I am greatly indebted to my colleague, Rev. George Addison, the ecumenical chaplain at Brock, for the information on the role of secular humanism in the university's early history.

5. Dickens, *Hard Times*, 1; quoted in Klassen and Zimmerman, *The Passionate Intellect*, 83.

PART THREE: APPLYING THE CRITIQUE

Already in the sixties, Teilhard de Chardin noted with uncanny foresight that a dramatic and unprecedented shift was occurring in the way we thought about God when he wrote: "The fact remains that for some obscure reason something has gone wrong between Man and God as in these days he is represented to Man . . . Hence . . . the impression one gains from everything taking place around us is of an irresistible growth of atheism."[6] It was also a time when, across the Atlantic, the Death-of-God Theology made headlines and even reached the front cover of Time Magazine; while in Rome, the cardinals and bishops attending Vatican II were—wittingly or unwittingly—setting the Catholic Church on a path of unprecedented change. It was the fresh breeze they felt emanating from the Council that inspired many young South American theologians to develop a theology of liberation.

A half a century later, the paradigmatic shift that began with the Enlightenment was entering another new phase which some are now calling postmodern and which represents, in many important respects, an open revolt against many of the most cherished principles of men like Descartes, Hume, Kant, Voltaire, and Rousseau. If anything, this change does not seem to have slowed down the deepening crisis in which Christianity in the West has been finding itself since the eighteenth century. On the contrary, the postmodern hostility towards all absolutes seems to undermine Christianity's claim to absolute truth even further, as well as the claim of every other religion for that matter.[7] In fact, even the word "absolute" seems to have different meanings in different contexts these days. But for many Christians, Christianity is all about absolute truth.

Of course, the question of truth relates not only to Christianity's position vis-à-vis atheism or agnosticism, but also, in an increasingly pluralistic society, especially in Europe and North-America, to its position as one among a whole smorgasbord of religions. Doubt in an absolute truth would seem to undermine the very *raison* for Christian evangelism and world mission.

The university may be an academic ivory tower, but when it comes to faith it not only reflects, but often intensifies the contradictions and

---

6. de Chardin, *The Future of Man*, 260; quoted in Zahrnt, *What Kind of God?*, 5.

7. See the somewhat alarmist comment in Wells, Above *All Earthly Pow'rs*, 11: "The two motifs which are transforming culture—the emergence of the postmodern ethos and the new, growing tidal wave of religious pluralism—are deep and powerful currents that are flowing through the nation."

Saving the Whale or Dancing with Dolphins?

tensions experienced in society at large. Furthermore, by their very nature, the lecture hall and the seminar room encourage, or at least are supposed to encourage difference of opinion in pursuit of the "truth." For these reasons, university chaplains these days often find themselves in the frontlines when questions arise regarding the relationship between faith and reason, or the relationship among the different faiths. These questions are not merely of intellectual interest to us, but of existential importance. More often than not, our very *raison d'être* is at stake.

My paper is therefore an effort not to resolve the issue; to attempt to do so would be both presumptuous and completely outside my field of expertise. Instead, I shall endeavor to arrive at some guidelines for a campus ministry in the multi-faith context of a secular Canadian university in the twenty first century. My point of departure will be—admittedly at the risk of gross over-simplification—a very brief comparison between Hans Küng, the dissident Roman Catholic theologian formerly from Tübingen University, and the very much younger James K. A. Smith, whose work is the focus of the current volume.

I would be the first to concede that the reasons for a comparison may in many respects appear to be quite arbitrary. However, I chose Küng as a kind of counterpoint to Smith not in order to endow my comparison with a neat confessional balance between Catholic—that is, in so far as Küng can still be considered a Catholic theologian—and Calvinist, but because Smith is, to my mind, one of the very few courageous enough to try to give a substantial and theologically responsible account of both the challenges and the dangers facing Christianity in the postmodern era. As I shall now attempt to show, there are significant differences as well as interesting points of convergence between Küng and Smith.

In a book written just a few years before the fall of the Berlin Wall, Küng noted that Christianity found itself in an identity crisis. The only way, he argued, in which Christianity would be able to overcome this crisis, was "to give an account of the Christian faith in a manner that was *scientifically* responsible and conformed to the gospel and to our time."[8]

Already in the early seventies, another—albeit less well-known—German theologian, Heinz Zahrnt, observed that "theology at the present day has a duty to *verify* all its statements about God."[9] By their own

---

8. Küng, *Une Théologie pour le 3e millénaire*, 11 (emphasis added).
9. Zahrnt, *What Kind of God?*, 93.

admission, both Küng and Zahrnt hold in high esteem the powerful legacy of critical thinking inherited from the Enlightenment, the latter even stating that "What we need today is not less enlightenment but more enlightenment."[10] However, Küng also cautions against the reductionism of modernity and believes it is necessary to reject what he terms "the modern superstition of reason, science and progress, as well as all the self-destructive forces which the modern era has unleashed in the course of history. These include nationalism, colonialism and imperialism."[11] Furthermore, Küng argues, Christian theology needs to "transcend" modernity and take postmodernity seriously, in order to become credible again.

It should be clear that for Küng, as well as for Zahrnt, the issue of truth plays a critical role in any effort to resolve the crisis of Christianity.[12] For Zahrnt, this truth is the reality of God that must be demonstrated in the reality of the world, "within the sphere of experience of contemporary secular existence."[13] "The word 'God,'" Zahrnt writes elsewhere, "can never be uttered except in the context of human life. We can perceive what God is saying in the vertical plane only within our commitment on the horizontal plane."[14]

The present world of human experience also forms an integral part of Küng's conception of a theology that is able to surmount the crisis of contemporary Christianity. Borrowing a page or two from the work of Dutch theologian, Edward Schillebeeckx, he emphasizes that the source, the norm of this theology remains: (a) the revelation of the word of God in the history of Israel and of Jesus of Nazareth; (b) the human interpretation of this tradition; and (c) the person of Jesus of Nazareth.

But not only does this theology have to be completely faithful to the Christian truth, according to Küng, it also has to be ecumenical, in the

10. Ibid., 101.

11. Küng, *Une Théologie pour le 3e millénaire*, 21. Elsewhere (p. 175), he mentions in the same breath the traditionalism of the Catholic, Eastern Orthodox, and Protestant churches on the one hand, and the Enlightenment ("reason," "history") on the other.

12. See for example Küng, *Une Théologie pour le 3e millénaire*, 217: "La théologie chrétienne se veut résolument témoignage réfléchi de la vérité de la foi *chrétienne* . . . ," (the author's italics). He also describes this theology as a "théologie *véridique* . . . qui cherche et dise la vérité chrétienne en toute sincérité" (282, the author's italics).

13. Zahrnt, *What Kind of God?*, 93.

14. Ibid., 95.

sense that it does not regard a different theology as an adversary, but as a partner. Furthermore, it is ecumenical because it does not seek separation but reconciliation both *ad intra* (i.e., among the various Christian denominations) and *ad extra* (i.e., in the context of world religions, ideologies and the human and natural sciences).[15]

Küng seeks to develop this important ecumenical dimension of Christian theology in the twenty first century without putting at risk what he calls "the singularity of the Christian faith."[16] He is quick to acknowledge, however, that theological accommodation of religious diversity does hold the danger of a bland religious relativism.[17] Interestingly, Küng does not believe that Christian theology's responsibility to be faithful to truth necessarily precludes an ecumenical openness *ad extra*. In fact, in order for Christianity to relate to other faiths it first has to clarify the question of truth! Instead of leading to confrontation, Küng maintains, this is the only way to world peace, since there can be no question of peace among the nations of the world without peace among the religions of the world![18] At the same time, he readily admits that no other question in the history of world religions has given rise to as many bloody conflicts and even "wars of religion" as the question of truth.

In regard to the question of religious truth, Küng distinguishes four possible positions:

a. There is no true religion (i.e., all religions are equally false).

b. There is only one true religion (i.e., all the other religions are false).

---

15. Küng, *Une Théologie pour le 3e millénaire*, 225.

16. Ibid., 249.

17. On the other hand, a "super" religion that encompasses all other religions may be very inclusive, but not very useful as a religion. See the interesting remarks in Debray, *Le feu sacré*, 358: "Cette religion pour tous serait aux religions tout court ce que sont le volapuk ou l'espéranto aux langues naturelles: un ustensile inutilisable, un radiateur glacé." Elsewhere (366), Debray, makes the rather unexpected point that the person who believes that no religion has the monopoly in regard to the cultures and traditions of the world and who, consequently, is equally open to all of them, runs the risk of having an empty, incorporeal or disembodied faith. To choose the infinite (or abstract) above the finite (or concrete) is to accede to the temptation of emptiness, and perhaps even to renounce life itself.

18. "Pas de paix entre les peuples de ce monde sans paix entre les religions du monde . . . Mais la confrontation avec les religions du monde va au-delà de la question de la paix. Elle appelle imperativement une clarification de la *question de la vérité*." Küng, *Une Théologie pour le 3e millénaire*, 316 (the author's italics).

c. Every religion is true (i.e., all religions are equally true).

d. Only one religion is the true religion and all other religions share in its truth.

While he does not accept that Christianity has the monopoly on truth he also does not believe that Christians should renounce the faith they profess for the sake of the truth in the form of a religious pluralism of convenience. In the end, he suggests that in the case of each religion, the question of true or not-true can only be answered according to two criteria that apply equally to all religions, namely to what extent it a) serves the good of humanity and b) is authentic (i.e., in what measure does it still conform to its original message), and according to one criterion that is specific to each religion. In the case of Christianity this would be the extent to which it reveals "in its theory and praxis the spirit of Jesus Christ."[19] Using the distinction between external perspective and internal perspective, Küng draws the further conclusion that regarding the former one can state that there are numerous true religions, but that regarding the latter each religion is uniquely true for its own adherents. In this sense then, the Christian, for example, can claim that for her Christianity is the one true religion.[20]

Although Küng's reasoning has a very clear postmodern ring to it and does at least allow for fruitful ecumenical discussion between Christianity and other religions, is it possible that, as Smith's book seems to suggest, there could be another way to find a place for the Christian faith at the multi-faith table? And can this be done without the category of truth which only seems to bedevil the issue?

One of the aspects of postmodernism that may be an important consideration to keep in mind in any engagement across cultural and religious borders is its deep-seated suspicion of what it calls metanarratives. However, in WAP, Smith states that Christianity actually shares this suspicion towards metanarratives. How does he arrive at this conclusion? He interprets Lyotard's definition of metanarrative as meaning that they

---

19. Küng, *Une Théologie pour le 3e millénaire*, 342. On the need for certain criteria as a prerequisite for tolerance (as opposed to complete indifference), see the interesting comments in Hersch, "Tolerance: Between Liberty and Truth," 30.

20. "Et dans la mesure où le christianisme concret témoigne de cet unique Dieu et de son Christ, il peut être dit lui-même—en un sens dérivé et limité—pour les croyants *la vraie* religion." Küng, *Une Théologie pour le 3e millénaire*, 348 (author's own italics).

are stories that "not only tell a grand story . . . but also claim to be able to legitimate or prove the story's claim by an appeal to universal reason" (WAP, 65). It is at this point where the fault line separating modernity from postmodernity is most apparent according to Smith. Whereas modernity seeks to legitimate itself by means of reason, postmodernity has no such intention, but rather seeks to announce its claims "within a story" (WAP, 65). According to Smith, it really boils down to the question of legitimation. "Metanarratives are therefore false appeals to universal, rational, scientific criteria" (WAP, 68).

In what way, then, is Christianity not just another metanarrative? WAP argues that Christianity's legitimation is based not on an appeal to reason, but on an appeal to faith.[21] In fact, Smith warns against following a modernist approach in an effort to demonstrate the truth of the Christian faith.[22] Instead, he emphasizes the narrative character of the revelation of the Christian message. The Christian faith is "not a religion simply of ideas that have been collected, but is inextricably linked to the events and story of God's redemptive action in the world" (WAP, 75).

Smith further recommends a new apologetic (à la Francis Schaeffer) in which everyone will be invited to bring his or her presuppositions to the table, followed by a narration of the story of the Christian faith which would allow "others to see the way in which it makes sense of our experience and our world." He actually qualifies this apologetics as an "unapologetics," characterized by "faithful storytelling, not demonstration" (WAP, 74). And Christian worship is the *locus par excellence* where the re-enactment of the narrative of the gospel takes place "week by week in order to teach us how to find ourselves in the story" (WAP, 75).

In an earlier work (FI), Smith expresses himself in support of the idea of a pluralistic view of truth that has God's authority behind it. He finds scriptural support for his claim in the creation story in *Genesis*. The sin of Babel, he states, consisted in replacing the plurality of God's original creation with exclusion and violence. This reading of the Babel story is

---

21. Unlike atheism which McGrath would argue "has a disturbing tendency to see itself as the only true faith, and demands that everyone conform to its beliefs" (McGrath, *The Twilight of Atheism*, 232).

22. Cf. WAP 73: "We must be careful, however, not to continue to propagate [the Christian] witness in modernist ways: by attempting our own rationalist demon demonstrations of the truth of Christian faith and then imposing such on a pluralist culture." See also Keyes, *Seeing Through Cynicism*, 142: "Evidence can never compel belief, because evidence is always interpreted."

already found in Derrida's essay "Des Tours de Babel," and is repeated by Richard Middleton and Brian Walsh in their book, *Truth Is Stranger Than It Used to Be: Biblical Faith in a Postmodern Age*.[23] The destruction of the Tower of Babel was God's resounding "no" to humanity's presumption that it could obtain God's view of things.

My reading of Küng does not lead me to conclude that he would disagree with Smith on this point. On the other hand, I have the impression that Küng's conception of religious pluralism is significantly more radical than James K. A. Smith's. Küng's ecumenical theology embraces not only the wide variety of Christianities, but also the whole spectrum of world religions, of which each one is true *sui generis*. I am not sure Smith would be of the same opinion, although he would probably not have a problem with other religions also being allowed to bring their "presuppositions to the table."

We have already noted the importance James K. A. Smith attaches to the fact that Christianity is not about a system of propositions, but is rather a narrative that needs to be told, a narrative that is the continuation of the story that began with the Incarnation when the Word, the Divine Logos, in order to breach the insufficiency of human language to speak of God, became flesh in Jesus of Nazareth. It is his life that Christians should be embodying and incarnating in their own life. As we have already seen, Küng, too, recognized that Christianity's distinctiveness derives from the person of Jesus Christ. In this regard, the Christian truth is already a given. But in so far as the story is still being told, this truth also needs to be verified continuously in the way in which each Christian life responds in love to the Truth Incarnate.[24]

"In love" not only towards God, but also towards the neighbor, the other. This love as a love for the other has its basis in the divine love that unites the three persons of the Trinity. When God became flesh, he also became "other to himself . . . Christians can [therefore] proclaim that the ethics of otherness have their origin . . . in a universal Other beyond language, an Other whose very nature endorses love of the other, an Other who became same with us in order to demonstrate universal love."[25]

---

23. J. Derrida, "Des Tours de Babel", and Middleton and Walsh, *Truth Is Stranger Than It Used to Be*; quoted in Downing, *How Postmodernism Serves (My) Faith*, 161–162.

24. See Downing, *How Postmodernism Serves (My) Faith*, 110.

25. Ibid., 228–30.

Saving the Whale or Dancing with Dolphins?

From a campus ministry perspective, this conception of the Christian truth as a continuous narrative, distinctive yet at the same time aware of its incompleteness and human limitations vis-à-vis other religions and belief systems with equally strong claims to the truth, is extremely valuable. For the past few years, my Roman Catholic colleague in Brock Campus Ministry has organized trips for Brock students to Peru and Brazil to work in shanty towns in a program called Solidarity Experiences Abroad. The program is in many ways unique in North America. For two and a half weeks, the students live and work in disadvantaged communities, giving concrete expression to their compassion for people who had been marginalized by economic equality and poverty. Because every group represents a wide range of faiths and belief systems, the students return with a deeper understanding of pluralism and a genuine appreciation for views that are different from their own.[26] The aim is not to impose a particular faith or belief system on the students, but rather to make them aware that no matter from which religious perspective we look at things, we are united by the love that drives us to reach out to a fellow human being in need. It was interesting that the students who participated in the Solidarity Experiences Abroad program did not experience this strangeness when they were working in those communities, but when they returned to Canada.

To conclude, I would like to return to James K. A. Smith's application of the story of the whale rider, but in order to replace it with another marine image, one, which I believe, gives better expression to the role of a Christian campus ministry in a multi-faith context. Because of its size, the whale evokes in my mind a period in the history of Christianity when it ruled the waves and was often anything but loving. That period is now long gone. It also reminds me of one of the standard questions seminary students in my day were asked before they were admitted to the church, namely "Do you believe that the fish swallowed Jonah?"

The image of dancing with dolphins, on the other hand, is an allusion to the movie *Dances with Wolves* and its allegory of cross-cultural reconciliation. It is also intended to evoke both the paradox and the playfulness of the new and exciting context in which this age old story that is the Christian faith is being told over and over again among so many other stories on the Brock campus and elsewhere, a story in which, as one of my

---

26. For an enlightening discussion of this new form of incarnational ministry among especially the young, see Bessenecker, *The New Friars*.

particularly irreverent classmates put it so many years ago, it doesn't really matter whether the fish swallowed Jonah or Jonah swallowed the fish.

WORKS CITED

Bessenecker, S. A. *The New Friars: The Emerging Movement Serving the World's Poor.* Downers Grove, IL: InterVarsity, 2006.
Brown, Dan. *The Da Vinci Code.* New York: Doubleday, 2003.
Chardin, Teilhard de, *The Future of Man.* London: Collins, 1964.
Debray, R. *Le feu sacré: Fonctions du religieux.* Paris: Fayard, 2003.
Derrida, Jacques. "Des Tours de Babel." *Semeia* 54 (1991) 3–34.
Downing, C. L. *How Postmodernism Serves (My) Faith: Questioning Truth in Language, Philosophy and Art.* Downers Grove, IL: InterVarsity, 2006.
Dickens, Charles. *Hard Times.* New York: Harper, 1854.
Hersch J. "Tolerance: Between Liberty and Truth." In *Tolerance Between Intolerance and the Intolerable*, edited by Paul Ricoeur, 27–33. Oxford: Berghahn, 1996.
Keyes, D. *Seeing Through Cynicism: A Reconsideration of the Power of Suspicion.* Downers Grove, IL: InterVarsity, 2006.
Klassen, N. and Zimmerman, J. *The Passionate Intellect. Incarnational Humanism and the Future of University Education.* Grand Rapids, MI: Baker Academic, 2006.
Küng, Hans. *Une Théologie pour le 3e millénaire.* Paris: Seuil, 1989.
McGrath, Alister. *The Twilight of Atheism. The Rise and Fall of Disbelief in the Modern World.* New York: Doubleday, 2004.
Middleton, J. R. and Walsh, B. J. *Truth Is Stranger Than It Used to Be: Biblical Faith in a Postmodern Age.* Downers Grove, IL: InterVarsity, 1995.
Nault F. "La question de la religion [chez Derrida]." *Magazine Littéraire* 430 (2004) 36–38.
Ricoeur, Paul, editor. *Tolerance Between Intolerance and the Intolerable.* Oxford: Berghahn, 1996
Wells, D. F. *Above All Earthly Pow'rs: Christ in a Postmodern World.* Grand Rapids, MI: Eerdmans, 2006.
Zahrnt H. *What Kind of God? A Question of Faith.* Translated by R. A. Wilson. London: SCM, 1971.

10

Taking Derrida, Lyotard, and Foucault to Tim Horton's

Experiencing the Modern and Post-Modern in Canada

Stan Skrzeszewski

> Sitting here at the Hortons'
> So you know this is important
> —Gord Downie (Tragically Hip), *Vancouver Divorce*

WHY TAKE DERRIDA, LYOTARD and Foucault to Tim Horton's? One only has to imagine Sartre and de Beauvoir in a Parisian coffeehouse to see the link between philosophy and coffee shops. Howard Schultz, the founder of Starbucks writes that "Coffee houses have been a meaningful part of community life for centuries . . . they have been associated with political upheaval, writers' movements, and intellectual debate in Venice, Vienna, Paris and Berlin."[1] Salons, coffee houses, and philosophical societies are all part of the project of the Enlightenment. Coffee houses are a place in which "fleshy communal beings" (WAP, 136) gather hospitably to speak with one another, to break bread, and to share a unique drink, in an atmosphere that if not that of worship and love is resonant with community and affection. Coffee shops are a place of communion, and where two or three are gathered in communion, God is present and dwells among us.

The coffee shop is the embodiment of the linguistic turn, often linked with post-modernism and with a chain of philosophers who include Wittgenstein, Heidegger, Derrida, and Habermas. As humans, we

---

1. Schultz and Yang, *Pour Your Heart into It*, 24.

are "these beings who have *logos*, who have the ability to speak" (LT, 16). As humans, we have always gathered in communal places to speak, since language is a "public phenomenon—shared with others in a community—(and) is an essentially relational phenomenon and thus necessarily involves others" (LT, 17).

The coffee shop is also a socio-philosophical phenomenon. In the book by Giovanna Borradori, *Philosophy in a Time of Terror*, she reports "On 9/11 Derrida was in Shanghai...The news found him sitting in a café with a friend."[2] Why mention the café, which at first glance can be taken as a meaningless detail? Mentioning the café immediately creates a counter-balancing image to the violence of terrorism. The image transmits a measure of re-assurance that no matter what, at least part of the world is as we would hope it to be. There is an oasis of peace in a desert of terror. The café represents the utopian dream of peace and happiness and it also provides a measure as to how we as a global society are doing. As long as there are people sitting in cafés and drinking coffee there is hope.

From the perspective of creative space, coffee shops can offer "atmospheres that are operatic, bohemian, noisy, eclectic, and stimulating."[3] Tim Horton's is the Canadian and in some ways, the post-modern version of the coffee shop. It represents the daily experience of post-modernism for Canadians, a limited menu for a curtailed life with choices so simplified that anyone can feel comfortable with them. As a simple test, try and visualize the 'operatic, bohemian, noisy, eclectic and stimulating' nature of your last visit to Tim Horton's. Ask yourself what truths does Tim Horton's reveal about us and about our world?

In this paper the Derrida, Lyotard, and Foucault that we are taking to Tim Horton's are based on a reading of two books by James K. A. Smith. I have used Smith's unique interpretation of post-modernism to outline a framework with which to analyze Tim Horton's and other cafes in Canada. The technique is similar to the one used by Walter Benjamin in his Arcades project where he analyzed the culturally common place. I have also used Lyotard's methodology by going out to the Canadian tribe for input and conducting a series of field studies in developing this paper, including conducting Philosophers' Cafes on the topic and individual interviews.

2. Borradori, *Philosophy in a Time of Terror*, xi.
3. Schultz and Yang, *Pour Your Heart into It*, 84.

Taking Derrida, Lyotard, and Foucault to Tim Horton's

DIFFERENT COFFEE SHOPS = DIFFERENT WORLDVIEWS

In examining coffee shops in general, I discovered that different coffee shops represent different worldviews. Tim Horton's represents "a modern, scientistic worldview" to which I would add a rational, cost-effective, and efficient worldview, clean and with warm colors. Tim's clearly has grass-roots support, is ecumenical, and uses the aesthetic in telling its' story. In Smith's sense Tim's represents the "dumbed-down" version of the coffee house, where everything has been simplified to make it accessible, which makes it in a sense modern, while at the same time being post-modern. Tim Horton's provides an affordable café without unique truths, without radicalism, minimal space for debate, a rather indeterminate place, a neutral zone, that does not link to any particular system of beliefs or values.

Starbucks is more elitist, and uses aesthetics to tell its story, but it is also a mirror or representation of "an ancient postmodern, mythic worldview" (WAP, 63), to which has been added color, music and ritual. Starbucks affirms tradition in all its complexity and makes efforts to initiate people into the narrative of dark roast coffee and the joy of cappuccino, but at an exclusive price. Starbucks seeks converts and attempts to edify. James K. A. Smith also acknowledges the relationship between the Starbucks approach and "postmodern worship" which "orients itself by ancient, strange practices" (WAP, 79).

Singular gathering places, exemplified in my study by the Renaissance Café in Toronto, the Red Canoe Café in Wilno and the Niagara Gallery in Fonthill (and I suspect that Chesterton's Cheshire Cheese pub also falls into this category) are authentic establishments of the Enlightenment with a touch of Foucault's sexuality and deviancy. Dean Tedesco describes his Niagara Gallery as a place for non-linear thinking, as a place of refuge from the linear world. It is hard to imagine sex in Tim Horton's, while some claim that Starbucks is a good pick-up place, whereas in the singular cafes, sex, drugs and rock n' roll are part of the fabric. As described by James K. A. Smith, these singular coffee shops are the most likely to provide us with "the scent of good Sumatran (fair-trade) coffee—the new wine of the postmodern church" (WAP, 144). However, the warning label of a fearful society would advise that all coffee shops are based on addiction and caffeine-madness.

PART THREE: Applying the Critique

IS TIM HORTON'S A CANADIAN META-NARRATIVE?

Tim Horton's is a proclamation of contemporary Canadian life. Tim's has introduced new words, such as 'double-double' into the Canadian vocabulary and it has introduced new social rituals into the daily life of Canadians. There is no doubt that Canadians understand the personal relationship that we have to Tim Horton's and its social and economic impact. To paraphrase Stendhal, for Canadians Tim Horton's is a mirror along the way.

Pierre Berton observed that "in so many ways the story of Tim Horton's is the essential Canadian story. It is a story of success and tragedy, of big dreams and small towns, of old-fashioned values and tough-fisted business, of hard work and of hockey."[4]

Tim Horton's is built on our past in at least three ways. First, Tim's reflects the image of a hockey player that most Canadians have forgotten or never knew and therefore it must reflect an archetypal concept of hockey and the hockey player. Second, it reflects a preferred archetypal Canadian self-image of small town life, which has also largely vanished and does not really reflect the reality of Canadian suburbia. James K. A. Smith makes a similar point in his conclusion to WAP when he writes of the importance of place in Radical Orthodoxy and the overall modernist superficiality and disincarnate nature of the suburban, where it is difficult to create a parish or a community. Third, there is something of Derrida's "colonialisms of ethnocentrism" (LT, 38) that is part of Berton's "Canadian story" but we would have to deconstruct Pierre Berton in order to get at his colonialism.

If Tim Horton's is iconic of the Canadian meta-narrative, it is useful to consider what franchising does to meta-narratives. Tim Horton's is franchised, Starbucks is not. Starbucks is not franchised in order to retain a common culture that helps to maintain it's meta-narrative. Yet, Tim Horton's, although it is franchised, does maintain a meta-narrative, but it may be that Canadians, rather than the Tim Horton's Corporation, maintain the Tim Horton's meta-narrative in spite of Tim Horton's. Jean-Francois Lyotard claimed that "postmodernism is incredulity toward meta-narratives." Since, Tim Horton's itself does not create a Canadian meta-narrative, and since no other explanation could justify the position Tim's has been given in Canadian society, it does not fit Lyotard's

---

4. Quoted in Garnett, "The Hole Story," 26–27.

or Smith's concept of the meta-narrative. The reality of Tim Horton's in Canada is based on a general proclamation by the Canadian people themselves. It is an expression of Canadian tribal culture. Tim Horton's rose to Canadian prominence more as an act of faith and hope, and as an act of self-generating mythology, rather than through an imposed universal marketing scheme. Tim Horton's, in Lyotard's terms has produced "a discourse of legitimation" and that legitimacy is based on the ongoing inter-subjective discourse of Canadians.

We accept the unique reality of Tim Horton's because of the ongoing discourse both within and beyond Tim's. This reality is based on what Lyotard would call "narrative knowledge." As James K. A. Smith outlines, "narrative knowledge is grounded in the custom of a culture [Canadian *Volk*] and, as such, does not require legitimation" (WAP, 66). This reflects a process of self-authentication or auto-legitimation in which a people, collectively and truthfully speaks its own story and arrives at an agreed-upon consensus. It doesn't matter whether you as an individual like or dislike Tim Horton's because in either case you have entered into the discourse and are part of the narrative. Tim Horton's is a self-producing Canadian institution and as such can serve as a model for new institutional frameworks and for "institutions to come."

COMMUNITY AND TIM HORTON'S

Coffee shops inhabit the "third place" or Habermas's public sphere, which is described as a "comfortable, sociable gathering spot away from home and work, like an extension of a front porch,"[5] which connects family and community. Howard Schultz, describes the Starbucks outlets as "an oasis, a little neighborhood spot where you can take a break, listen to some jazz, and ponder universal or personal or even whimsical questions over a cup of coffee."[6]

Coffee shops are a place in which we gather to speak with one another and in this sense within the "world as the horizon of being ... Language creates community." By gathering together to speak with one another we create "the community of persons" which "is primarily a linguistic community" (LT 21 n.69).

---

5. Schultz and Yang, *Pour Your Heart into It*, 5.
6. Ibid., 12.

PART THREE: Applying the Critique

The Third Place as coffee shop is defined by "mixed opposites" or "binary oppositions" which are so popular with philosophers such as Derrida. For example:

- Affordable luxury (everyone can afford a cappuccino): This may apply to Starbucks but not Tim Horton's, where everyone can afford a coffee and donut. Tim Horton's does not provide luxury so much as it supplies freshness, convenience, and price.

- 15-minute romance: Tim Horton's is designed for the quick liaison, and not for any love-based anatomy lesson

- Personal but public oasis: a place for a quiet moment in which to gather your thoughts; Tim Horton's offers a short respite with no surprises

- Limited interaction: Tim Horton's offers a place for social interaction and we go there looking for social interaction, based on the coffee house stereotype, even though there is very little chance of meeting someone new; surveys show that "fewer than 10% of the people ... actually ever talked to anybody."[7]

- Open homogeneity: Tim's provides "the space of the social homogenous—a 'sphere of the Same'" (LT, 51) where although you may enter as a unique individual, once inside common rules apply, which make co-existence possible. Uniqueness is excluded.

- Answers to life and consumer needs: "A place where individuals come to find answers to their questions (through social interaction) or as one more stop where individuals can try to satisfy their consumerist desires" (WAP, 29).

Bryant Simon, a professor at Temple University in Philadelphia who spent a year studying Starbucks claims that "what Americans are really looking for in their cup of joe is a sense of belonging. 'We spent so much of the post [World War II] period in this country retreating inside suburban houses with fenced-in-back-yards," Beth Livedoti, owner of The Daily Rise Espresso states that 'Coffeehouses play to the desire to be out, even if

---

7. Ibid., 118.

you don't talk to anyone'... 'Some customers come in two to three times a day just to talk'... 'We are their little piece of sanity.'"[8]

According to these views Tim Horton's can be seen as transcendent space. Tim's is not a community killer or a kind of nihilistic space, where we are contained for a very short time in a very sterile space aimed at the maximization of sameness through a thousand versions of franchising sameness. Perhaps Tim's does foster "an ethical concern for the relation to the Other and the place of community in the constitution of the [Canadian] subject" (LT, 26).

If Tim Horton's does contribute to the constitution of the Canadian subject, then it probably reflects on Canadians as common place and local and as such is the antithesis of "cool." As Ron Joyce puts it "The taste of Tim Hortons' coffee was actually quite calculated—largely a middle-of-the-road flavor that would not be too strong or off-putting"[9] served with 18% cream. Apparently Western Canadians like weaker coffee than do Canadians in Ontario so at one time the coffee was adjusted according to our regional subjectivity, but now there is one standard across the country.

EXISTENTIALISM OR THE SEARCH FOR FREEDOM AT TIM HORTON'S

Tim Horton's can be associated with Bentham's panopticon or with Foucault's view of society as prison. The architectural design of Tim's is similar to that of Bentham's panopticon. They are usually dominated by windows and built on an open concept with a central control point, which makes the buildings transparent and open to a type of Foucault's surveillance and are part of the "system of control and domination."

By comparison, Starbucks is less open and less visible. There are a few seats that are tucked away. Perhaps for this reason, as we were advised at one of the Philosophers' Cafes, Starbucks is a better "pick-up" place than Tim's.

The Renaissance Café is opaque and full of nooks and crannies, in a less desirable neighborhood, and in some ways close to deviant. Here all activity is hidden away, and freedom of action and authenticity is encouraged. As Randall Clark, the owner of the Renaissance Café put it, "It is

8. "Coffeehouses," 84.
9. Joyce and Thompson, *Always Fresh*, 116.

all about originality and authenticity—authentic coffee, original music, poetry and performance." Singular cafes are much closer to the Garden of Eden than the fallen atmosphere of Tim Horton's or the sinful nature of a Starbucks. No Tim Horton's would be evocative of the description given to the Princess Café by Walter Benjamin: "[T]here is something that brings back to memory that most uncomprehended room in the old Princess Café. It was the back room on the first floor, with couples in the blue light. We called it the 'anatomy school,' it was the last restaurant designed for love."[10]

Traditional churches tend to be designed along the lines of the singular café. They are not transparent and are generally very solid and opaque. They also focus on love. Unlike Tim's, there is never room to park. The new and huge evangelical churches tend to be built on a Tim Horton's model with high visibility and efficiency. There is always room to park. Perhaps modernity can be clearly identified and measured by using a "parking lot" rule.

However, Tim Horton's can be a place of existential freedom. It provides the possibility of buying a coffee instead of making one. This in itself is a form of protest against the power of money and commercialization. We choose the less economic route as a protest against commercialism. By consuming we protest against the imposition of consumerism. One of my first steps in my search for freedom which has lead me here today, began with an attempt to take back my time, and I started with giving myself the freedom to have a daily coffee break at Tim Horton's.

Of course, according to Foucault, we may escape to Tim's and even consider it a place of freedom, but Tim's is part of the system of control and the discipline society. As Paul House, the current CEO at Tim Horton's recently admitted in the manner of Foucault, "Any big company has to be run with discipline."[11]

As Canadians we have come to think that Tim's is OK. A break at Tim's becomes sufficient, necessary, and imposed—it is just one of the "innumerable mechanisms of discipline" (WAP, 93). In Foucault's universe our freedoms are clearly prescribed. Since Tim Horton's is an institution and is part of normal, productive society and part of the system of control, they are flourishing. Singular coffee houses are not institutionalized

---

10. Benjamin, "Surrealism," 176.
11. Pitts, "This CEO's Mom Taught Him Everything He Needs to Know."

and are perceived by many as abnormal or deviant and even as a threat to society and are therefore marginalized and are in decline, as are the mainstream churches. Much of what is associated with the "Enlightenment project of freedom" is suspect and in decline.

POLITICS AND TIM HORTON'S

> Because the Eastern giant was frightening, they stuck to their tables in the coffeehouses—Czeslaw Milosz

Long before Tim Horton's became the coffee shop of choice, the small cafes across Canada were collectively defined as "coffee row." It was along "coffee row" that politicians could come to check the pulse of the community and to conduct polls on local issues, long before polling became a mainstay of Canadian political life. Coffee shops are part of the Canadian democratic and political tradition.

To use the language of Levinas and Derrida, coffee shops are part of the hospitality industry, and hospitality consists of "making room for the Other" (LT, 66). Under "*the* Great law of hospitality," which "requires unconditional welcome" and which enables an ethic of hospitality (welcoming the other) "is, rather, the condition of possibility for ethics...ethics is hospitality"(LT, 70).

Justice, for Derrida, is hospitality—welcoming the other. "Those institutions which are called to be paradigmatic sites of welcome" and which are systems of openness and hospitality by including the other can also be models for "democracy to come" and for "a new 'cosmopolitics' oriented around the core value of hospitality" (LT, 68–69).

Democracy requires "another kind of institution—hospitable institutions that make room for the other." In a sense, the Niagara Gallery, the Renaissance Café, and there like, more so than Tim Horton's represent the kind of democratic institution which also stands in opposition "against all the hegemonic organizations of the world" and provide a home for "messianicity without messianism" (LT, 84, 114).

It is relevant to note that fair trade coffee has become emblematic of a just globalization and of positive cosmopolitan action. Fair trade has made it to Starbucks, but not to Tim Horton's, while it is a staple at the Renaissance Café.

PART THREE: APPLYING THE CRITIQUE

TIM HORTON'S AND AESTHETICS

In Tim Horton's the person behind the counter is an unskilled worker in spite of the claim made by Tim's that it is a very good place to work. According to Foucault, Tim Horton's employees are "merely technicians" (WAP, 83). In counterpoint, the server in an Italian coffee bar or in Starbucks becomes a barista, an artist when he prepares a beautiful cup of coffee with ritual and respect. The coffee barista occupies a position of respect and even admiration.

Starbucks consciously tries to be ancient, to recover tradition, and to implement a specific ritual or liturgy.[12] Starbucks represents a celebration of coffee. Its Shamanism is found in the fantastic blends of drinks and teas and the exotic nature of some of its coffees.

Randall Clark at the Renaissance Café takes great pride in his original coffee blends and in his fair trade coffee. He asks his customers to "awaken to the coffee, and to the world, as it should be."

Tim Horton's tends to be iconoclastic where even iconic pictures of Tim Horton are only occasionally displayed. Starbucks is iconic and it includes murals and posters intended to induce memories of Tuscany and outdoor coffee shops. The Renaissance Café and the Niagara Gallery have elements of "New Age" Gnosticism but are also shamanic and idolatrous.

THE MUSIC TEST

So why do they play music at some cafes and not at others? Arthur Kroker and David Cook in their exploration of post-modern aesthetics write, "Everywhere music creates the mood, the energy level, of the post-modern scene"[13] so music is a measurement of post-modern enthusiasm. James K. A. Smith concludes that the "postmodern church affirms the role of the aesthetic in telling the (gospel) story . . . through images and dance." Surely, the day-to-day human story should also be accompanied by images, dance and music.

The celebration at Starbucks and their unique language of coffee includes music, so that you will regularly hear Dean Martin crooning Amore or some world music tune while you are encouraged to purchase a special musical compilation of iconic tunes.

---

12. For more on this approach see WAP 25.
13. Kroker and Cook, *The Postmodern Scene*, vi.

Taking Derrida, Lyotard, and Foucault to Tim Horton's

There is only background music at Tim Horton's. This may be because in the language of Kroker and Cook, the surveillance society has only "ocular sounds." We see and are seen, but are otherwise silent.

The postmodern church can learn from Starbucks—don't dumb down the story; keep the menu distinctive; needing to learn is not a bad thing; orient the ancient, strange rituals of the Barista and the priest "in a way that invites not only the faithful but also the searching into the story's rhythms and cadences" (WAP, 79).

The Renaissance Café and the Niagara Gallery present live music and live performance. Again, the authentic enlightenment institution or the 'institution to come' goes beyond the institutionalized coffee shop.

A THEOLOGY OF TIM HORTON'S

> This idle talk at a restaurant was to exert a very great influence on him as the whole thing grew and developed. It was as though there had really been something pre-ordained here, a kind of sign . . .
> —Dostoyevsky, *Crime and Punishment*[14]

At a very basic and ancient level going to Tim Horton's is about people gathering to break bread and to share a drink—if this was the Mediterranean, it could easily be wine or at least espresso. Any act of eating and drinking, especially one that includes more than just family or other residents in the same house, is an act of communion. This reflects on a social covenant among people in which you are encouraged to be at peace, to chill out and share a story. For a few minutes the cares of this world are put aside in a moment of brotherhood and a celebration of being with others.

The coffee shop is a contemporary temple. One of the participants at a Philosophers' Cafes spoke of participating in a 24-hour vigil at Tim's—"We went to Tim's to be renewed and refreshed and to be together with other members of our community." Going to Tim's is an ongoing "simple but radical practice of friendship and being called to get along with those one doesn't like." Going to Tim's means exposing yourself to others including friends, people that you don't know and people you may not like. At a very modest level, it is also a place for random acts of kindness, where holding the door for someone with a tray of coffee cups, gives

---

14. Dostoyevsky, *Crime and Punishment*, 85.

you the opportunity to do something nice, to participate in the good, and to recognize that in spite of everything else, basic civility still thrives.

Coffee shops and Tim Horton's in particular tend to be ecumenical, since everyone feels welcomed there. Because most Canadians claim adherence to some spiritual belief when we gather at Tim's, we are gathering as a spiritual people, whether we recognize it as such or not. It is no accident that so many of us stop into Tim's after going to church to join in communion with others, a communion which is much more inclusive than that of our churches.

As per the ecumenical Derrida, Tim's is a deconstructed institution, which makes room for the other and for those who are marginalized. It is not uncommon to see groups of marginalized people, gathering together in coffee shops, where they find common and welcoming space. Tim's celebrates Derridean *Différance*. Within Tim's distinctions are blurred and there is a clear pluralism and a welcoming of diversity, more so than Starbucks, since Tim's does not proclaim an objective truth whereas Starbucks does. As Fresh Prince exclaimed "the brothers don't go to Starbucks." Tim's opens "up spaces for that (and those) which have been excluded" (LT, 47) whereas Starbucks operates on the basis of exclusion by privilege and education.

The following is a very brief theological genealogy of coffee shops:

- Tim Horton's: A Protestant institution (Weber) with minimal ornamentation, iconography and ritual.

- Starbucks: "enlightened Catholicism" with considerable ornamentation, iconography and ritual. Starbucks has a mission. Starbucks undertakes to evangelize people and to convert them. Through education consumers are converted which leads to redemption as people are reborn as dark-roast or as fine coffee drinkers. With Tim Horton's there is no process of conversion or redemption.

- The Renaissance Café: The pagan and Shamanic Coffee Shop. The Shamanic always has something of the past and the future in it. Tim Horton's calls upon a long dead ancestor. All coffee shops rely on an addictive, narcotic substance—caffeine.

I cannot conclude this section on theology without referring to the drive-thru, which allows a person to almost entirely avoid community or any sense of communion. It provides for instant gratification, speed and efficiency. As one of my correspondents wrote "Passing by the local Timmy's today, I counted 19 cars lined up at the drive-through. Nineteen!!! And today isn't much different than any other day. There is just so much wrong with this on so many different levels." Singer-Songwriter David Celia in his song "Evidently True" writes, "I can't believe that there's a drive thru, and I'm sitting in my car. I'm gonna order up some coffee. My arms and legs don't work apparently. The world has come so far."

The drive-thru and "Roll-up-the-rim" present a metaphor for theology based on easy entry and low price—the cherry-picking or buffet-style version of spirituality: low price rather than quality, consistency rather than richness.

TRUTH AND TIM HORTON'S

Even though Ron Joyce, the man behind Tim Horton's, states, "Today, very few people who go to the restaurants relate the Tim Hortons name to the Hall of Fame hockey player," and the chain "had to have broader appeal than simply relying on hockey,"[15] it is clear that Tim's starts with a basic Canadian truth—hockey. Hockey represents a set of values that are interpretive for Canadian life.

Tim Horton, the defenseman, dates from a time when most players in the NHL were Canadian and before the "influx of European mercenaries"[16] and before high salaries. Tim Horton represents a memory of hockey before expansion and its ongoing commodification. He represents Canada as it was, when for many of us, life seemed much simpler and hockey was a game, not a franchise and Tim Horton was "not yet synonymous with an impersonal chain of donut restaurants."[17]

Hockey is not a source of objective or absolute truth, but it is a fallible and inter-subjective source of truth; it has validity and it can be justified by its self-evident acceptance in Canada. Since the truth of hockey is more than that of any individual hockey player, fan or Canadian, it represents a transcendent truth, although not a revolutionary truth or a revealed truth. Belief in the truth of hockey requires faith, but not the faith of the Holy Spirit, but rather convictional power that the faith that so many of our fellow Canadians exhibit and share cannot be wrong. Of course, it is

---

15. Joyce and Thompson, *Always Fresh*, 49–50.
16. MacInnes, *Remembering Tim Horton*, 7.
17. Ibid., 71.

also clear that not all Canadians agree on the truth of hockey so it is not a universal or an objective truth. Therefore it is clear that Canadians have an ongoing role in placing both hockey and Tim Horton's in context as they continue to interpret their places in Canadian society. Here there is "the role of community in interpretation" (WAP, 52). It is the "the community of interpreters who come to an agreement about what constitutes the true interpretation of" (WAP, 53) hockey as truth and Tim Horton's as Canadian institution that relies on the identification of hockey as truth. We accept hockey as part of the Canadian truth. By extension and by contemporary practice, both hockey and Tim Horton's have become a part of "our horizon of perception and our presuppositions," that is they are part of the "interpretive framework" (WAP, 54) through which we understand the world.

CONCLUSION

James K. A. Smith wrote WAP for students and practitioners. As both a student and practitioner of philosophy, I want to thank him for his work. His books provided the insights that gave me the courage to consider the "foolishness" of Tim Horton's and to attempt to speak with philosophical seriousness about the Canadian post-modern condition as it were "from the margins" (WAP, 58).

During our discussions leading up to this conference someone asked the question, "Does it matter whether Derrida, Lyotard and Foucault go to church or to Tim Horton's?" This question has fascinated me all along. On the one hand I want to say "yes," that it does make a difference. Making a choice between going to church and Tim's does matter, just as it matters whether we regularly go to Tim Horton's, Starbucks, or the Renaissance Café. By choosing one over the other we self-identify with a self-image and set of values that we obviously want to endorse and which define who we are.

Choosing between going to church or to Tim's, indicates whether we are emblematic of post-modern spiritual amnesia or whether we are still capable of making conscious decisions. When we chose to go to church, we select the "catholic difference" and a commitment to our traditions which reflects a turning away from modernity.

On the other hand, both going to Tim's and to church represent an act of faith, an act of faith as communion and as openness to community, to hospitality, to dialogue and to affection, if not love, and ultimately both places represent the holy and the sacred. After all, the truly enlightened drop in to Tim Horton's on their way home from church.

WORKS CITED

Benjamin, Walter. "Surrealism: The Last Snapshot of the European Intelligentsia." In *Critical Theory and Society: A Reader*, edited by Stephen Bronner and Douglas Kellner, 172–83. New York: Routledge, 1989.

Borradori, Giovanna, editor. *Philosophy in a Time of Terror: Dialogues with Jurgen Habermas and Jacques Derrida*. Chicago: University of Chicago Press, 2003.

Celia, David. "Evidently True." From the album *This Isn't Here*. Self-released, 2007.

"Coffeehouses." *Entrepreneur* (December 2006). Online: http://entrepreneur.com/magazine/entrepreneur/2006/december/170426-2.html.

Dostoyevsky, Fyodor. *Crime and Punishment*. New York: Penguin, 1951.

Garnett, Glenn. "The Hole Story." *The Toronto Sun* October 29, 2006. Online: http://www.calgarysun.com/cgi-bin/publish.cgi?p=160748&x=articles&s=lifestyle.

Joyce, Ron, and Robert Thompson. *Always Fresh: The Untold Story of Tim Hortons by the Man who Created a Canadian Legend*. Toronto: Harper Collins, 2006.

Kroker, Arthur and David Cook. *The Postmodern Scene: Excremental Culture and Hyper-Aesthetics*. 2nd ed. New York: St. Martin's, 1988.

MacInnes, Craig, editor. *Remembering Tim Horton: A Celebration*. Toronto: Stoddart, 2000.

Pitts, Gordon. "This CEO's Mom Taught Him Everything He Needs to Know." *Globe and Mail* February 19, 2007, sec. B.

Schultz, Howard, and Dori Jones Yang. *Pour Your Heart into It: How Starbucks Built a Company One Cup at a Time*. New York: Hyperion, 1997.

PART FOUR

Critiquing the Critique: Questions Moving Forward

11

Is James K. A. Smith Afraid of Postmodernity?

Wendy C. Hamblet

JAMES K. A. SMITH's *Who's Afraid of Postmodernity?* is addressed to Christians, students as well as vocational practitioners of Christian thought such as pastors, campus ministers, and lay worship leaders. The objective of this excellent little primer in postmodern philosophy is to put to rest Christian fears about disconcerting new trends in philosophy, especially its three core themes emanating from the "Devils from Paris," Jacques Derrida, Jean-Francois Lyotard, and Michel Foucault. Smith's clear rendering of difficult postmodern concepts is refreshing to any audience that has gazed into the abyss of Derrida's *Gift of Death*, scaled the heights of Lyotard's metanarratives, or dangled from the bloody scaffolds of Foucault's genealogies of disciplinary society. Smith's contribution to postmodern discourse is not to be underrated but I would not be a good postmodern if I failed to deconstruct Smith's postmodern religiosity. Ultimately I wonder if Smith has been fearless enough to risk a truly skeptical postmodernism.

I was struck from my first reading of WAP that students from most religious traditions, including the religion of atheism and the religion of materialist consumerism, would benefit from reading this book, not simply to allay their fears about scandalous postmodern claims, but to demonstrate that religion per se, humbly undertaken, has nothing to fear from philosophy per se. Fervent religious believers worry that philosophy's dogged questioning of all things represents a challenge to the truth value of the things they hold sacred—holy scripture, revelation, and confession—a challenge that is impious and offensive. Postmodern philosophy is held in greatest contempt because its challenge to modernism lies precisely in its radical skepticism; postmodern philosophers contend that modern philosophers wander off from the skeptical tradition of philosophy that, following Socrates, calls for a humbling self-examination, an appreciation of the limits, rather than the heights, of human wisdom.

Smith not only calms the believer's fears about core postmodern ideas; he demonstrates that those ideas, rightly understood, offer renewal and healing to Christian communities, pointing to a new "Radical Orthodoxy" that reclaims founding notions of the Christian tradition in new and exciting ways. Smith commandeers postmodern ideas to construct a more vital Christianity, a healthier religiosity that can overcome the sectarianism that separates Christians.

DERRIDA

Smith first considers Derrida's claim, "there is nothing outside the text" (*Il n'y a pas de hors-texte*).[1] Christians fear this claim because it renders their beliefs and their sacred scriptures mere interpretations. Smith explains that Derrida is simply demonstrating a fact to which experience testifies every day—nothing meaningful presents itself to understanding independent of a meaning con-text. This is not to say that interpretation is a voluntary condition, as though people willfully impose meaning upon the brute facts they encounter. Rather, things arise as meaningful phenomena of a world because interpretive possibility serves up a sense of coherent reality.

Derrida's claim that all is text does erode the modernist confidence in rationality as determinant and guarantor of truth (and this is indeed Derrida's intention). Postmoderns share a deep suspicion of science's pretensions to be the "objective authority" imparting the absolute truth about everything.[2]

The textual nature of experience does not guarantee truth, but, Smith assures his religious fearful, neither does it exclude its possibility. Interpretations differ in truth value: some are good and true interpreta-

---

1. Derrida, *Of Grammatology*, 158.

2. In the tradition of Edmund Husserl and Georg Wilhelm Friedrich Hegel, Derrida is demonstrating a phenomenological fact—that even the most supposedly "objective" scientist accesses the world as a subject; her "truth" is subjective experience.

tions and some are not. In the imagery of Disney's Little Mermaid, Smith offers, "We all bump into the same stuff; it's just that some see it as a dinglehopper, others as a fork" (WAP, 50). Smith shows that the believer's feared corollary to the interpretative status of experience—that Christian truth becomes impossible—is a non sequitur. As long as interpretation happens in the context of "necessary conditions" comforts Smith, Christians may be reassured that their interpretation is reliable. Religionists have nothing to fear from the erosion of the possibility of objective knowledge; their knowledge, explains Smith, is not ratified by the powers of human rationality. Christian truth is sought in faith, granted in grace, delivered in the form of revelation, and guaranteed by the power of its divine source.

LYOTARD

Next, Smith considers Lyotard's rejection of metanarratives.[3] Religious folk fear this rejection because, states Smith, they mistakenly believe their belief system to compose a metanarrative. Smith explains that Lyotard is referring to grand theories of reality that claim to be self-evidently true, demonstrated and verifiable by a universal and autonomous Reason. For Smith, Hegel's unfolding dialectics of Spirit or Marx's (r)evolutionary history of the working subject fit the metanarrative mold, but the Christian worldview does not. In fact Lyotard's critique raises the status of religious truth where, in the modernist scheme, religion is relegated to the realm of (mere) myth; Lyotard shows that the Western dichotomy of truth and myth is a false dichotomy. There exists no universal reason that stands outside history, guaranteeing across the vicissitudes of time the validity of some narratives (scientific truth) and not others (myth or religion).

Christians have nothing to fear from Lyotard's rejection of metanarratives, states Smith, because Christian stories are not metanarratives but local narratives that record an individual people's story. Their story is distinct from metanarrative on two counts: theirs makes no claim to universal validity and no pretensions to rational verifiability. Smith posits the notion of the incommensurability of mythical traditions as an opportunity to the Christian church to embrace its role as "witness among the plurality of competing myths" (WAP 70).

---

3. Cf. Lyotard, *The Postmodern Condition*.

PART FOUR: CRITIQUING THE CRITIQUE: QUESTIONS MOVING FORWARD

FOUCAULT

Finally, Smith treats of Foucault's concept of "disciplinary society." Christians greatly value the notion of discipline, because the daily regimen of a believer is ordered according to disciplines of worship, prayer and service. Foucault's genealogy of punishment demonstrates that the supposedly freest societies are "disciplinary" in nature.[4] In schools, hospitals, workplaces, and at home in front of their televisions, the individual is immersed in rigorous insidious systems of control that mirror the workings of the penitentiary. Social-scientific systems of constant asymmetrical surveillance measure the populace according to predetermined notions of normalcy, locate the deviants, and, through the subtle mimetic power of images and stories, "discipline" their desires into conformity with the requirements of the system.

Discipline and Punish: The Birth of the Prison is not a mere critique of the prison but reveals the prison as the microcosm of the system's social reality. All institutions, for Foucault, are networks of power-knowledge relations that dictate, convey, and educate members into "right" ways of being and behaving. By documenting the covert structures of domination, Foucault exposes that the goal of a disciplinary society is to serve and affirm the mechanisms of power; discipline is not simply negative, the dishing out of undesirable desserts to the social deviant, but is positive and productive. Western disciplinary societies are dedicated to producing docile, mindless, productive consumers who are obedient laborers, faithful materialists, and, when necessary, submissive soldiers. Mass media, advertising campaigns that invest products with social, sexual, and religious meaning, and subtle political propaganda (that of the superiority of the Western materialist way of life) provide mechanisms of control that impose the dominant structures of reality upon their populations and normalize the desired vision of "what is good" in life and what makes for a "good citizen."

Smith shows his fellow religionists that they have nothing to fear from Foucault's critique of disciplinary society. The effectiveness of disciplinary measures for shaping certain kinds of human beings should point the way for Christians to break free from consumer disciplines. Unveiling the disciplinary conspiracy, Christians are freed to pursue Christian dis-

---

4. Cf. Foucault, *Discipline and Punish*.

ciplines. They may form, Smith states, "disciples who are countercultural agents of redemption" (WAP 107).

Smith's treatment of the three postmoderns lands him in the territory of a new religiosity, a "Radical Orthodoxy." He ends WAP with a compelling account of a new kind of liturgy, rich with ritual practices drawn from diverse religious traditions, amalgamated in a new "catholic" unity, pioneering in its comprehensive embrace. Rejecting Derrida and Jack Caputo's "religion without religion," Smith champions the particular in his new orthodoxy. Religion without religion jettisons the "radical alterity" of religious particularity, whereas Smith's new liturgy redeems the "incarnate particularity" of Christian traditions in a cross-denominational smorgasbord of sacred practices.

DECONSTRUCTING SMITH

The value of Smith's contribution to the discourse of a postmodern religiosity is not to be underrated. Ultimately, however, I worry that Smith does not go far enough. Smith flirts with postmodern skepticism, indulges in, let us say, postmodern foreplay. But ultimately, when the bedroom door closes and the flirtations risk the serious "play" of radical skepticism, I fear that Smith cannot, shall we say, get out of the missionary position.

Postmodernism attempts to recapture the humble wisdom of Socratic unknowing with a radical skepticism that ungrounds the arrogant self-certainty of the rationalist scientific worldview that begins with Descartes. When Descartes posits the rational as the essentially "human"—human beings as mere "thinking things"—the human mind becomes the veritable Archimedes' point of certitude, guaranteeing the edifice of human knowledge, rightly investigated according to his method.

The elevation of the rational is a major focus of postmodern critique. But dangerous self-certainties go beyond the merely rational structures of the human mind, and configure as well the ontological landscape of Being across the history of philosophy. Radical self-certainty is grounded and fed by ontological assumptions. Colonialism, imperialism, and Nazi "new world orders" rely upon idealized worldviews, grand ontological constructions—"metanarratives"—that order the world hierarchically and eclipse the fragile concerns and defective knowledge of perceiving and suffering subjects. Science tells that higher vertebrates advance by ranking and ordering. Philosophers, scientists and religionists construct their

PART FOUR: Critiquing the Critique: Questions Moving Forward

peculiar worldviews, but they are all ontological and morally-significant. Top-down, often coercive, hierarchical orderings leave some people, some "lesser beings," on the bottom-most rung of the ladder; what is morally owed to each grows dramatically depleted as the ladder descends.

Immanuel Kant, meditating upon the Great Chain of Being, tracks truly fundamental ontological differences separating the species of "possibles" that evolve across history. He launches the philosophical notion that ontological distinctions explain diversity not merely among animal species but within species as well; the human world becomes ontologically divided. Kant states: "fundamental is the difference between the two races of men [black and white] and it appears to be as great in regard to mental capacities as in color."[5] Racist ontology also finds blatant expression in David Hume: "I am apt to suspect the negroes, and in general all the other species of men (for there are four or five different kinds) to be naturally inferior to whites. There never was a civilized nation of any complexion than white."[6]

The phenomenology of Georg Wilhelm Friedrich Hegel is generally accepted as the most blatant reformulation of the Great Chain of Being that elevates white European reason above other diverse ontological kinds. For Hegel reality does not simply have a logical structure; it is logical structure unfolding into the incontestable excellence of logic. Reason is history. For Hegel, one need only note the cultural differences in the world to witness reason's unfolding into its differing historical moments. The world's various cultures mark the notches of reason's development. For Hegel, as for Kant, simple tribal people suffer ontological inferiority.

> The characteristic feature of the negroes is that their consciousness has not yet reached an awareness of any substantial objectivity—for example, of God or the law—in which the will of man could participate and in which he could become aware of his own being. The African, in his undifferentiated and concentrated unity, has not yet succeeded in making this distinction between himself as an individual and his essential universality, so that he knows

---

5. Kant, *Observations on the Feeling of the Beautiful and the* Sublime, 110–31. See also the discussion of this passage in Serequeberhan, *The Hermeneutics of African Philosophy*, 61; and Popkin, "Hume's Racism," 218.

6. Hume, "Of National Characters," 252nc. See also the discussion of this passage in Serequeberhan, *The Hermeneutics of African Philosophy*, 61 and Popkin, "Hume's Racism," 213, and further discussions of Hume in McGreal, *Great Thinkers of the Western World*, 266–70.

Is James K. A. Smith Afraid of Postmodernity?

nothing of an absolute being which is other and higher than his own self.[7]

In Hegel, the Cartesian *cogito* becomes governor of the world, and since every governor needs its subordinates, simple tribal peoples serve nicely as the primal point of reason's unfolding. Hegel's grand ontological schema is the exemplary "metanarrative," a Great Chain of Being that captures the spirit of modern times, permitting white Europeans to name themselves winners in the ontological race, teetering on the brink of perfection. A very small and predictable step separates Hegel's unfolding Reason from Adolf Hitler's overblown nationalisms and Aryan fantasies.

Postmodern philosophers have simply connected the dots from metanarrative to fascism. Now they labour to unseat the arrogance and return philosophy to the radical skepticism of its Socratic roots. Derrida's insistence that everything is text reminds thinkers that their ideas are infinitely removed from "objective" knowledge; all knowledge must be seen as subjective "phenomenal" experience, interpretation, text, hermeneutic elaborations of a concrete immediacy that is never securely grasped and remains ever vulnerable to error. Lyotard shows that secure knowledges have a way of rising up into formidable edifices that weigh heavily upon individuals and freedom. Foucault demonstrates that the societies that most celebrate individualism and freedom may be the most "disciplinary" of all, because their oppressive structures of citizen control have grown subtle, cunning and seductive.

Smith concurs with the postmoderns that much harm has been done in the name of Western truth and science. He agrees with Derrida that all human knowledge is text, but his concurrence does not land him in the cognitive humility of our three "devils." Rather, for Smith, the textual nature of knowledge and the failure of reason simply deliver the Christian back into the camp of revelatory truth. Since all text is con-textualized, cognitive error for Smith is the failure to make judgments according to reliable parameters, right context. "What is required to interpret the world well is the necessary conditions of interpretation—the right horizons of expectation and the right presuppositions" (WAP 49). These necessary conditions, continues Smith, are a gift to Christians: "grace gifts that attend redemption and regeneration." Smith cites a pageant of holy scripture to affirm his position (Rom 1:18–31; 1 Cor 1:18—2:15; Eph 4:17–18).

---

7. Hegel, *Lectures on the Philosophy of World History: Introduction*, 177.

PART FOUR: CRITIQUING THE CRITIQUE: QUESTIONS MOVING FORWARD

Right horizons and right presuppositions, says Smith, reclaim the "truth of Christian confession" (WAP 51) and the "truth of the gospel" (WAP 51). Smith's redemption of truth rescues Christians from the skeptical vertigo that postmoderns like Derrida deem ethically essential. This rescue evidences something further: the metanarrative quality of the Christian worldview. Smith trusts that the Christian worldview escapes metanarrative status because its knowledge derives from divine revelation and not rationality; it is not a "collection of . . . facts." "not propositions. . . not bullet-points" (WAP140). Christian truth, states Smith, is not metanarrative but "narrative—a grand, sweeping story from Genesis to Revelation . . . a story unfolded within the biblical canon" (WAP 74–75).

But this defense is faulty. Narratives are not something distinct from, and more legitimate than, metanarratives, any more than forks are something distinct from and more legitimate than dinglehoppers. This distinction resurrects the false dichotomy between truth and myth. Metanarratives are narratives grown grand. They are the "grand sweeping stories" of a particular people that seek to explain more than those people—human beings, human history, the nature of the world, truth. Metanarratives are texts that forget their textual status, "grand sweeping stories" that ignore the heterogeneity of human existence, the naturally existing chaos of the universe, and the latent diverse passions of human beings that make it impossible for them to be marshaled under a single theoretical doctrine. "Grand sweeping stories" express local reality postulates that have forgotten their local origin. Worse, grand sweeping stories are created and reinforced by power structures. They serve particular agendas, somebody or some group's interests. They are, therefore, not to be trusted.

Smith shares Lyotard's attack upon philosophical and historico-scientific metanarratives—the unique status of the individual, the ontological unfolding of Reason; the techno-evolutionary march of civilization, history as progress—but he places religious metanarratives—existence as creation, history as god's plan unfolding, human error and suffering as the salvational opportunity of a fallen humanity—safely outside of the critique. But any narrative that grants order and meaning to world, history, and human thought composes a metanarrative. What grounds and configures the ordering schema is not the issue, but the fact of its grounding, its presuppositions, its horizons, its universal scope. Its totalizing structure makes metanarrative dangerous.

Is James K. A. Smith Afraid of Postmodernity?

Finally, Foucault's treatment of "disciplinary society" offers Smith the opportunity to reflect upon disciplinary regimens, so important in the religious life, an import that will drive Nietzsche to name the religious spirit "camel." In bringing to reflective consideration what one chooses to practice and why, one breaks the hold of blind disciplines of control that can serve dangerous agendas of power-knowledge. Mere habit undermines personal responsibility. If Smith fully appreciates Foucault's concerns about the insidious power of discipline, he must not simply use Foucault to confirm Christian routines; he must use it to challenge Christian disciples to a rigorous and self-conscious examination of their ritual practices.

Since daily disciplines shape human beings and determine their communal culture, bringing disciplinary practices into reflective critique helps people make sounder choices. Replacing the silent insidious disciplines of school, work, and television ads with the mystical seductions of sacred practices is insufficient to the task of a post-Holocaust ethics. Rigorously trained "disciples who are counter-cultural agents of redemption" (WAP 107) may convert Nietzschean camels to lions, destructive of current realities, but lions cannot create. Lions make good crusaders and holy warriors but it takes a childlike tolerance and affirmation to build a better world. No empirical evidence thus far in history suggests that religious culture is less "disciplinary" or is disciplined toward more excellent ends than the current consumer society.

Blind discipleship must be broken and brought to a reflective, critical self-awareness that questions the things we hold sacred and the ends we aspire to achieve. Hegel's Lectures on the History of Philosophy celebrate Socrates' ethical discipline because it represents a profound overturning of the blind devotion and thoughtless "untrained morality" of the divine law of the ancient world, exemplified in the old man Cephalus in Plato's Republic.[8] Conscious self-disciplinary practice prevents Socrates' inner life of wonder from closing in on itself, permitting desire to pass beyond the marketplace of worldly economics, beyond the blind devotion to jealous gods, and beyond the arid intellectualism of sophistry. Christian disciplinary regimens must become truly Socratic, truly self-critiquing and self-limiting, if they are not to be a thoughtless blind adherence to

---

8. Hegel, *Hegel's Lectures on the History of Philosophy*, 384.

an externally-dictated law that can culminate in the horrors of holy war, witch-burnings, and Crusades.

CONCLUDING REMARKS

Smith's postmodern religiosity may, as Smith claims, empower Christians "to question the interpretations of trigger-happy presidents and greedy CEOs" (WAP 51), but the willingness to deconstruct other people's truths is insufficient to the task of a truly skeptical postmodernism. Deconstruction must be self-ungrounding; one's own most fundamental truths must be placed at risk. Will Smith's narrow Christian postmodernism permit Christians to question their own moral failures—their Nazi-supporting popes and Lutheran ministers, their Crusading holy armies, their colonial-supporting evangelists, their imperialist Conquistadors? Can a grounded deconstructionism undermine the self-certainty of fanatics the world over, dissuade them from their bigotry, their pogroms, their bombings of abortion clinics, their wars against "infidel" civilizations?

Smith may be taking Derrida, Lyotard, and Foucault to church, but I fear that he first converts them. A truly postmodern church would admit not only the radically orthodox, but the radical skeptics too. I am certain that Smith's new religiosity sets out to celebrate Christian difference and disarm the dangerous tendencies that culminate in religious fanaticism. All discourses have moral fault-lines and my deconstruction is simply meant to point out a few dangers. Smith's ideas for a postmodern religiosity can force a rethinking of religion's role in the sponsorship of peace and global justice. But these same ideas in the hands of unscrupulous leaders could have frightening consequences. For religion to safeguard its role as peacemaker, it must be willing to assume the most extreme risk—the risk of a truly skeptical postmodernism. I fear that the most radical postmoderns are still too fearsome, too scandalous, too threatening to Christian truth, to be permitted inside the hallowed halls of many churches.

WORKS CITED

Derrida, Jacques. *Of Grammatology*. Translated by G. Spivak. Baltimore: Johns Hopkins University Press, 1976.

Foucault, Michel. *Discipline and Punish: The Birth of the Prison*. Translated by Alan Sheridan. New York: Vintage, 1977.

Hegel, G. W. F. *Hegel's Lectures on the History of Philosophy*. Translated by E. S. Haldane and F. H. Simson. New York: Humanities Press, 1974.

———. *Lectures on the Philosophy of World History: Introduction.* Translated by Hugh Barr Nisbet. Cambridge, U. K.: Cambridge University Press, 1989.

Hume, David. "Of National Characters." In vol. 3 of *The Philosophical Works of David Hume,* edited by T. H. Green and T. H. Grose, 224–44. London, 1882.

Kant, Immanuel. *Observations on the Feeling of the Beautiful and the Sublime.* Translated by John T. Goldthwait. Berkeley: University of California Press, 1965.

Lyotard, Jean-Francois. *The Postmodern Condition: A Report on Knowledge.* Translated by G. Bennington and B. Massumi. Minneapolis: University of Minnesota Press, 1984.

McGreal, Ian P., editor. *Great Thinkers of the Western World.* New York: HarperCollins, 1992.

Popkin, Richard H. "Hume's Racism." *The Philosophical Forum* 9, nos. 2–3 (Winter 1978) 211–26.

Serequeberhan, Tsenay. *The Hermeneutics of African Philosophy.* New York: Routledge, 1994.

12

Who's Afraid of Theology?

A Conversation with James K. A. Smith on Dogmatics as the Grammar of Christian Particularity

Mark Alan Bowald

MY INTENTION IN THIS paper is to open up a conversation with James K. A. Smith on the positive function of theology as the grammar of the language and speech of Christian particularity.[1] This desire is motivated by two things:

1. First, my own interests in Philosophy, Theology and Hermeneutics overlap to a remarkable degree with Smith's, with the one caveat that I consider myself to be a theologian first and a philosopher second and he would say the reverse for himself. In light of this I am interested in coaxing Smith into a deeper conversation on the issues he raises with regard to the role of dogmatic theology in his books; particularly comparing his views in *Speech and Theology* with *Who's Afraid of Postmodernism?*

2. Second, my reading of Smith's writing has led me to conclude that, amid the constants, that there are potentially significant shifts in his thinking on the positive role of theology from *The Fall of Interpretation* and ST (2002) to WAP (2006). I am genuinely curious about these shifts; whether they are real or apparent, and how he himself would confirm or correct my reading.

---

1. The idea of theology as a "grammar" is indebted to the work of the two fathers of postliberal theology: Hans Frei and George Lindbeck.

Who's Afraid of Theology?

The primary shift that he indicates is from viewing theology as a violent oppressive mode of speech to one that genuinely projects the constructive and faithful character of the Christian faith. Finally, in light of this shift, I will close the paper asking whether this tension in Smith's writing would not require a subsequent evaluation of his employment of the idea of "incarnation" as a concept for describing the "appearance of transcendence."[2]

To begin: we can examine some of the main features of WAP and its view of theology then bring those retrospectively into comparison with ST. I begin by committing a cardinal sin of public speaking or writing; apologizing to the audience. I regret to inform you that I am nearly entirely in agreement with the main ideas in WAP. Unfortunately this reduces the prospect for fireworks or flying sparks at his point; things that conference-goers and readers secretly hope and wish for. I do have questions and minor quibbles though, and this will hopefully sustain interest and spur reflection.

Smith's exposition of the main lines of the postmodern philosophers in WAP is excellent. Smith has a rare gift to represent the ideas of these difficult and opaque writers clearly and, more importantly, fairly to a more lay-level reader (lay in both the philosophical and theological sense of the word). I have seen this consistently in his other books as well.[3] Smith's assessment in WAP that Derrida, Lyotard, and Foucault present a varied admixture of resources for the church is correct. I will not make any more specific comment on the first four chapters of WAP except with regard to Lyotard.

I agree with his exposition of Lyotard and suggestions that what he probably meant by "metanarrative" was specific to a certain form of narrative that functioned (and functions) as a mechanism of justification for certain theoretical frameworks. It nevertheless remains the case that the popular on-the-ground interpretation of what his incredulity towards them means typically bears the character of suspicion towards *any* "big story" that claims to have special purchase on the whither and whence of the human story in the world.

This sort of thing happens all the time with influential books. George Lindbeck, the postliberal theologian, once remarked that the common

---

2. This is the way it is used throughout ST.
3. Including his IRO.

misreading of his book *The Nature of Doctrine*[4] had come to be so influential that over time he became conscious of a drift for him to come to read it those ways himself.[5] In the case of Lyotard, then, a "pastoral" interest might be better served by giving fuller redress to the form of the misreading rather than to correcting it.

We turn now to Smith's own proposal in chapter four: "Applied Radical Orthodoxy: a Proposal for the Emerging Church" (WAP, 109–146) and will compare this with his earlier writings. We set the stage for this by way of Postliberal Theology, particularly the Yale theologian Hans Frei's lesser known (and unfinished) book *Types of Christian Theology*.[6] Frei's analysis is focused on the tension between the Christian community's internal self-understanding and self-description and the descriptions of Christianity which originate externally to it. He uses spatial metaphors of internal and external to represent the two alternate milieus to be related in the typology. Frei's five types occupy positions along a line or continuum. Their position represents different weightings of the internal and external descriptions. Types 2 and 1 give greater and greatest weight respectively to external descriptions of the Christian faith primarily by way of philosophy or social sciences. Type 1 is at the extreme left end of the line and is represented by the work of the theologian Gordon Kaufman as an application of the method of Immanuel Kant (*Types*, 28–30). Type 2 sits just next to it but still left of the center of the line and is represented by the work of David Tracy (*Types*, 31–4). This could be viewed as the location that Hegel, as a more illustrative figure for this approach, would also occupy. Alternately, types 4 and 5 increasingly rely on Christianity's self-understanding by way of confessions, dogmatics, and theology to name or describe itself the exclusion of those that come from outside it. Type 5 is at the extreme right side of the line and is represented by the philosopher D. Z. Phillips (*Types*, 46–50). This position would also, in another sense, be occupied by certain forms of Anabaptist theology. Type 4 sits just to the left of type 5 but still to the right of the center of the line and is represented by Karl Barth (*Types*, 38–46). Frei's Type 3 attempts something of a balancing act between external and internal descriptions for the

---

4. Hereafter cited as *NOD*.
5. Related in personal conversations.
6. Hereafter cited in text as *Types*.

Christian faith and sits right in the middle of the line and is represented by Friedrich Schleiermacher (*Types*, 34–8). This is illustrated below:

Hans Frei's Types of Theology

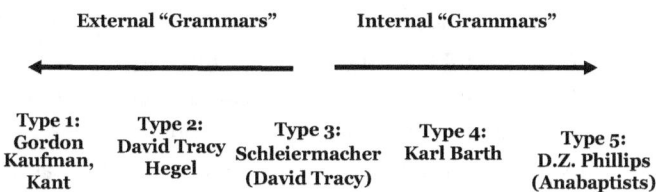

With this typology in place we can discern where Smith's writing in WAP would be situated. His assertion that "the critique of modernity reopens a significant role for tradition" (WAP, 109) sets up the question that frames his closing constructive chapter; how is it possible, in a postmodern setting, to be faithful to tradition. This is consistent with a theme that runs throughout his books in which Smith suggests that "we are traditioned creatures"[7] and that this feature of our creatureliness is not attributable to some fallen or sinful condition. So, being traditioned does not inevitably mean that we are violent and oppressive. In fact, turning other purported forms of postmodernism on their heads, he insists that to deny our traditionedness results in "self-alienation, even self-destruction" (WAP, 110). This is the most significant point of contrast between Smith and the prophets of philosophical postmodernism and emergent movements that he expounds with such clarity and ease.

Smith rightly points out that the deep suspicion of tradition that is often indicated by these so-called postmodern thinkers, including many in the emergent movement, is not really post modern at all. That this suspicion trades on a strong link between knowledge and some kind of ideal certainty and rejects *any* link between them. This results in a fundamental opposition between faith and knowledge. The deepest irony emerges here; that this brand of postmodernism is actually a form of hyper-modernism.

7. An idea that appears in his first book FI.

PART FOUR: Critiquing the Critique: Questions Moving Forward

I would, however, not quite put my own conclusion the same way as Smith when he writes that we should then "confess knowledge without certainty, truth without objectivity" (WAP, 121). Calvin believed that faith produced a certainty that was actually higher than that which issued from our senses and physical science. Likewise, pre-modern notions of objectivity which traded on the belief that things are endowed with the power to make themselves present to our minds and faculties in ways that are more or less faithful to their natures, is a more acceptable notion of objectivity.[8] So, terms and ideas like certainty and objectivity, in my mind, are redeemable and well worth redeeming and should fall *within* the pale of the work of Christian theologians and philosophers.

From this point Smith unpacks several constructive ideas about the church that coalesce around two key ideas (cf. WAP, 116–46):

1. He promotes the unapologetic reclamation of pre-modern church practices. An Ecclesiology that proceeds from "thick confessional identities" (WAP, 117).

2. A retrieval of a "Robust confessional theology," a "postmodern" or "postcritical dogmatics of second naiveté" (WAP, 117).

A quote from his book sums up these ideas:

> A more persistent postmodernism embraces the incarnational scandal of determinate confession and its institutions; dogmatic theology and a confessionally governed church. Perhaps in its most scandalous form there is nothing more postmodern than hierarchy! And nothing more modern than autonomous, nondenominational anarchy. (WAP, 122–23)

I concur with both the assessment of the nature of the implications of postmodernism and the response that should be promoted in the Church here and throughout WAP. The impulse to escape, repress or discard the traditioned aspect of our creatureliness is, *in nuce*, the kernel of modernity. So called "postmodern" movements that repeat or mimic this stance continue to move within the modern tradition in this important respect.

In correcting this impulse his proposal in WAP invests the self-identity and the self-identifying and self-describing language of the church with greater weight than the alternate vernacular and descriptions

---

8. On this, see Bowald, "Objectivity."

that arise from without. So the church derives greater self-determination by way of the "grammar" of its confession and doctrine than it does by way of the analysis of a third person perspective of the typically construed modern religious studies perspective.

Smith's proposal in WAP gives every indication of falling somewhere to the right of type 3 in Frei's typology. He advocates for "a robust appropriation of the church's language as the paradigm for both thought and practice" (WAP, 123) and associates his approach with postliberal and radical orthodox theology.[9]

A pressing question, however, emerges here: Does Smith's proposal in WAP indicate a significant shift in the value he attributes to the grammar of particularity in the Christian tradition, as compared to the views he expressed in his earlier books? Returning to the typology, Smith confirms that his proposal falls somewhere to the right of type 3 in that he is critical of postmodern and emergent church forms that derive from a "correlation" model of theology. He cites David Tracy as the purest form of the correlationist model he has in mind (WAP, 123). Tracy and Schleiermacher represent the two quintessential versions of type 2 and 3, respectively, in Frei's book and later writings.[10]

One key point where I see this tension between WAP and earlier writing appears in *Speech and Theology* where Smith calls for a reconsideration of the question of the appropriate use of "concepts" in order to stage his own proposal there:

> Could there be a kind of concept, and therefore a kind of theory, which does not treat objects as present-at-hand, but rather both honors the transcendence and answers the call for reflection? That is, could the violence of the (traditional) theoretical concept signal the development of a new kind of concept and set of conceptual categories, precipitated by a fundamental redirection of philosophy to pretheoretical experience…The construction (or recovery) of just such a third way is precisely the task of this book: to provide an alternative interpretation of concepts which do not claim to grasp their object, but rather signal the phenomenon in such a way

---

9. It should be noted that postliberal theology, particularly the contributions of George Lindbeck, Hans Frei, and now their legion of students, created a space for the possibility of something like radical orthodoxy. The debt should be acknowledged.

10. Frei initially uses Tracy as a quintessential type 2 but later insisted Tracy would be more properly located as a Type 3.

that respects its transcendence or incommensurability rather than collapsing the difference and denying otherness. (ST, 6)

The idea of conceptual realm that is derivative of "pretheoretical experience" is a proposal in favor of a correlating framework, or mediating theology, which locates this project much more towards Type 1 or 2 in Frei's typology. We can fill out this picture a bit more with further examples from SAP.

Smith links the possibility of pretheoretical concepts to the work of Derrida: in "formalizing the problem of negative theology, in order to open up new a dialogue with phenomenology . . . to provide an account of how phenomenology can recognize religious experience and the appearance of transcendence" (ST, 3–4). Smith also appeals to the work of Jean-Luc Marion who indicts Kant as a co-conspirator in the reduction to immanence (ST, 33–34). As appreciative as Smith is of Marion, he is also severely critical in that:

> Marion's "religious phenomena" is collapsed into a theological phenomenon; correlatively, his (albeit impossible) phenomenology of religion slides toward a very possible, and very particular, theology. The result is both a reduction of religion to theology, and also a particularization of religion as Catholic or at least Christian—which, of course is also a kind of reduction, a reduction which reduces the size of the kingdom and bars the entrance to any who are different. (ST, 95)

Smith sees Marion's Christian particularization as an injustice. Smith continues,

> But what if we were to delineate religious phenomena differently, in the plural? My goal is to argue that just such a space for difference is opened in the work of the young Heidegger . . . [in which he] wants to recover or liberate (*relever*?) religion, as a pretheoretical mode of existence, from its theoretical sedimentation as a "science of God" in theology. The phenomenology of religion, as a *Religionswissenschaft* distinct from theology, brackets committed participation in a faith community and analyzes the intentions or meanings of a religious community or tradition. As such, it stands in contrast to theology, which investigates religious existence from within the commitments of the community . . . Thus Heidegger's attention to the distinctions between phenomenology and theology in fact opens the space for a distinct science of religion of "religious studies"—which would be precisely a phenomenology

Who's Afraid of Theology?

of religion distinct from both phenomenology (as ontology) and theology. This is a space for the study of religion for which Marion provides no account. Further, and perhaps more importantly, this distinction between theology and religion opens the space for an understanding of religion or religious experience as a pretheoretical mode of being-in-the-world, rather than a "theologized" body of dogma. In other words, religion is a matter of the heart, whereas theology is a matter of cognition. While this does not exclude the latter, we ought not reduce religion to a theology. (ST, 95–6)

The advantages of the early work of Heidegger with respect to these issues are ones which Smith sees as important and helpful for his own argument in ST. Smith advocates the study of religion which discerns the nature of religious life as a "pretheoretical mode of existence."[11] The former, violent ways that Smith seems to wish to "bracket" in relation to this pretheoretical religious phenomenon are "theology" as well as the role that the "committed participation in a faith community" plays. The critical attack on Marion in particular illuminates this. He writes:

> Thus for Marion, as for Aquinas, the phenomenology of religion remains tied to the God of Abraham, Isaac, and Jacob as its horizon ... The result of this rather insidious movement is two-fold: first, this conception of a phenomenology of religion reduces religion to theology; that is, it effects a leveling of the plurivocity of (global) religious experience and forces it into a rather theisitic, or at least theophanic, mold. Religion, for Marion, turns out to be very narrowly defined and, in a sense, reduced to its theological sedimentation. Second, and as a result of this, Marion particularizes religion and the religious phenomenon as quite Christian—at best, monotheistic, and at worst, downright Catholic. (ST, 98)

Smith continues:

> [F]or Marion, though the phenomenology of religion is without faith, it nevertheless remains tethered to the God of faith; the "God of phenomenology" is, of course, behind the veil, the God of Abraham, Isaac, Jacob, and Pope John Paul II. Marion's reduction, then, is also a particularization which reduces the size of the field and restricts both entry and appearance ... The result is that religion itself is reduced and particularized—or, more aptly, colo-

---

11. This is a revised version of his commitment to "empirical transcendentals" in FI, 169–70.

nized in the name of a Christian imperialism.[12] ... Marion's piety leaves no room for difference and will not permit any other gods to appear. (ST, 101)

Marion is too restrictive in not allowing for "other gods" to appear. Smith appeals to the early work of Heidegger to begin to make the necessary corrections to Marion at this point, "[L]iberating religion from such colonization ... and providing space for plurality and alterity—though I would also suggest that his mission fell short of a radical liberation of religion from theology, since he retains a focus on Christian religion" (ST, 102). Heidegger's rescue of "religion" from the oppression of "theology" was not as exacting as Smith here suggested it needs to be. These examples illustrate both the negative tone toward the particular grammar of Christian theology in Smith's earlier book as well as his investment in the primacy of an external location from which to describe religious phenomenon, including Christianity. These two combine to locate his work up to and including ST somewhere on the left side of Frei's typology; as a kind of correlating theology near Type 2.

This stands in considerable tension with his proposal in WAP for which key points are summarized in the following quote:

> [T]hat a more persistent postmodernism, articulated by Radical Orthodoxy, begins from a primary affirmation of the incarnation ... I argued that if our theology and practice are going to be fundamentally incarnational, then they should be the catalysts for a reaffirmations of the particularities of Christian dogma, confession, and ecclesial practice ... the incarnation should entail a deep affirmation of time and history, which should translate into church practice that is catholic and traditional (though in a postmodern mode). (WAP, 127)

Further, that "the most persistent postmodernism should issue in a thickly confessional church that draws on the very particular (yet catholic) and ancient practices of the church's worship and discipleship" (WAP, 25). And,

> a more properly postmodern theology will reject the very terms of [Derrida and Caputo's religion without religion] critique and, in fact, be much more hospitable to both dogmatic theology and the institutional church. (WAP, 120)

---

12. On Marion's "Christian imperialism" see also ST, 98.

Who's Afraid of Theology?

The tension, here, is apparent. This illustrates what appears to be a shift in his writing that is a substantial changing of his mind on these questions. Whether this is the case or there is some larger framework to reconcile these approaches, which this author cannot foresee, would be for Smith to assess and indicate.

Assuming that there is, in fact, a substantial tension between Smith's earlier and later writings in their general attitude toward theology, we can now turn to the final task of this paper: to evaluate his use of incarnation as a "principle" for accounting for the appearance of transcendence.[13] His use of incarnation as a principle or paradigm persists throughout his work and continues in WAP. The analysis of his use of this term for this purpose is a helpful exercise to illustrate the tensions that emerge between internal and external grammars in expounding Christian particularity and theology.

Returning to SAP we see that his proposal comes to its constructive point of expression in the notion of an "incarnational paradigm" which is "both the paradigm and condition of possibility for the proper understanding of language in general and theological language in particular" (ST, 154). He gives the following succinct definition:

> My goal . . . is to outline an understanding of philosophical (and theological) "concepts" as "incarnational" (following Augustine) "formal indications" (following Heidegger). By this, I mean to suggest that such revised "concepts" are able to indicate that of which they speak without claiming to make them objectively present . . . I mean to show that the transcendent phenomenon is not reduced to the sphere of ownness; rather . . . we see an appearing which is at the same time a withholding, such that the Other is both present and absent. I will describe this as "incarnational" insofar as it bears analogy to the appearance of God within humanity, such that the Other appears within the sphere of immanence without giving up its transcendence. (ST, 10)

---

13. As an apology or correction: In the manuscript of *Rendering the Word in Theological Hermeneutics*, I discussed these shifts in Smith's writing. The deadline for my final manuscript submission was December 2006. In the fall of 2006 Smith's book WAP appeared, I hurriedly read it, and included a brief discussion of it. Then, I read WAP and attempted to reconcile it with Smith's earlier writing, which I read and still read as a Type 2 project of correlational theology. I then (mistakenly) assumed that Smith's thinking had largely remained unchanged. I now believe he has shifted considerably on these questions and would qualify and correct my analysis of his work in that book by what I have written here.

PART FOUR: Critiquing the Critique: Questions Moving Forward

This "concept" underwrites all language and even all "appearances" of transcendence, potentially in any and all human religious experiences. The question posed here is: Is Smith, in his use of the incarnation as a paradigm in this fashion, giving greater determinative weight to grammars internal or external to the Christian tradition and faith?

A generic definition of the word "incarnation" is "enfleshment" or "becoming flesh." In this usage there are two aspects to consider. First, there is the thing that in some prior state was not flesh. Second there is the particular moment or event when this thing takes on fleshly form. One common use of incarnation can be illustrated by way of drama. After viewing a particularly impressive performance of Tennessee Williams' *Glass Menagerie* one might offer the review that the actress was the "incarnation of Laura Wingfield." In this example the literary character, previously only living transcendently in the midst of the pages of the script, is viewed to be given a physical voice and presence in the performance of the actress. This is a common use of the term that emerges in generic English speaking contexts.

The ambiguity that emerges with Smith's use of the term is whether what he describes as Incarnation, "the appearance of God within humanity," takes its primary cue from internal grammars of Christian particularity or from this generic extra-Christian grammar. So, when Smith writes:

> God's incarnational appearance is precisely a condescension to the conditions of finite, created perceivers. How could he appear otherwise? The Incarnation signals a connection with transcendence which does not violate or reduce such transcendence, but neither does it leave it in a realm of utter alterity without appearance. (ST, 126)

The principle of incarnation that Smith describes is, strictly speaking, limited to the possibility and necessity of transcendence "appearing" in immanence (ST, 156, 164, 176). This may be indicated by something as minimal as a sign, a gesture, or as the appearing of transcendence in some perceivable form. This would apply to any "appearance" that would make some impression on human senses: "appears" as a sight, sound, physical touch, or smell. Any one of these, on this account, would qualify. If this is God's appearance, it could, in some of these cases, also be called revelation, depending on what one determines revelation to be and whether that event qualifies.

Very early on in ST, he indicates in a more specific way the function that his use of the term is intended to serve:

> I will concede that my employment of the notion of "incarnation" draws on a theological understanding, rather than a merely philosophical notion of "embodiment"... By describing my account as "incarnational," I mean to invoke the analogy of the Incarnation, of the appearance of God within humanity in the person of the God-man, Jesus of Nazareth... This is an instance of the transcendent appearing within the immanent, without sacrificing transcendence. In the Incarnation, the Infinite shows up within the finite, nevertheless without loss. My task, however, in no way involves the defense of a Christology, though it perhaps presupposes one. I invoke the Incarnation as a metaphor, bracketing strictly christological questions, but nevertheless pursuing a question about the philosophical possibility of theology itself. (ST, 10)

The internal-external grammar problem is evident here. He desires to use the particular Christian grammar of the incarnation of God in the person Jesus Christ. However, at the same time, he insists on "bracketing strictly Christological questions" and employs incarnation as an "analogy" or "metaphor" reducing incarnation to the succinct definition of the "transcendent appearing within the immanent."[14]

Smith continues to employ incarnation in these terms in WAP. In it he refers to his approach as an "incarnational strategy" which he defines as "attempting to accommodate thought to language that is accessible to an audience" (WAP, 21); film, as well as both the Eucharist and the "arts in general" are all "incarnational medium" (WAP, 24; 77–8); worship is "incarnational"; "A more persistently postmodern church must be radically incarnational" (WAP, 78).

But, again, the question to be asked here is whether the specificity of the term "incarnation" as it is defined by the description of the *internal* grammar of the Christian tradition which begins with the affirmation of God's *becoming* a human being: while having several points of continuity with all of the above things, has as its most defining feature a singular point of discontinuity. God does not just appear within immanence but

---

14. This "move" is the primary point of discussion for Hans Frei in his groundbreaking *The Identity of Jesus Christ: The Hermeneutical Bases of Dogmatic Theology*. Frei concludes, persuasively, that the incarnation, as attributed to Jesus Christ, cannot be reduced to a principle without compromise and loss. The following analysis is indebted to Frei's writing.

becomes immanent. Further, and even more radically, in the thickest of Christian self descriptions, the ecumenical creeds, the central claim of Christian particularity turns on the confession that the second person of the eternal Trinitarian Godhead becomes *this particular person* and no other: Jesus the Christ.

The doctrine of the incarnation is defined in these terms according to Christian confessional and dogmatic grammar. This stands in rather stark contrast to Smith's use of incarnation in ST in which he "brackets strictly Christological questions" (ST, 10) to employ it as the conceptual idea that transcendence appears immanent in language. There are a host of resultant theological problems that emerge here that time and space just will not allow exploring, save a few we will look at now.

Returning to our drama analogy, the difference between an "incarnation" in external versus internal Christian categories is initially signaled in the difference between an actress "embodying" the literary figure of Laura Wingfield in some sense that can be recognized as uniquely faithful to the character of that figure and an actress, *one* actress, actually *becoming* Laura Wingfield. That difference, already profound, is amplified exponentially when we consider that the Christian doctrine of the Incarnation is defined not by the embodiment of some idea or character but of God becoming flesh; *this* person.

Smith's employment of the concept of incarnation in ST does not take its primary cue from the particularity of the Incarnation of God in Jesus Christ: a particularity that surpasses Smith's purely formal and perpetually deferred logic in ST at the very point of its adequation *and* finality.[15] There is a radical identity in God becoming *a* human, becoming *this* man Jesus Christ and not just "appearing" or "becoming immanent" or even simply "becoming human." There is a finality of identity of God and man, and of all humanity in the Messiah, in Jesus Christ. By nature of its finality and adequacy (full-filment) it cannot so easily be reduced to serve as a general analogy of a general and forever deferred possibility (for all language) by way of external grammars.

The preceding analysis, limited to this specific example and to the time and space allowed for this presentation, is sufficient to, minimally;

---

15. For another criticism of the kind of formalistic and universalist (as opposed to material and particularist) use of terms like "incarnation" that Smith (and many others, their name is legion) employs see the brilliant analysis in Hart, *The Beauty of the Infinite*.

illustrate the tensions that one must wrestle with as a theologian or philosopher if one is working out of a perspective or worldview that takes seriously its religious and confessional shape. In this important sense this exercise illustrates a tension that would be compelling for persons working out of any religious tradition or worldview.

There are a series of other questions that could be raised in a more specific way for Smith: Is there is a more grammatically precise way to talk about how Christians manifest their faith without the complications of "incarnation"?; How does one maintain the "critical" or antithetical edge which should contrast the Christian faith from the "powers and principalities of this age" if one uses incarnation as a formal underwriting principle?; How does one account for the radical particularity of the incarnation of Jesus Christ as well as the lines of the creature/creator distinction so basic to a Reformed worldview if one uses incarnation in this sense? Others follow. It is enough for now, however, to illustrate one important tension that is so fundamental to how one answers them.

WORKS CITED

Bowald, Mark Alan. "Objectivity." In *Dictionary for Theological Interpretation of the Bible*, edited by Kevin Vanhoozer, 544–46. Grand Rapids: Baker Academic, 2005.

———. *Rendering the Word in Theological Hermeneutics*. London: Ashgate, 2007.

Frei, Hans W. *The Identity of Jesus Christ: The Hermeneutical Bases of Dogmatic Theology*. Philadelphia: Fortress, 1975.

———. *Types of Christian Theology*. Edited by George Hunsinger and William C. Placher. New Haven: Yale University Press, 1992.

Hart, David Bentley. *The Beauty of the Infinite: The Aesthetics of Christian Truth*. Grand Rapids: Eerdmans, 2003.

Lindbeck, George A. *The Nature of Doctrine: Religion and Theology in a Postliberal Age*. Philadelphia: Westminster, 1984.

13

Unlike Any Other Hope

The Eschatological Structure of Hope

James H. Olthuis

IT WAS MY PRIVILEGE to be James K. A. Smith's mentor when he began his graduate studies at the Institute for Christian Studies in Toronto. Ever since then we have kept in touch. Jamie, as I know him, is a wonderful friend, a co-worker from whom I have learned much in our ongoing quest to become letters of love, witnesses of the Spirit, in a world awaiting the fullness of Christ's coming. So I freely admit to fatherly feelings of pride as we celebrate his work in this volume.

James K. A. Smith, it strikes me, could aptly be called a post-postmodern Christian academic. In his earlier work, to be more specific, I read him as intentionally and strategically positioning himself as a Pentecostal in the vicinity of Derrida/Caputo. In his more recent work, he seems to have repositioned himself intentionally and strategically as a Pentecostal in the vicinity of Radical Orthodoxy. As I was writing this, a friend emailed that he espied an even earlier deployment on James K. A. Smith's part: a Pentecostal in the vicinity of Dooyeweerd/Olthuis. That naturally heightens the intrigue, not the least for me. What accounts for the movement? Where is he heading? Why? How?

Even though in the recent past he has been quite critical of Derrida/Caputo, in 2005 he wrote a wonderfully engaging, accessible, and even-handed exposition of Derrida entitled *Jacques Derrida: Live Theory*, which he likened to "returning to a first love." In the second preface to this book, the exergue written after Derrida died, he exhibits remorse for the brashness of his "fairly blistering critique" of Derrida's notion of hope that he offered at an American Academy of Religion meeting in Toronto (LT, xii, xvi).

I was at that meeting, and it was then and there that I first became acutely aware of his growing discomfort with Derrida/Caputo. Indeed, as I began to prepare this essay, my mind immediately went back to that morning and that paper. What I particularly recall is that—even though I in no way think or thought that Derrida is beyond criticism—I felt uncomfortable with this particular paper and its critique.

So in this essay as former teacher, now friend and colleague of James K. A. Smith, I want to pay particular attention to the published version of this speech, entitled "Determined Hope, A Phenomenology of Christian Expectation." In this article he critiques Rorty's hope as lacking sufficient grounds, and Derrida's hope for lacking determination. He ends by concluding that the Christian hope is, epistemologically, "not unlike any other kind of hope"(DH, 226).

Succinctly put, in this essay I want to suggest otherwise. I want to suggest that the hope of faith—and thus the hope of the Gospel in a world broken by sin and evil—is unlike any other hope. My concern is that Smith's insistence on the determination of hope, such that the Christian hope is epistemologically not unlike any other hope, could lead to, or is in danger of, risk-proofing Christianity, in effect defusing the unforeseeable surprise, unpredictable mystery, and extraordinary hope of God's coming realm of love, peace, and justice. Since I am sure that domestication is not his intent, I say this with hesitation and trepidation. After all, who am I, a Calvinist, to wonder whether James K. A. Smith, a Pentecostal, takes the newness of the eschaton seriously enough!

Smith argues that Derrida's hope for the impossible does not qualify as hope because it lacks determinate content. He tries to show this by doing a Husserlian phenomenology of hope as a "particular way of 'intending' the future." Three elements are emphasized. Consciousness is always consciousness of ... something. The intended object is constituted by the ego. The process of constitution happens within horizons of meaning. "Without the horizons, there is no constitution, without constitution, there is no object of hope; and, without an object of hope, there is no hope" (DH, 207). Moreover, according to Smith, all hopes, whether ultimate, penultimate, or mundane have the same formal structure.

Armed with his Husserlian phenomenology, he examines Derrida's "messianic eschatology" with its opening to the future as the advent of justice and finds it wanting because, "without horizon of expectation" and "absolutely undetermined," Derrida's hope lacks an object. Since it is "impossible to think of hope as lacking an object," how, asks Smith rhetorically, does one "wait for who-knows-what?"(DH, 219). "One cannot wait for (literally) nothing" (DH, 223). In the end, Smith claims that Derrida's messianic hope which awaits without horizon is phenomenologically impossible, even *Unsinning* (DH, 223), since any mode of consciousness such as hope cannot escape the conditions of horizonality.

Smith then proceeds to describe the determinate elements of Christian expectation in contrast to the indeterminate messianic hope of Derrida as well as the liberal utopia of Rorty. The advent of Christian hope will not take us by surprise. It is a waiting of sanctified impatience whereas "Derrida's hope delights in waiting"(DH, 224). He ends by referring to Moltmann for a comprehensive vision and exposition of Christian hope, and by noting that there is an important degree of indeterminacy as well as discontinuity in Christian eschatology

JUSTICE MUST NOT WAIT

I remain perplexed by Smith's critique of Derrida. To me his critique is slightly out of focus, resulting in a much too fast and facile dismissal of Derrida. At points it even seems uncharitable, as when he says that Derrida's hope delights in waiting. The messianic hope for Derrida is an "urgency, an imminence"[1] calling for change, allowing no complacency or patience with injustice. Justice "must not wait," and a just decision is "required *immediately*, 'right away'"(FL, 26). It is not an experience of paralysis or complacent waiting, but rather constitutes the very conditions of decision, affirmation, and responsibility.

Indeed, for the "surplus of responsibility" that is, according to Derrida, ours by nature of the "unconditional, imperative and immediate ... affirmation that motivates deconstruction" a "waiting period is neither possible nor legitimate." Since the affirmation is "ceaselessly threatened," it "leaves no respite, no rest."[2]

---

1. Derrida, *Specters of Marx*, 168. Hereafter cited in-text as S.
2. Derrida, *Points*, 286.

Unlike Any Other Hope: The Eschatological Structure of Hope

Moreover, it is not that Derrida fails to see that hope takes shape in terms of determinate horizons. His central concern is that since horizons contain the future within the reach of the past, they actually prevent anything truly novel from happening. They set limits and define expectations in advance (FL, 57). Moving into the future, then, is to arrive at and actualize that which was potentially already there. The horizon is in fact the "always-already-there" of a future.

Contrary-wise, genuine expectation for Derrida must move through our horizons, disturbing and disrupting them—horizon with/out horizon—because horizons belong to the formal structure of intentionality in terms of which we are able to predict, program and foresee the future. For that reason Derrida (and Levinas) are reluctant to talk of justice in terms of a "horizon of expectation." While horizons have to do with "space" and periods of "waiting" which involve strategies of delay, justice is at this very moment required.

What is particularly intriguing is that James K. A. Smith knows and recognizes all this at other points. As he says in LT, "if the space of the political is to remain *really* open to the other—and to the future *to come* (which is not simply programmable or foreseeable—then our waiting must not be conditioned by any particular, determinate horizon of expectation. If we specified beforehand what we are looking for, we would have already set up blinders to an alterity that would have surprised us" (LT, 87; cf. also 112).

"Faith, of course, is madness," says Derrida.[3] It is to hope against hope that something will break in and push us beyond the realm of the same with its built-in exclusion of the other. "Faith *par excellence*" is to "only ever believe in the unbelievable" (S, 143). Undecidability is structurally an ingredient of faith, or it is not faith. Here there is an obvious analogy to the way faith is described in Hebrews: "Faith is the assurance of things hoped for, the evidence of things not seen" (11:1).

For that reason, if Derrida's messianic hope is *Unsinnig*, as Smith suggests, I as a fellow Christian believer am worried. After all, Derrida's dreaming and praying for the coming of an absolute future that suspends, breaks, interrupts our ordinary horizons of meaning seems to me analogous structurally to my praying and longing for the coming of God's kingdom of love and justice.

---

3. Derrida, "following theory," 36.

My guess is that James K. A. Smith's reliance on Husserl has led him astray. What puzzles me is why he didn't rather refer to Moltmann's eschatology of hope in more detail when attempting to come to grips with Derrida's messianic hope. For, I wager to say, it is in Moltmann that you find a Christian approach to hope which is structurally rather congenial with and analogous to Derrida's quasi-Jewish "atheistic" messianic hope.

For the rest of this paper I want to flesh out my wager a bit more and invite James K. A. Smith and all of you to think along on the way to exploring the structure of the hope of faith.

FUTURUM AND ADVENTUS

The hope of faith, says Jürgen Moltmann, contradicts the way things are. In Christian eschatology "present and future, experience and hope, stand in contradiction to each other" so that we are "drawn into the conflict between hope and experience."[4] In the linear conception of historical time there is a tendency to focus on movements in time towards a future at the expense of a fuller experience of an eschatological future time beyond our control. However, it is this eschatological hope—a future all-embracing, life-anticipating outlook—that brings to light how open all things are to the possibilities of life, beyond death.

In working this out, Moltmann's theology of hope emphasizes the need to distinguish the future that is (not yet) (*futurum*) from the future as *adventus* which is not (yet). *Futurum* (as the present future of historical time) we can extrapolate towards and foresee. We only need to bring it about programmatically. It's only a matter of time. By contrast, the *adventus* (as a future present of eschatological time) is not a matter of something determinable, programmable, or foreseeable. The *adventus*, a future present coming we know not when, will come like a thief in the night, discontinuous, surprising.

The *adventus* is not a *telos* that we move towards out of the past, it is rather the coming future brought into existence through hope. Whereas the future present (*adventus*) is imminent, it is not implicitly immanent as present future (*futurum*). Since the historical horizon (closed down by sin and evil, opened up in redemption) is still beclouded, it is in hope that we know the not-yet of the future when God will be all-in-all.[5]

---

4. Moltmann, *Theology of Hope*, 18.

5. See Ansell, *The Annihilation of Hell* for a comprehensive and trenchant treatment of Moltmann's eschatology.

Unlike Any Other Hope: The Eschatological Structure of Hope

For Moltmann (and for myself) the movement between the already and not-yet of the Kingdom of God is not a simple linear movement of continuity. The eschaton is not simply about a future yet to come, but it is the adventful future which is not-to-be-predicted-from-the-actual. The future as advent is an unprogrammable gift, rather than the realization or fulfillment of something potential in reality.

In fact, Derrida, following the lead of Levinas, also sharply contrasts the "future modality of the living present" (S, 65)—a future that belongs to the regime of the present and can be programmed—and the future which is to break in, the advent of messianic time. Such a future, says Levinas, is "not my anticipation of a present that is already waiting for me, all ready …'as if it had already arrived.'" Rather this "future is the time of pro-phecy, which is also an imperative, a moral order, herald of inspiration."[6] This future does not reach us as "the horizon of my anticipations or pro-tentions" and contrasts "strongly with the synchronizable time or re-presentation, with a time offered to intentionality, in which the *I think* would keep the last word" (EN, 173). For Levinas and Derrida the kind of vigilance which characterizes our longing for the coming of justice marks a rupture with the formal structure of intentionality with its usual kind of waiting.

Levinas even sees this imperative as a "rupture of the natural order of being" that is "improperly called super-natural?" The "futuration of the future … is the singular intrigue of the duration of time … time as the to-God [*à-Dieu*] of theology!" (EN, 173). It is the "infinity of time … the very movement of the to-God, and that time is better than eternity which is an exasperation of the 'present,' and idealization of the present" (EN, 115).

Indeed, it is in relation to this adventful future that one encounters for Levinas and Derrida the limits of phenomenology. In his exchange with Marion at Villanova, Derrida insisted that, although he is "very true to phenomenology," when he agrees "on the necessity of suspending the horizon, then I am no longer a phenomenologist."[7]

Although it is no doubt true that Christians know how the story ultimately ends, in an equally important sense they do not. And it's important, as Merold Westphal reminds us, "to keep clear what we know and don't know."[8]

---

6. Levinas, *entre nous*, 115. Hereafter cited in text as EN.
7. Caputo and Scanlon, *God, the Gift, and Postmodernism*, 66.
8. Westphal, *Overcoming Onto-theology*, xii.

PART FOUR: CRITIQUING THE CRITIQUE: QUESTIONS MOVING FORWARD

We receive life both as gift (grace of the already) and promise (grace of the not-yet). In the giving-over of faith, in hope against hope, we precisely take hold of the promises of God and risk seeing through the horizon of the end of the world into the new coming of the kingdom of God. That is to say, we count on the coming of God's kingdom not as something that will happen because it *must*, but we have confidence that it will come because we trust the *promises* that it is to come.

What *must* happen is related to the present transcendental conditions, horizons, and possibilities for existence, conditions that have been affected by sin and evil. In the renewal of creation, these will be transformed, and the primordial conditions will be opened up to its eschatological fulfillment beyond what was implicit in beginning, although not out of line with it.

"Behold I make all things new" (Rev 21:5).

Somehow. All things will be new. That is to say, the present fall-affected conditions will be transformed and the primordial creational conditions will be eschatologically opened up and fulfilled. Redemption is then not only a restoration of the original blessing of creation, but also the opening of history to its eschatological fulfillment.

The advent to come is linked to what will be, but it is more than that. "For what is to come does not emerge out of the forces and trends of growth and decay, but comes in liberation to meet what is becoming, what has become, and what has passed away."[9]

In other words, there is the future as coming that builds on and fulfills the gift and call of creation, but there is also the future as *adventus* that comes to us as the promise and call of the eschaton.

Although the reformational tradition of Calvinism to which both James K. A. Smith and I belong is known for its emphasis on redemption as restoration (grace restores nature), it is noteworthy that the influential Dutch Reformed theologian Herman Bavinck was alert to the "more" of redemption. "Grace restores nature," he says, "and raises it to its highest fulfillment, but does not add a new, heterogenous element to it."[10] Or again, "There is a movement from creation through redemption to sanctification and glorification. The point of arrival returns to the point

---

9. Moltmann, *The Church in the Power of the Spirit*, 130.
10. Bavinck, *Gereformeerde Dogmatiek* III, 666 (my translation).

Unlike Any Other Hope: The Eschatological Structure of Hope

of departure, and is simultaneously a high point elevated high above the point of departure."[11]

THE HOPE OF FAITH

Even though it appears obvious that hope as a conscious mode of intending the future cannot be without horizon, it seems to me of the utmost importance to distinguish the structure of ultimate or messianic hopes—the hopes of faith—and their horizons from the structure of penultimate and mundane hopes and their horizons.

In the horizon of faith, unlike the social, economic, aesthetic, political, or ethical horizons et. al. (although these horizons in themselves may anticipate and be led by the faith horizon), there is not only a horizon of trust that sets limits, defines hopes and expectations in advance, but there is an opening up, a reaching out beyond any horizon in hope.

As a structural element of faith, to hope is to hope-in . . . (whatever one takes to be ultimate), a giving-over in faith to that which is beyond proof, demonstration, or expectation. *Spero ut intelligam.* I hope in order to understand. Such hoping is not in a specific object, envisioned against a determinate horizon, but an (ad)venturing, a faithing, a total giving over of one's life with a view to living life to the full. Epistemologically "I hope-in" with its cosmic range and scope is structurally to be distinguished from "I hope-that" with its determinate objects.

In Paul Ricoeur's words, "hope is not a theme that comes after other themes, an idea that closes a system, but an impulse that opens the system, that breaks the closure of the system; it is a way of reopening what was unduly closed."[12]

In fact, in hope (depending on and correlated with what is accepted as revelation), we move prayerfully beyond, disrupting, and interrupting our horizons in the promise of something more.

Historically, we live not only in hopeful anticipation, we also live in fear of death. However, if our hope is in God, there is a "more," an excess or surplus of God's promise that breaks through our ordinary historical horizons. We long and desire the break-in of a different future, God's future.

---

11. Bavinck, *Our Reasonable Faith*, 144.
12. Ricoeur, *Figuring the Sacred*, 211. Hereafter cited in text as FS.

Hope is not the hope of faith if you can calculate the outcome in linear progression, or see on the horizon what you are hoping for. The hope of faith is hope against hope, in spite of the killing fields, in spite of our doubts when we don't see a way out. It is not that hope is without horizon, but it is not bound by any horizon, hope is beyond mastery.

In faith we connect to both our origin and destiny. Foundationally, faith is empowerment rooted in trust in God as origin of creation out which we move into the future. Here the future is the space in which we attempt to cultivate the gift we have received by nourishing, releasing and enhancing already existing potential. Transcendentally, faith is hope in God beyond creation. Here we receive as promise that which is yet to come. Receiving the promise in hope we seek innovation beyond development of past trends, as we open ourselves to the risk and surprise of the unknown. Our lives are guided into the future both by faith as a founding trust in the God of creation, and by faith as a clinging in hope to the promise of God's coming kingdom. Trust and hope: trust in God as origin even as we hope for God as destiny.

CROSS-EYED

Pushing towards and waiting for the future, desire and hope.

We hope and wait even as we work earnestly for God's coming again. We strive to live lives of holiness and justice as we move into the future. And we hope for a promised future yet to come.

We are cross-eyed, out of focus, one eye fixed on God's coming, and one eye fixed on our task. Waiting and hastening: waiting, we keep open the present for the future; hastening, we extend the present into the future as we work for justice and mercy (II Pet 3:12, 14).

Indeed we are to plan for the future in hope, all the time realizing that the future is God's. Which is to say that the second coming will be visited upon the world. The kingdom of God is not of our doing, although we are to work for its coming. God's coming will happen in terms of a horizon of expectation, but it will not be contained by it, rather precisely it will interrupt, overflow and shatter our horizons of expectation. Indeed, the kingdom comes against a horizon of expectation that it breaches.

It will be the gift that tears open the closed economies of this world.

We can protest—and I think we must—that the economies of this world need not be invariably closed and structurally exclusionary of the

Unlike Any Other Hope: The Eschatological Structure of Hope

stranger, the widow, and the orphan. In the hope of the Gospel in which we trust in God's redemptive faithfulness, there can be the beginnings of an economy of love and justice in this present world. However, it is equally true that, although violence is not inevitable—and here with James K. A. Smith, I question Derrida's conflation of finitude and violence—the historical record continues to be rife with injustice, violence, and evil. For that reason alone, the breaking through of our closed-down horizons that Derrida insists upon and prays for needs to be honoured. If, with Kant and Husserl, horizons demarcate zones of possibility and intentionality, and if, with Derrida, these horizons are always exclusionary and repressive, then the kingdom of God belongs to the impossible and surprising.

For Derrida this aporia regarding our inability to give the gifts of love and justice even though we are called to do so neither leads to nihilism nor to paralysis. It is the call to responsible action. We are to give economy its chance, in the hope that miraculously in the aleatory moment a gift may be given.

Christian believers too are caught in an analogous aporia between the already of God's rule and the not-yet of the coming Kingdom. Our temptation too is double: triumphalistically, we can act as blessed possessors, our future in hand, predicting, planning, and enacting the kingdom, or, resignedly, we can abandon the world to its own devices and wait for the life to come.

In both cases, the aporia is to be energizing, calling us to work for justice, practicing mercy. In both cases, we are called to adopt what Kierkegaard and Ricoeur call the "absurd logic ... of hope as opposed to the logic of equivalence and repetition" (FS, 206). This absurd, messianic logic of hope for the impossible implies no illusion nor is it utopian. We live in a future marked not only with a "not yet," but also with the "much more" of grace (Rom 5:16–17). In the hope of faith, we do not look to the future as the source of the time to come, but to the future as the Age to Come, a new age in which God's promises will be fully actualized. We are called to work out our salvation with fear and trembling, awaiting the resurrection, knowing that "all resurrection is resurrection from among the dead, that all new creation is in spite of death"(FS, 206).

So help us God, help us in our unbelief.

PART FOUR: Critiquing the Critique: Questions Moving Forward

WORKS CITED

Ansell, Nicholas. *The Annihilation of Hell: Universal Salvation and the Redemption of Time in the Eschatology of Jürgen Moltmann.* Milton Keynes: Paternoster, forthcoming 2008.

Bavinck, Herman. *Gereformeerde Dogmatiek* III 3rd edition. Kampen, Kok, 1918.

———. *Our Reasonable Faith.* Translated by Henry Zylstra. Grand Rapids: Baker, 1977.

Caputo, John D., and Michael Scanlon, editors. *God, the Gift, and Postmodernism.* Indiana Series in the Philosophy of Religion. Bloomington: Indiana University Press, 1999.

Derrida, Jacques. "following theory." In *life.after.theory*, edited by Michael Payne and John Schad, 1–51. New York: Continuum, 2003.

———. *Points . . . Interviews 1974–1994.* Edited by Elisabeth Weber. Stanford: Stanford University Press, 1995.

———. *Specters of Marx: The State of the Debt, The Work of Mourning and the New International.* Translated by Peggy Kamuf. Routledge Classics. New York: Routledge, 1994.

Levinas, Emmanuel. *Entre Nous: Thinking-of-the-Other.* Translated by Michael Smith and Barbara Harshav. New York: Columbia University Press, 1998.

Moltmann, Jürgen. *The Church in the Power of the Spirit.* Translated by Margaret Kohl. Minneapolis: Fortress, 1977.

———. *Theology of Hope.* Translated by James Leitch. London: SCM, 1967.

Ricoeur, Paul. *Figuring the Sacred.* Translated by David Pellauer. Minneapolis: Fortress, 1995.

Westphal, Merold. *Overcoming Onto-Theology: Toward a Postmodern Christian Faith.* Perspectives in Continental Philosophy 21. New York: Fordham University Press, 2001.

14

Is the Grace that Calls Whale-Riders Back to Catholicism any More Amazing for Smith than for Derrida and Caputo?

David Goicoechea

> For Christ plays in ten thousand places,
> Lovely in limbs, and lovely in eyes not his
> To the Father through the features of men's faces.
> —Gerard Manley Hopkins

INTRODUCTION: HAS NOT SMITH RECEIVED AN AMAZING GRACE?

Reading the two books of James K. A. Smith, WAP and LT, has been for me a major event. For twenty-five years I have been thinking with the postmodernists. But Smith has deconstructed them in a significant way that never occurred to me, and I totally agree with him. He has shown how, if we want a true Catholic universalism that is not exclusivistic we have to go back to the particularity of the incarnation in order to guarantee a non-exclusivistic universalism. Smith focuses on the way in which the incarnation of the Logos implies a new logic of the incarnation that opens out so that "all flesh might see the salvation of the Lord" (Luke 3:6). To explore this, I would like to think with Smith about: (1) the word becoming flesh, (2) the word becoming Church, and (3) the word becoming scripture-tradition.

However, I must say that I am not totally at ease with Smith's application of the incarnational logic. I think that there is great positive and not only critical value in the Levinasian hospitality that welcomes widows, orphans, and aliens, and that suffers for our persecutors. I think that Derrida's deconstruction as justice is needed between the many voices of the institutional church. I think that Caputo's Derridean religion without religion does not indicate a false humility but that it keeps the weakness of God before the mind of the church, which too easily becomes militant and triumphalistic. But after Smith uses their theories to be critical of modernity and get back, as a Shamanistic Whale-Rider, to the traditional Catholic Church I do not see that he adequately reconciles himself with them or continues to have a major positive role for their philosophies. To think further with Smith about the incarnational logic I would like to explore how it can revitalize the Torah before Sinai, deconstruction as justice, and religion without religion in the emerging Catholic Church that is calling Smith to call others to it.

It strikes me that Smith is like a new Cardinal Newman of the 21st century, starting his Oxford movement at Calvin College in Grand Rapids, Michigan. As a Shamanic whale-rider he is called to recover his roots in the incarnation and logic of the incarnation. What is this incarnation? It is God becoming man or the creator becoming creature. The God of Jesus is Yahweh or I am who I am. When I am who I am became flesh so that God could say I am my body there was the event of the incarnation. Smith is careful to say that when persons are material we do not just inhabit flesh and blood, but we *are* flesh and blood. Jesus the God-man does not have a body. The God-man *is* his body. The word for body in the Hebrew Bible is *Bashar*. When translated into the Greek of the Septuagint *Bashar* becomes both *soma* and *sarx*. When translated by Jerome into Latin *soma* and *sarx* become *corpus* and *carnis*. Jesus is both: he is the corporal and the carnal body. The word of God becomes a corporal-carnal body. This incarnation of the logos implies a logic such that God must be a trinity of Persons: God the Father or the loving *Amans*, God the Son or the beloved *Amandum*, and God the Holy Spirit Who is the *Amor* or love between Father and Son. The logic of the incarnation in revealing how the word of God becomes flesh also reveals the trinity in which God is complacent love which becomes caring in the flesh for suffering creatures.

The logic of the incarnation has to do with the incarnation of the God-man, the resurrection of the God-man, and the Pentecost of the Holy Spirit of the God-man empowering his church. It also has to do with His Holy Mother who is the Mother of God because her child is God

Is Grace Any More Amazing for Smith Than for Derrida and Caputo?

become man. God gets his flesh from his mother, Mary. So there is the Holy I am Who I am. And that Holy I am Who I am in becoming flesh is the Holy Lord Jesus. The Holy Spirit incarnated the Son in the womb of Mary so that she became Holy Mary. So the logic of the incarnation is calling Smith to love the Holy Mother, the Holy Father, the Holy Spirit, and the Holy Lord Jesus. The Holy Christ Jesus lived a Holy life in being able to say in truth, "I am the Good Shepherd who lays down his life for His sheep." The flesh of the Holy Lord is then crucified, resurrected, and comes a second time in the power of His Holy Spirit. In recovering the incarnation, James K. A. Smith recovers all of this.

BODY

Has Not Levinas Received and Handed on an Amazing Grace?

So what is this logic of the incarnation such that it is calling James K. A. Smith from his Calvinist Church back into the arms of Holy Mother Church? How is it calling him to a radical orthodoxy and, thus, to the One, Holy Catholic Apostolic Church? The logic begins with the created creatrix of playful delight (Prov 8: 22–31) or Lady Sophia who is the mirror image radiatrix (Wis 7:22–30) and the word-breath mediatrix (Sir 24:1–39) becoming incarnate in the womb of Mary by the inseminating power of the Holy Spirit. This is a logic of the Holy. I am who I am, the Holy One, at the moment of the incarnation said "I am my body." Then she- become he- said, "I am my Church." The Church is the Body of Christ. And who belongs to the Church? One could say that outside the Church there is no salvation. But how does all flesh see the salvation of the Lord? It is through baptism of desire. Those who will the good are baptized with desire. And as Aristotle says, all must will at least the appearance of the good. Given the logic of the incarnation are not all carnal creatures members of the Body of Christ? With Christ's life, death, resurrection and Pentecost is there not the destruction of hell? Jesus-Sophia in his-her incarnation has redeemed all flesh. Through the incarnation does not Christ play in ten thousand places, lovely in limbs, and lovely in eyes not his, giving glory to the Father through the features of men's faces?

But does not the logic of the incarnation get also articulated by Levinas and his Torah before Sinai? Is there not a Golden Rule of hospitality rooted in the identity of the Hebrew word for womb and mercy? Is not Smith called to cultivate a womb that embraces all sinners, widows, orphans, aliens, and persecutors without any resistance? Does not the orthodox church of Smith need to show the older brother that his way is more important in order that there might be reconciliation? Is not Levinas showing us the natural law of love with his merciful womb? Is this not like the Chinese welcoming that says I will let his ship sail in my stomach? In the particularity of the incarnation has Smith not found a way of universal love and justice that should be especially welcoming to the insight of Levinas and the law before Sinai or even to the love before the incarnation? As Smith rightly argues there was not an adequate and consistent logic of embracing all before the incarnation. But once that particular way is revealed by the God-man and embraced by his followers then the law before Sinai can be seen as enhancing even the logic of the incarnation. Is this not what is happening with Smith? Has he not discovered the incarnational law of love after Sinai and does this not bring him to embrace the law of love before Sinai? Can the law before Sinai not help him to flesh out his own philosophy of love?

The Skeptical Ethics of the Derridean Nietzsche's More-than-Socratic, Franciscan Jesus

Smith is called to return to the Catholic tradition. But does he feel called to return primarily to the Augustinian voices within the tradition and does he resist the Franciscan voices? Augustine did love God in order to be happy. Francis loved in order that others might be happy. "I seek not so much to be consoled as to console." As his Holiness Benedict XVI has shown in his book, *Bonaventure's Theology of History*, Bonaventure went against Augustine's theory of history with the seeds of history as a *multiformes theoriae* that could sprout forth in unlimited, unpredictable ways. Scotus took this up with his principle of haecceity that let each single individual be singularized by unlimited differentiations. Ockham saw the implications of this and went against Augustinian Platonic ultra-realism and Thomistic Aristotelian realism and Abelardian Stoic conceptualism to the Socratic skepticism of nominalism in order to protect that singularity with its unique dignity of unlimited differences.

Do Smith and Milbank and the radical orthodox resist the Franciscan stream of the Catholic tradition, because they have not caught up with the Kierkegardean logic of the incarnation? Kierkegaard writes:

Is Grace Any More Amazing for Smith Than for Derrida and Caputo?

> The greatest good, after all, which can be done for a being . . . is to make it free. In order to do just that Omnipotence is required. This seems strange, since it is precisely Omnipotence that supposedly would make [a being] dependent. But if one will reflect on Omnipotence, he will see that it also must contain the unique qualification of being able to withdraw itself again in a manifestation of Omnipotence in such a way that precisely for this reason that which has been originated through Omnipotence can be independent. That is why one human being cannot make another person wholly free . . . Only Omnipotence can withdraw itself at the same time it gives itself away, and this relationship is the very independence of the receiver.[1]

The nominalism of Ockham comes right out of his theory of God's omnipotence. When God became incarnate He showed how He steps back from Himself. This revealed how He also does it in creating free creatures. So there is a third kind of complexity at the heart of postmodernism as it was already there in the Franciscans. Augustine found it hard to connect all the dots of complexity but he could do it beginning with his "*Si fallor, sum*" that gave him a foundation for certitude. The Socratic skeptic knows that becoming is too complex for the human mind to connect the dots. But with Ockham and Kierkegaard even God cannot connect all the dots because of love's gift to the creature of freedom. This is the basis of Derrida's pure giving that lets him get beyond the give and the take of Calvin, Adam Smith and Benjamin Franklin in which time is money. It is also the basis of Lyotard's reading of the many voices in scripture that does not let there be a meta-narrative. When Nietzsche comes to humankind's highest affirmation of *amor fati* and loving all of existence with a Yes and Amen he is thoroughly Franciscan in his following of the non-resentful Jesus as the overman-child.

Caputo's Augustinian Modernity from the Prayers and Tears of Monica to Descartes through Husserl

Is James K. A. Smith living up to his radical, incarnational, Catholic orthodoxy as a philosopher or is he becoming "wiser than thou" so that he cannot accept the Catholic philosophy of John D. Caputo, David Tracy, and maybe even of John Paul II? He has written his wonderful book on Derrida and I am sure Derrida would value it highly just as would anyone

---

1. Kierkegaard, *Journal and Papers*.

who highly values Derrida. He has made his telling criticism of Derrida and the postmodernists that they do not get back to the root of our tradition, namely, the radical root of the incarnation. They are not radically orthodox. Good. His criticism is as wise as is his explication of Derrida and the postmodernists. But is not the incarnational logic such that it is affirmatively open to all singularities? Is not Gilson right in his *Unity of Philosophical Experience* that the four main philosophies are always thinking together in an open interplay of questioning and inquiring questing? Thus, is not Catholic philosophy always a dialogue between radically orthodox, Platonic, Augustinian ultra-realists; and conservative, Aristotelian, Thomistic realists; and liberal, Stoic, Abelardian conceptualists; and skeptical, Socratic, Franciscan nominalists?

Smith is obviously cool toward the Franciscans and the postmodernists who are nominalists. He is also against Kant and modern conceptualists. He claims to agree with Aquinas. But does he do that fully? Does he bring the many voices around the disputed question and draw bits of good in an affirmative way from each? Does Gilson not see Augustinian and medieval roots in Descartes? From a Bonaventurean perspective are not the *multiformes theoriae* of Socratic, Platonic, Aristotelian, Stoic, and Epicurean insights all to be affirmed? Was not Woytila this open? Even though Scheler did not replace Aquinas for him, given Aquinas, Scheler could be very affirmative. The catholic tradition never became modern and thus it is not postmodern in a non-incarnational way. But it is postmodern in that the incarnation is the root of its logic of mixed opposites and its openness to all.

CONCLUSION: SO THAT EVEN ST. LUTHER AND ST. CALVIN CAN BE LOVED AND APPRECIATED IN SMITH'S EMERGING CATHOLIC CHURCH

James K. A. Smith with the shamanic whale-rider, Paikeia, has been graced to get in touch with the metaphysical, logo-centric presence of his-her premodern traditional roots. For Smith the radical root is the Holy God-man Christ Jesus (*tu solus sanctus*) in his incarnation. This root in the logic of the incarnation is radically connected with three other roots: the Holy Father, the Holy Spirit and the Holy Mother. Then the logic of the roots unfolds into the Church which becomes the trunk of the tree.

Is Grace Any More Amazing for Smith Than for Derrida and Caputo?

Next, the branches of the tree emerge and bear fruit. Are the radical roots something like this?

1. The life and works of Jesus, his manner of death, resurrection and Pentecost reveal that he is the logos-word, who is God, who became *sarx*-flesh.
2. So the Hagia Sophia of the Holy I am who I am, of the burning bush, is flesh and Mary is the Mother of God.
3. He founded his Church upon Peter (Thou art Peter and upon this rock I build my Church) and at Pentecost the Holy Spirit of the Risen Lord Jesus activated that Church.

In his reading of the incarnational logic of the trunk of the tree does Smith not see the Church, the Scripture, the Eucharist to be something like the following?

1. The Holy I am who I am in the Gospels not only says I am my body; but says I am my Church.
2. This Church brings forth the word of God in the Scripture and says with its authority: "This is the Word of God."
3. These Scriptures and the Church reveal how the incarnated God-man lives on in his real presence not only in his church, and in his scripture but also in his real presence in the Eucharist. Through the authority of the church in its Petrine line the bread and the wine are validly consecrated into this body and blood of the incarnate God-man.

In his reading of the incarnational logic does Smith not think that a return to the orthodox Petrine line (for "*orthos*" means "straight line") will recover the branches of the liturgy and art and philosophy of the Holy Catholic Church in all of its Augustinian, Benedictine, Franciscan, Dominican, Jesuit and Carmelite fruits?

But is there not some Franciscan postmodern truth with its vision that this incarnational logic is not only an arboreal logic of meaning, but also a rhizomatic logic of sense? In clarifying the weakness of God is not Caputo showing in what way he is a beloved member of the fragile and vulnerable incarnate Church? And even if Luther founded modernity by breaking away from the orthodox Petrine line and if Calvin did not keep the real presence, are not the political and economic fruits of their modernity still to be highly valued? Outside the Church there is no salvation. But even if St. Luther and St. Calvin do not have the Petrine orthodox validity, they still must be very special members of the body of Christ through their baptism of water and their Eucharist of desire.

WORKS CITED

Gilson, Etienne. *Unity of Philosophical Experience*. New edition. Fort Collins, CO: Ignatius, 1999.

Hopkins, Gerard Manley. "As Kingfishers Catch Fire, Dragonflies Draw Flame." Online: http://www.bartleby.com/122/34.html.

Kierkegaard, Søren. *Journal and Papers*. Vol. 2. Edited and translated by H. V. Hong and E. H. Hong. Bloomington: Indiana University Press, 1970.

PART FIVE
Responding

15

Continuing the Conversation

James K. A. Smith

MY FIRST RESPONSE IS one of gratitude. I would like to especially thank David Goicoechea and Andre Basson for their work organizing the conference at Brock University—the first stage of the conversation, which has now become this book. Their hospitality, interest, and passion for wisdom were the impetus for drawing together a wonderfully diverse array of scholars and practitioners to think together about the shape of both philosophy of religion and ministry in our contemporary context. It was a special privilege for me to see my work engaged in this space between the university and the church, particularly since much of my own labor has tried to inhabit that precarious place between the narrow academic conversations of the guild and the gritty, messy, and challenging shape of ecclesial life. My thanks, also, to each of the contributors here, as well as other speakers at the conference, for honoring me by taking my work seriously. I learned much from the conversations, was challenged by thoughtful disagreements and criticisms, and glimpsed new vistas and possibilities because of this dialogue. Finally, I am also grateful to Neal DeRoo and Brian Lightbody for their hard work in bringing these conversations into the light of print, so to speak.[1]

---

1. Permit me to note one other special delight: In a way this volume represents three generations of intellectual formation and friendship. Jim Olthuis, as he notes, was my teacher in Toronto; I, in turn, was Neal's teacher when he was an undergraduate at Calvin College (before also going on to study with Jim at ICS). Part of the fun of this book, for me, is seeing this play of intellectual generations. My hope is that, in the process, we might model how to *dis*agree in love.

PART FIVE: RESPONDING

Each of the contributions offers a number of different themes, critiques, and possible trajectories of conversation. I couldn't possibly take up all of them, though I have learned from them all. Instead, at the invitation of the editors, and with some pressure for compositional haste, here I will simply offer some responses and impressions as a way of continuing the conversation. Some of the contributors have provided excellent opportunities to correct misunderstandings; others have been an occasion to indicate my more recent thought on matters; still others have pointed to places where I need to retool my thinking, and I have made some step toward doing so here, at least as a start. So while my response is by no means comprehensive or exhaustive, I hope readers (and the contributors!) will find it constructive and fresh. I leave it to readers to follow up on other paths and avenues of questioning, suggested in the preceding chapters, which I have been unable to pursue here. And lacking any overarching agenda, I will simply respond to each chapter in turn, taking up Aquinas's venerable strategy of replying to (*ad* . . .) objectors and objections (*sed contra*).[2]

AD DEROO: WHY "MESSIANICITY?"

Neal DeRoo is asking important questions that get at the heart of two competing schools of thought regarding what might be called "postmodern religion," though his own position seems to occupy a kind of middle space (somewhat akin to the work of Richard Kearney, perhaps). I appreciate his desire to take us back to the basics, so to speak, and especially to get us to face up to texts—though I think there are texts that DeRoo has not addressed (both by Derrida and others by myself) which make his more charitable reading of Derrida a little more difficult to maintain. But he helps us to appreciate just how complicated and messy this debate is. While his careful contribution deserves a fuller response, let me say just a couple of things in reply.

First, while he has attended to various facets of the critique, I'm not sure that DeRoo has delineated my critique of Derrida correctly. In particular, I don't suggest that Derrida's position is problematic because

---

2. Though a number of these contributors are friends and acquaintances with whom I am familiar, here I will follow academic convention and refer to them by their last name. This is not meant to be any indication of distance, but rather of respect and protocol, and stems from a concern of not wanting anyone to feel "left out" if I didn't feel comfortable addressing them by their first name.

he somehow advocates, affirms, or celebrates violence (as if he was "OK with violence"), nor do I ever criticize his "messianicity" for merely being empty or lacking "meaning." Let me clarify this. With respect to violence, my claim has not been that Derrida is somehow pro-violence, but rather that Derrida makes ontological assumptions that won't let him have what he wants (yes, I'm humming along with Mick Jagger in the background). I certainly think that Derrida wants institutions and policies that minimize violence; but I think he's committed to an ontological picture that sees violence as somehow inherent to creation.[3] In this respect, I think DeRoo's reading misses just what *motivates* Derrida to even posit a messianicity without messianism; that motivation is precisely Derrida's concern that the determination and specificity that characterizes messianisms is violent and leads to violence.[4] So showing that Derrida is opposed to violence, for instance, does not refute the critique. Similarly, I don't think I ever criticize Derrida's messianicity for being "empty." Rather, my claim is that, in fact, such emptiness is an impossibility—that what parades itself as messianicity is always already a messianism[5] (despite Derrida's protests to the contrary), and it's precisely because such emptiness is impossible that the very goal of elucidating or appealing to a "messianicity without messianism" is misguided at best.

Second, DeRoo and I both seem to share a similar hermeneutic strategy when it comes to reading Derrida's corpus, namely, a desire to deconstruct Derrida by reading Derrida against himself, which strikes me as a way of being faithful to Derrida. It's just that we seem to have different goals in doing so: DeRoo wants to save Derrida's later talk of messiancity without messianism by showing how Derrida affirms determination, context, and specificity elsewhere in his corpus, whereas I think it is just these analyses of context and determination which implode what *moti-*

---

3. Thus I think DeRoo seems too quickly dismissive of Milbank's claims (for instance, in *Theology and Social Theory*) without much evidence of taking them seriously. I find Caputo and Kearney also fail to really appreciate the sort of claim Milbank is making.

4. This is perhaps most clearly articulated in *Specters of Marx*, which doesn't seem to quite show up on DeRoo's radar. Furthermore, I think DeRoo fails to appreciate the nuances of my critique because he relies almost entirely on the articulations of it in my (relatively "popular") books, but doesn't attend to the more sustained arguments in Smith, "Determined Violence," and Smith, "Re-Kanting Postmodernism?".

5. In this respect, Derrida's messianicity is a bit like Rawls' "original position": it pretends to a kind of purity and decontamination which is, in fact, just a masking of a particular configuration.

vates the whole notion of messianicity.[6] In short, if DeRoo was right about determinacy and determination, it would seem to me that there would be no motivation for Derrida to start trotting out later notions of "religion without religion" and "messianicity without messianism." But he does. Why? Because there is a *logic* that motivates him to extol a messianicity, because this logic entails an identification of finitude, particularity, and determination with violence. I think DeRoo has failed to address those texts (as well as my own detailed criticisms) which make such a reading of Derrida plausible, and thus which make the critique of Derrida plausible.

Finally, I applaud DeRoo's attempt to envision what this means "on the ground," so to speak. But what I find is that those practitioners who are quite taken with Derrida—and particularly Caputo's rendition of Derrida—tend to find in Derrida a comfort and an excuse for their anti-institutionalism, giving them a license to escape what they perceive to be the clutches of determinate religious traditions, etc. I see such as the flowering—or rather, the going to seed—of modernity and as nothing short of a flight from finitude. So while I, too, have found an engagement with Derrida to be a constructive catalyst for imagining the shape of faithful discipleship in postmodernity, I don't find the resources for that in Derrida's notion of messianicity. Indeed, I think it's when Derrida actually starts talking about religion that he is most unhelpful to the church.

AD STAN: CATHOLICITY AS PARTICULARITY

Writing a book like *Jacques Derrida: Live Theory* is always a tricky affair: in it I'm trying to be a conduit, a translator; and while I have no illusion of being unbiased or objective in doing so, nonetheless, the primary goal is to enable readers to be confronted by Derrida, not Smith. I think Leo Stan's contribution fudges that distinction a bit. Throughout he tends to attribute positions to me that are rather those of Derrida. And though I'm articulating them in LT, that doesn't mean I'm affirming them. Indeed, as other contributors have pointed out (and some have lamented), I'm quite critical of Derrida on just some of these points. So in some ways, Stan's contribution is better aimed at Derrida than Smith. I won't here try to referee the disagreements between Derrida and Stan about Kierkegaard

---

6. For my positive reading of Derrida's affirmation of "interpretive police," see Smith, "Limited Inc/arnation."

and Abraham, except to say that I, too, have marshaled Kierkegaard's embrace of particularity as critical for articulating what I've called the logic of incarnation (see ST, ch. 5). Kierkegaard's Abraham is certainly not Derrida's Abraham, precisely because the Other that encounters him is not just "every other" wholly other, but a *particular* Other, Yahweh. The Christian vision Kierkegaard articulates is one of a Catholic particularity—that is, a very specific way of envisioning a universal community. While Kierkegaard's Lutheran individualism sometimes tends to minimize the importance of community (though not entirely), the Christian confession of "one holy, catholic, apostolic church" is, I take it, just such a particular catholicity. I don't think this can be sufficiently generated from Kierkegaard, but I agree that the impetus of his thought points in this direction.

AD LIGHTBODY: ON READING DERRIDA CAREFULLY

It has been one of the unfortunate realities of academic philosophy since the early twentieth-century to be fractured into two competing, and often hostile, camps: "analytic" (Anglo-American) philosophy and "continental" philosophy (inspired by a particular subset of European sources). The result has been a similar bifurcation of figures and texts such that, for too long, "analytic" philosophers would never touch Hegel or Heidegger or Derrida, and continental philosophers would never engage Frege or Rawls or Plantinga.[7] In some ways, Richard Rorty was singular in refusing these dichotomies. But recently, as I noted in LT, there have been "analytic" philosophers willing to engage Derrida seriously as a philosopher, and I see Brian Lightbody's contribution as yet another example of how reading Derrida "through" analytic philosophy, as it were, can be illuminating, even if also heuristic. I think he makes a helpful contribution that crystallizes some issues for long-time readers of Derrida, while also serving to introduce the originality of Derrida's ethical intuitions for analytic philosophy. I'm happy to have him defend a stronger claim than I make, namely, that Derrida's ethical thought is almost wholly dependent upon and derivative from Levinas. I intentionally kept my claims about influence to a minimum, mainly because I didn't have space to properly address critics who would contend that such a reading fails to do justice to the independence of Derrida's thought—and I won't try to defend Lightbody against

---

7. There have been interesting shifts in this regard; consider, for instance, Robert Brandom's careful readings of Hegel and Heidegger.

them here.[8] I would only suggest that if one takes this strong reading of Derrida's dependence upon Levinas, then one also runs into a problem internal to Derrida's corpus: the fact that Derrida also seems to have been significantly influenced by Nietzsche, and yet Levinas' project seems very much concerned with countering Nietzsche (as in the opening of *Totality and Infinity* where Levinas wants to consider whether we have really been "duped" by morality). Perhaps there is an account that could explain such an apparent schizophrenia in Derrida's corpus; Lightbody's contribution helps crystallize why this would be an important question to ask next.

AD ZLOMISLIĆ: ON FEASTING

It would seem a bit wrongheaded, even perverse, to write a "response" to Zlomislic's contribution, which, in many ways, is much more like Derrida in its *performative* aspect than my rather buttoned-down expositions. Aside from sharing an enthusiasm for Hopkins and Ted Hughes, I will just say that I think the focus on "taste" gets at something that's hard for us to articulate with our philosophical lexicons: that there is a way of relating to the world that is prior to, and irreducible to, knowing. One senses this in Derrida's intuition that we often make our way in the world less by sight than by touch (a key theme in *Memoirs of the Blind*)—that there is a kind of know-how that is irreducible to the register of "knowledge." The metaphor (and sense) of taste is suggestive in this regard because other senses (sight, hearing) seem readily commensurate with the existing categories of epistemology, whereas taste indicates a way of relating to the world that is not easily subsumed by something like the correspondence theory of truth. Both Hopkins's and Hughes's poetry strain for a lexicon to try to communicate the tactile sense of being in the world to which "ordinary language" fails to do justice—and in Hughes especially, this isn't an excuse for flying off into flights of ethereal abstraction, but rather for adopting a kind of guttural, gritty speech of north Yorkshire that makes one almost

---

8. One of the questions that Derrida's intellectual biographers will have to tackle is just *when* Derrida began to read Levinas. This is a particularly important question for those (like me) who want to contend that there is no massive *Kehre* in Derrida's thinking about ethics and justice, but rather a development from more implicit to explicit formulations. (One of my central goals in *Jacques Derrida: Live Theory* was to make a case for the continuity of these themes in both early and later Derrida.) If one takes Lightbody's "strong" stance regarding Derrida's dependence on Levinas, then either one has to argue that Levinas had this impact on Derrida's thought very early on, or one would have to argue for a significant shift or "turn" in his later thought.

feel—almost taste—a hawk in the rain or frozen-still horses oozing steam on a quiet winter morning. Derrida, too, I think, was often trying to "communicate" a sense of taste (a "taste for the secret"), which is precisely why his language and lexicon—his entire philosophical performance—was so anathema to the guild taken in by "ordinary language philosophy."

Might the same not also be true of the church's witness? Might it be the case that the peculiarity of the wafer on my tongue is a better testimony of the Gospel than an apologetic defense in three syllogisms, or an alliterated "message" on PowerPoint slides? This is why I've suggested that the church, if she will be authentically postmodern, must also be Catholic—because the Catholic tradition is a full-bodied tradition that activates all the senses (this clearly informs Hopkins's poetic sensibility that Zlomislic draws upon).[9] Unlike Protestant talking-head Christianity, which mimics modernity's epistemological fixation by centering worship on a 45-minute didactic sermon, Catholic Christianity centers worship around a meal, where the smell of wine delights and tingles, where even the tongue and nose hairs are called to participate in praise. A Catholic postmodernism has a *taste* for the mystery.

AD WOLF: WHOSE PARTICULARITY? WHICH UNIVERSALITY?

Since I am almost completely ignorant about Bahái (and what I do know I learned from Wolf at the conference), I feel quite unequipped to respond in any sort of constructive way to Wolf's contribution. From the hip, I wonder whether, in fact, the Bahái account of dispensations might actually diminish particularity in a kind of Hegelian story of progress and/or universal *telos* such that all of the different, particular religions are taken up (*Aufhebung*) toward one overarching telos. Radical Orthodoxy, on the other hand, while it is unapologetically Christocentric, would nevertheless be radically pluralist and thus would, in a sense, honor other religious faiths precisely by conceding their own difference and particularity, rather than narrating an overarching account that unifies all faiths. I suppose if I was pressed on these matters, I would suggest that religious diversity (what Richard Mouw and Sander Griffioen describe as "directional pluralism"[10])

---

9. For a lucid account of this point, see Ratzinger, *The Spirit of the Liturgy*, 171–224 (on "The Body and the Liturgy").

10. See Mouw and Griffioen, *Pluralisms and Horizons*, 87–109.

PART FIVE: RESPONDING

is, in the Christian story, not something inherent to finitude or humanity as such, but rather is in some sense an effect of the fall. Thus the Baháí account of religious diversity is just one narration or *mythos* that is just as "unfounded," we might say, as the Christian account of religious diversity. As such, they share the same epistemic standing. Wolf's critique, then, constitutes a "transcendent" critique, rather than an immanent critique that seeks to implode the Christocentric account from within.

What I mean to suggest is that the "Radically Orthodox" account of religious difference, though it is unapologetically Christocentric and even missional, might nonetheless better respect the differences between religions than the quasi-Hegelian Baháí account. Furthermore, the particular Christian story *about* religious pluralism should seek to do justice to other religions by *not* subsuming them into the Christian story (though I think it is equally important for Christians to listen to and learn from those of other traditions[11]). In that spirit, I appreciate Wolf's contribution and criticisms.

AD SCHUURMAN: DERRIDA'S VISIT TO THE EMERGING CHURCH

As a practitioner with his feet close to the ground, as well as a cultural expositor who is attuned to currents in culture and the church, Peter Schuurman has put his finger on something that already concerned me in *Who's Afraid of Postmodernism?*, and the concern has only increased: precisely those sectors of the "emerging church" that are most taken with Derrida, Caputo, and deconstruction also tend to be those sectors which exhibit a hyper-modern allergy to structures, institutions, and authority and incline toward a sloppy pastiche of "spiritual" activities as a substitute for the gathered work of the people (*leitourgia*). In short, they tend to celebrate the proliferation of Lockean voluntary associations of individualist pursuit, unhampered by traditions or bishops—which is just to say that they look like consummate American pods of self-construction ("Long live Thoreau!"). And even when such emerging churches do show an interest in the tradition, it is eclectic and selective, picking and choosing *from* the tradition without submitting *to* the tradition. Anyone who's read

---

11. See the excellent articulation of the importance of "hospitality" in inter-religious dialogue in Yong, *Hospitality and the Other*.

Continuing the Conversation

Kant's *Religion Within the Limits of Reason Alone* could have seen this coming 300 years ago. Remind me again, just *how* is this *post*modern?

AD VANDERBERG: MEA CULPA

If the postmodern church is called to be anything, surely it is called to be a community of forgiveness—a people who bears witness to the fact that God was in Christ reconciling the world to himself by being a people that reconciles itself to one another (and its enemies). In this respect, Vanderberg is right to find in Derrida's rich quasi-phenomenology of forgiveness something of a call and invitation for the church to be stretched and pulled, to no longer be comfortable with a counterfeit forgiveness that operates on the basis of a miserly economy, willing to forgive what's easy or what never happens, rather than entertaining Jesus's hyperbolic call to forgive the unforgivable—times seventy. I think he's right that there is something about Derrida's rhetoric here that is important, even therapeutic and corrective for a comfortable and complacent church. I certainly find that my students are quite moved and motivated by such. That said, I think Derrida's account of forgiveness (like his accounts of justice, hospitality, the gift, etc.) is conditioned by a logic of determination that we do well to recognize and reject—not in order to remain comfortable, but so that we don't buy into a logic that ultimately undercuts the call to tangible, concrete forgiveness. The resources needed for a radical call to forgiveness are available within the logic of incarnation (cp. Col 3:13), since this is the logic of the one who humbled himself to the point of death (Phil 2:8), dying for us while we were yet enemies (Rom 5:6–11), and could utter from his brokenness on the cross, "Father, forgive them for they know not what they do" (Luke 23:34). Such radical forgiveness comes not from a "pure" and impossible forgiveness always and only to come, but from the determinate space of the cross. Its very specific shape is cruciform.

AD BASSON: AN ECUMENISM OF CONTESTABILITY

I very much appreciate where Andre Basson works; that is, I appreciate the unique challenges and opportunities for campus ministry situated at a public or state university, right in the heart of the supposed "marketplace of ideas."[12] On the one hand, postmodernism's critique of Enlightenment notions of objectivity—which often fueled aggressively secularist campaigns to exclude religion from the university—would seem to open the door for the university to be properly *pluralist*, recognizing and making room for a multiplicity of voices and perspectives.[13] And yet this has not often been the case; the university remains worried and suspicious about religion (particularly if the religion in question is Islam, but also if it is Christianity). On the other hand, others note that this has given rise to a sort of tribalism in which each "interest group" retreats to its own enclave, shutting down the sort of dialogue that is crucial to the university.[14] I appreciate Basson's concern and call for campus ministry to speak into, and above all minister to students, in this situation.

To that end, I think he is right to put the question of ecumenism and inter-religious dialogue on the table. And while I have not discussed this much in my heretofore published work, over the past couple of years I have become particularly interested in dialogue with Jews and Muslims, and even more convinced that the university campus—and campus ministry, in particular—is an important site for such inter-religious conversations to take place (and increasingly, this must include conversations with "new atheists").[15] However, the goal of such ecumenism is not the sort of

---

12. I have some suspicions about such claims made by the university for itself. All too often such a claim to diversity masks a militant secularism that is quite happy to rule certain voices out of court. It is perhaps an irony that, despite academic departments touting "postmodernism," the university remains one of the last bastions of modern secularism (and Religious Studies departments in particular!). Though, as Basson notes, the very fact that this conference took place at Brock University is a sign that things might be changing.

13. This is basically the argument of George Marsden's excellent little book, *The Outrageous Idea of Christian Scholarship*, see especially pp. 44–58.

14. We could add to this the concern that the postmodern critique of objectivity feeds right into the revisionism of fascism that would suggest 2+2=5 if Big Brother says so. See Hitchens, *Why Orwell Matters*, 193–204.

15. So contra DeRoo's suggestion (note 30 of his chapter), my Radical Orthodoxy or Catholic postmodernism does not lack reasons for engaging in inter-religious dialogue—though I should also note that, unlike DeRoo's rather rosy (and Bahái-ish) picture of world religions, my account also doesn't give up on the task of missions and evangelism, whereas DeRoo seems to suggest that "respecting" other religions requires not challenging them. (Would anyone ever undergo a conversion in DeRoo's world? Being myself a convert, I'm suspicion of accounts that are suspicious of conversion.)

But are there "reasons" for inter-religious dialogue beyond evangelism and "using" the religious other for self-understanding? Yes, certainly: I would articulate this in an

liberal, modernist search for lowest-common-denominator banalities so that "we can all get along." Rather, I would advocate what we might call an "ecumenism of contestability." This requires, first, a leveling of the playing field (and thus the displacement of secularism that is part of the postmodern critique of Enlightenment objectivity) such that all come to the table with an honest appreciation for the fact that we begin from confessional standpoints, even if we are new atheists. In short, each recognizes that they're account of the world—they're confession of faith—is *contestable*.[16] Second, such a leveling of the playing field must also entail a denial of any "Constantinian" pretensions to impose a particular story on the university;[17] this might even require giving up the desire of coming to the table to win the argument and thereby shut down all other confessional traditions.[18] But that said, we don't then just come to the table of conversation apologetically and sheepishly, embarrassed about the particularities of our faith. Rather, given the first two moves, the third should be that

---

Augustinian fashion. As Augustine outlines in *City of God*, to inhabit a *saeculum* is to inhabit a *time* between times where we find ourselves in the same spaces (the same empires, the same nations, the same neighborhoods) with those who have fundamentally different visions of the coming kingdom, so to speak. In other words, though we see ourselves journeying toward different destinations, we find ourselves on the same road together for now. In this time between times and situation of co-pilgrimage, we need to find ways—as far as possible—to collaborate on the (albeit penultimate) common good. This requires careful *listening*, but not just deference. I have explored this in a little more detail in Smith, "The Politics of Desire." In addition, I think it is important for Christians to be in conversations with Jews in order to find wisdom about how to live as an exilic people, and I think we should be in conversation with Muslims in order to be reminded why Christians shouldn't be so comfortable with Western liberalism. In short, I think there are all kinds of reasons to engage in inter-religious dialogue, whereas DeRoo seems to think one can only be properly motivated if one also holds that all other revelations are authentic in some sense. Such a claim has serious internal problems. For a related discussion, see Abraham, *Crossing the Threshold of Divine Revelation*.

16. I'm drawing here on the work of William Connolly, especially *Why I Am Not a Secularist*.

17. I suppose I see the "university" as an inherently pluralist institution, whereas the "college" is more focused on education as formation. Thus what I say here about the university does not preclude also affirming a very thick and specific confessional identity for a college. In short, I think it makes more sense to speak of a Christian *college* than a Christian *university*. However, these distinctions are only meant to be heuristic.

18. This might mean that fundamentalisms of various stripes excuse themselves from being part of this conversation. I worry that philosophies of campus ministry which are bent on "taking the university for Christ" seems to be tinged with such Constantinian pretensions.

each comes to the table with a "thick," unapologetic account of the world informed by the specificity and scandalous particularity of their faith. And while we should come to this table in humility, with the goal of listening and learning, we should also be free to proclaim, testify, and witness—to make our case for our story as the *best* story, the most comprehensive and coherent story, the story which best accounts for the phenomena that we bump up against and that push back on us. Such an ecumenism of contestability avoids triumphalist pretensions without sacrificing evangelistic mission and kerygmatic zeal. It also provides a rationale for a common pursuit of truth and wisdom; so the postmodern recognition of ultimate contestability does not entail giving up on the pursuit of truth, nor does it necessarily entail a tribalistic retreat to insulated enclaves.

Finally, I think it is important that such inter-religious and inter-confessional conversations take place at the level of *practices*. To put this starkly, I think the engagement between religions would do well to stop being focused on "truth"; I think we need to try to imagine an engagement between religious traditions that does not take place on the register of knowledge, but rather at the level of practices—of justice, or worship, or prayer (if possible).[19] At the end of the day (or rather, at the beginning of the day!), "religion" is not primarily an epistemology, or even a body of doctrines. It is a way of life, a set of practices.[20] We do well to envision inter-religious dialogue on our campus not first and foremost as a matter of word, but of deed.

AD SKRZESZEWSKI: CANADIAN RELIGION

First and foremost, Stan Skrzeszewski wins my personal prize for best title. American readers might fail to appreciate the centrality of Tim Horton's coffee shops in Canadian self-identity (perhaps a close second to Hockey Night in Canada and just ahead of the Mounties). That said, I don't think we're likely to run into Charles Taylor and Michael Ignatieff sipping a double-double and munching on timbits at the Timmy's on the corner. That's just to say that this isn't exactly the Left Bank; Tim Horton's seems

---

19. Amos Yong helpful articulates how Christian participation in inter-religious dialogue should not be primarily governed by doctrines but should flow from distinctive Christian practices, particularly the practice of hospitality. See Yong, *Hospitality and the Other*.

20. I have made this point in more detail in Smith, "Philosophy of Religion Takes Practice." See also Smith, "How Religious Practices Matter."

to exhibit a kind of working-class culture that feels a long way from those quaint cafes outside the Sorbonne. However, I think Skrzeszewski provides a wonderful anthropological foray into Tim Horton's as a Canadian cultural phenomenon, and I'm tickled that my work might have been an occasion for such a delightful and illuminating venture. He leaves me wondering to what extent the emerging church has been taken to Tim Horton's.

AD HAMBLET: BEYOND MODERN SKEPTICISM

Does my rendition of a postmodern Catholicism remain too timid, unwilling to go "all the way," so to speak, with postmodernism? Wendy Hamblet finds my engagement with postmodernism to be a bit prudish—engaged in coquettish play and flirtation, but all as a bit of a tease, finally resisting with an emphatic "No!" when things really get serious. She thus suggests that I'm still afraid of postmodernism because I'm afraid of *skepticism*.

Unfortunately, I think such a criticism is common and fails to understand the crux of my critique. To run with Hamblet's suggestive metaphor, I don't find skepticism tempting or terrible; I find her modern, boring, and just a bit sophomoric—I hardly give her a first look, let alone a second. I'm not even flirting with her because the core of my argument is that postmodernism is *not* a skepticism; rather, I have tried to argue that what Hamblet calls "postmodern skepticism" is really just *hyper*-modern skepticism because it is the outcome of an epistemology that remains haunted by the ghost of Cartesian certainty. Having accepted the Cartesian standard of "clear and distinct" certainty as the bar for what counts as "knowledge," and then having concluded that such is impossible, skeptics like Hamblet thus conclude that knowledge is impossible.[21] But in both ST and WAP, I have rejected the major premise of this argument. On this account, skepticism is not postmodern at all; it is the flipside of modernism and is constrained by a distinctly (inadequate) modern imagination. Whereas I'm arguing that postmodernism is not just a rejection of modernity certainty (leaving us with only uncertainty and skepticism) but a radical critique of the very identification of knowledge with certainty. So Hamblet's "truly skeptical postmodernism" is neither tempting nor

---

21. And it turns out that Hamblet seems to *know* at least a few things: that fascism is a bad thing, that the Religious Right is abhorrent, that witch burnings were wrong, etc. She also seems not to be too skeptical about the truth of democracy, feminism, and the "naturally existing chaos of the universe."

terrifying for me.²² This skepticism looks like every other predictable, cookie-cutter "woman" on offer in modernity. If I find any "woman" tempting, it is the Holy Mother, the Queen of Heaven, who cuts a line that I find much more distinctly counter-cultural; she is *post*-modern in a way that refuses to play by modernity's rules, whereas the harlot of skepticism is ruined modernity.

AD BOWALD: TAKING SMITH TO CHURCH

Mark Bowald has caught me skipping church, as it were—like an elder or deacon who accosts you on a Sunday morning and says in that vaguely accusatory tone, "Jamie, we *missed* you last Sunday." But in this case, through careful reading, Bowald has pointed out something that has become painfully clear to me over the past couple of years, and not a little embarrassing: the complete absence of the church in my earliest work, particularly *The Fall of Interpretation* and *Speech and Theology*. Bowald is absolutely right to find a shift from these earlier books to IRO and WAP. One might say that FI and ST were insufficiently post-liberal; that is, I think they glimpsed the issues, and I think they make a start to refusing the logic of determination, but I hadn't yet worked out the implications of what I then called a "creational hermeneutic." In part this is because I still largely envisioned the "interpreter" as a lone Protestant in her closet. Despite my emphases on traditionality and intersubjectivity (FI, 152–57), it is curious that community never really makes a showing in FI, and the church as an interpretive community never makes it onto the radar.²³ But slowly

---

22. Oddly, Hamblet suggests that it is skepticism that induces humility, and yet her critique sounds stridently confident and confidently dismissive. I would suggest that it is not skepticism that induces humility, but rather a recognition of what I've described above as *contestability*. As William Connolly points out, one needn't give up making strong claims to knowledge in order to foster humility: "You merely need to come to terms viscerally and positively with the extent to which it must appear profoundly *contestable* to other inducted into different practices, exposed to different events, and pulled by different calls to loyalty." See Connolly, *Pluralism*, 32.

23. This partly stems from the fact that the book—which was originally penned as my Master's thesis—was written from a context of having been wounded by the church. It was written shortly after I was systematically barred from continuing to preach in a circuit of Plymouth Brethren assemblies in southwestern Ontario, by councils of elders who were confident that they were just *reading* the Bible while I was "interpreting" it. So existentially, one might say, I wasn't in a place to be very affirmative about interpretive communities or the church (as I knew it). I consider it to be a sign of grace that despite these experiences, I did not spiral into the sort of anti-institutionalism that characterizes so much of the emergent reaction to fundamentalism.

I started to see where my core intuitions would lead.[24] So while I think Bowald is right to discern significant tensions between the earlier and more recent work, I hope that the emergence of the "postliberal" emphasis on the church as an interpretive community (i.e., on the ecclesiological conditions of interpretation) can also be seen as an outworking of earlier intuitions whose implications were inadequately grasped.

I think (sheepishly) that he's also right about a lingering correlationism in ST. This is particularly clear when one recalls that this began its life as my doctoral dissertation (under John D. Caputo) and was then entitled, "How to Avoid Not Speaking: On the Phenomenological Possibility of Theology." I had rumblings of discomfort with the project as I was progressing, and as I was reworking it into a book for the Radical Orthodoxy series, but I couldn't quite put my thumb on it. I would now say that there is an internal tension in the book: on the one hand, I argue—in postliberal and Radically Orthodox fashion—that philosophical reflection on language should begin unapologetically from the logic and wisdom embedded in the specificity of the Incarnation; that our thinking about words and speech should be fundamentally shaped by the Word made flesh. But on the other hand, the project is framed as one where philosophy somehow clears the space for theology to have the right to speak; phenomenology "makes possible" theology. As such, there remain traces of an apologetic project in ST.[25] It is this latter aspect of the project which Bowald rightly notes as a lingering correlationism.[26] And Bowald is right

24. A turning point here was my participation in a summer seminar on hermeneutics at Calvin College in 2002, led by Kevin Vanhoozer. My project related to that seminar pushed me to consider these issues more closely, and though Vanhoozer and I continue to disagree about some of these matters, I do owe him a debt for pushing me to work through these issues. The opening and conclusion of the resulting article shows the signs of this "postliberal" shift. See Smith, "Limited Inc/arnation."

25. I think Pascal's *Pensées* was characterized by a similar internal tension: on the one hand, he was laying out an epistemology that would call into question the very project of "apologetics;" on the other hand, his notes and jottings were made with a view to creating a work on apologetics.

26. I'm also particularly embarrassed by my critique of Marion on 94–98 of ST (though I stand by the critique on 157–61). This was partly due to my lingering "liberalism," one might say, which also tended to be dismissive and disdainful toward Marion's role for bishops in the last part of *God Without Being*. Such a response has been common in continental philosophy of religion where scholars have been enthusiastic about chapters 1–4 of *God Without Being*, but then think Marion goes off the rails in chapter 5. (In an analogous way, I have found that many "emerging" Christians have enjoyed chapters 1–4 of *Who's Afraid of Postmodernism?* but then think chapter 5 is a regrettable

to see this evidenced in my bracketing of "strictly Christological questions." In sum, he has helped me to better discern my own discomfort with earlier stages of my project; I hope other readers of my work will find his contribution here and suspend judgment until reading his account of these shifts.

AD OLTHUIS: HOPING DIFFERENTLY THAN DERRIDA

I appreciate that Olthuis has taken up one of my more scholarly engagements with Derrida, rather than just the more "popular" readings in WAP and LT. This, however, introduces a level of complexity that requires us to be careful and precise. In particular, I think we need to sort out just what gives Olthuis pause and thus where we disagree. Or more specifically, I think we need to sort out what Derrida thinks from what we should think *about* what Derrida thinks. On the one hand, Olthuis suggests that I've perhaps misread Derrida. On the other hand, he seems to think that as a Christian I shouldn't be so quick to disagree with Derrida. Let me try to sort out these two layers of disagreement.

First, one of the threads of concern is whether I have properly interpreted Derrida. Olthuis suggests that my reading is overly critical, perhaps uncharitable, and even puzzling because at other places (for instance, in *Jacques Derrida: Live Theory*), I seem to get him right (on Olthuis's account). This provides an opportunity to make a clarification: often in more expositional works like LT and WAP, my primary concern has been to encourage critics of Derrida to read him well and to read him charitably. Thus in those places, particularly in LT, I have tried to be a sort of translator of Derrida in a way that is as faithful and charitable as possible. And to do so (again, especially in LT), I tried to set aside my

---

appendix.) I now see Marion's account of the bishop as a logical outworking of his position and would be much more affirmative of his ecclesiological framework as integral to his project. My criticism of Marion on pp. 94–98 was also partly due to a brief flirtation I had with "Religious Studies" as a possible vocation, and I regret that evidence of that survives in this form. That said, I do think there can be a kind of phenomenology of religion that need not *just* reduce to theology; that is, there can be a phenomenological investigation of how religious communities "intend" their world. Granted, I think such phenomenologies of religion might be best undertaken by *practitioners* of the religion, but I also think that I, for instance, could engage in a phenomenological exploration of Islam. So I think we can maintain a distinction between theology and phenomenology of religion, and I think Marion's phenomenology of religion might still risk being a bit "colonial" in this regard.

critical voice; instead, I have reserved the critique for scholarly articles such as "Determined Hope." So I don't think there's any contradiction or inherent tension between rightly articulating what Derrida thinks or says (e.g., in LT) but then elsewhere criticizing what he thinks or says in other contexts. Indeed, I think one of the disturbing tendencies in the continental philosophy of religion "industry," so to speak, is to simply remain at the level of commentary or exposition of Derrida, leaving him almost immune to critique.[27] We need to sort out two different tasks: the expositional work of doing justice to Derrida by trying to charitably and correctly understand what he thinks, and the critical work of evaluating what he thinks. Unfortunately, a number of Derrida's admirers confuse the two; in response to any criticism of Derrida, they retort that one has misunderstood Derrida. I don't think I have misunderstood Derrida; rather, I just disagree.

So second, we come to the matter of evaluation: What should we think about what Derrida thinks? Should we—Christians—agree with him regarding the conditions of eschatological hope as hoping for the impossible? I won't rehash my criticism here, but will only say that Olthuis's concerns don't convince me to abandon it. There is some irony in the fact that I see the criticism as being informed by much that I absorbed from Olthuis's own Reformational emphases on the goodness of creation, which were the core impetus behind *The Fall of Interpretation* and almost all of my subsequent work. I take the increasing Catholicity of my thought, including the embrace of determinacy, particularity, and even hierarchy characteristic of the logic of incarnation as the logical extensions of this Reformational emphasis on the goodness of finitude. And, I take it that it is just this "goodness of finitude" that is rejected by Derrida's logic of determination. Though Olthuis thinks Husserl has "led me astray," I think Husserl has rightly delineated the conditions of finitude as ineluctably heremeneutic. Indeed, I take my critique of Derrida's notion of hope to just be an extension of my critique of Derrida in ch. 4 of FI, as well as my critique of Marion and Levinas's notion of revelation in ch. 5 of ST. Insofar as hope is the hope of finite creatures, then the conditions of finite perception, projection, reception, and interpretation still hold (the focus of ST, ch. 5). In a way that is analogous to my critique of Pannenberg in FI (63–77), I think Derrida paints a picture of hope that seeks to tran-

---

27. For instance, could we find any *criticism* of Derrida in Caputo's work after 1997?

scend the very conditions under which we hope. *Who* could hope in such a way?

Finally, when Olthuis worries that I overemphasize *continuity* between the present order and the eschaton, I'll admit to being a bit puzzled by his emphasis on the eschaton as "truly novel" according to the conditions set down by Derrida (though he inserts important qualifiers—qualifiers which I think should trump his enthusiasm for Derrida's claims). I find this puzzling since it was precisely the Reformed tradition that taught me that redemption could only be properly understood in relation to creation. Olthuis, following a Moltmannian reading of Derrida, emphasizes that the *adventus* is unpredictable, unprogrammable, and cannot be predelineated; in short, the eschaton is characterized by a deep discontinuity. He also seems to think that my critique of Derrida is offered in the name of a "simple linear movement of continuity." But I think this way of putting it smuggles in two problems. On the one hand, I certainly nowhere advocate a "simple linear movement" towards the eschaton. The systemic, ubiquitous brokenness of the world means we are hoping for a new heavens and a new earth that is radically new and radically renewed. On the other hand, I don't think the Christian understanding of "newness" should be equated with "novelty." The Christian logic of the new is different from the clean-slate notion of the novel. And the biblical narrative emphasizes this precisely by articulating the new creation as a restoration of the creational garden—albeit also characterized by the "more" that Olthuis rightly notes. I think Olthuis (like others) is taken with Derrida's emphasis on novelty because he is worried about triumphalist eschatologies—parading themselves as Christian—which overemphasize continuity. In this respect, Derrida's (non)eschatology is adopted as an anti-fundamentalist therapeutic. But I don't think we need to buy into Derrida's logic of determination (with all of its attendant problems) in order to criticize such over-realized eschatologies. Properly Christian and Catholic eschatology has its own resources for criticizing such over-determined conceptions.

Ultimately, I agree with Olthuis that it is a Christian eschatological vision of the coming kingdom—of the advent of *shalom*—which should fund our prophetic critique in the here and now. But such a prophetic critique of "the economies of this world" finds its criteria not in some indeterminate hope for who-knows-what, but in the quite (though not completely) determinate vision of what the world (and its economies, nations, families, etc.) are *called to be*. It is from this quite determinate vision of human flourishing that a prophetic critique can then say, "That's not the way it's supposed to be!" And it is the same quite determinate vision that leaves us asking, "How long, O Lord?" and hoping and praying, "Maranatha! Even so, Come, Lord Jesus!"

AD GOICOECHEA: TOWARDS A CATHOLIC PARTICULARISM

David Goicoechea's engaging and playful response to my work rightly grasps that what's at stake here is how we think about universality (catholicity) and particularity. These are themes that have occupied continental philosophy of religion over the last several years, including something of a backlash against postmodernism from figures such as Alain Badiou and Slavoj Žižek. Seeing the postmodern celebration of "difference" as a sophomoric relativism, Badiou notes how amenable this is to the flow of the market:

> What inexhaustible potential for mercantile investments in this upsurge—taking the form of communities demanding recognition and so-called cultural singularities—of women, homosexuals, the disabled, Arabs! And these infinite combinations of predicative traits, what a godsend! Black homosexuals, disabled Serbs, Catholic pedophiles, moderate Muslims, married priests, ecologist yuppies, the submissive unemployed, prematurely aged youth! Each time, a social image authorizes new products, specialized magazines, improved shopping malls, "free" radio stations, targeted advertising networks...[28]

Nothing is more interested in difference than the market. Thus in the face of postmodern difference, Badiou and Žižek assert a new "universalism."

In a similar vein, Goicoechea wants a non-exclusivistic yet Catholic universalism, and he finds in my logic of incarnation hints toward something like that. In particular, he suggests that such a Catholic universalism is unique because it emerges from the particularity of the Incarnation. But precisely because of this, Goicoechea is worried that my Catholic postmodernism remains a bit of an insider club, a little too exclusive. It would seem that a Radically Orthodox universalism is a bit miserly and stingy, even a bit unbiblical, not open to the prophetic hope that "*all* flesh might see the Lord" (Luke 3:6).

---

28. Badiou, *Saint Paul*, p. 10.

But here's the thing: I think embracing a Catholic particularity means that we don't get to be selective in our affirmation of that particularity. That is, I think the logic of incarnation entails owning up to particularity in all its scandal, including the scandal of even election and exclusion.[29] Thus I might describe this as an *Abrahamic* universality which is closely linked to the logic of election. In the biblical narrative, Yahweh's vision for a redeemed people is channeled through the election of a particular person—or rather, a particular *family*—in Abraham (Genesis 12) through whom all the nations of the earth will be blessed. But it seems to me that the logic of election continues, with all its scandal, into the Book of Revelation. There we see the Bride of Christ, composed of martyrs and saints "from every tribe and tongue and people and nation" (Rev 5:9). But they do not constitute the totality of all people; they are a peculiar people *from* every tribe and tongue and nation. This is, we might say, a "representative" universality, an elected catholicity.[30] This is because the logic of Incarnation, in a Trinitarian formula, cannot be separated from the work of the Spirit who indwells some but not all. While I might hope that it is otherwise, I feel that embracing the logic of incarnation requires embracing this scandalous logic of election. This, however, is not reason for pride or self-congratulation: it is a function of grace, of gift, and it is an election *to* responsibility—for the nations and for the Other.

---

29. My take on this should not be attributed to "Radical Orthodoxy" in general (whatever that might be). In fact, in response to Goicoechea's question, "Given the logic of the Incarnation are not all carnal creatures members of the Body of Christ?," he would perhaps find Graham Ward and John Milbank to be more amenable to his proposal. I have criticized Ward and Milbank on this point; see IRO, 257–59.

30. My friend Amos Yong tends to read the prophet Joel's vision of the Spirit poured out on "all flesh" (see Acts 2:17) in a way similar to Goicoechea. I have pressed Yong on this point, analogous to my suggestion here, in Smith, "The Spirit, Religions, and the World as Sacrament," 254–55.

Continuing the Conversation

WORKS CITED

Abraham, William J. *Crossing the Threshold of Divine Revelation*. Grand Rapids: Eerdmans, 2006.

Badiou, Alain. *Saint Paul: The Foundation of Universalism*. Translated by Ray Brassier. Stanford: Stanford University Press, 2003.

Connolly, William. *Pluralism*. Durham, NC: Duke University Press, 2005.

———. *Why I Am Not a Secularist*. Minneapolis: University of Minnesota Press, 1999.

Derrida, Jacques. *Specters of Marx: The State of the Debt, the Work of Mourning, and the New International*. Translated by Peggy Kamuf. New York: Routledge, 1994.

Hitchens, Christopher. *Why Orwell Matters*. New York: Basic Books, 2002.

Marion, Jean-Luc. *God Without Being: Hors-Texte*. Translated by Thomas A. Carlson. Chicago: University of Chicago Press, 1991

Marsden, George. *The Outrageous Idea of Christian Scholarship*. Oxford: Oxford University Press, 1998.

Milbank, John. *Theology and Social Theory: Beyond Secular Reason*. Oxford: Blackwell, 1990.

Mouw, Richard J., and Sander Griffioen. *Pluralisms and Horizons: An Essay in Christian Public Philosophy*. Grand Rapids: Eerdmans, 1993.

Benedict XVI, Pope (Joseph Cardinal Ratzinger). *The Spirit of the Liturgy*. Translated by John Saward. San Francisco: Ignatius, 2000.

Smith, James K. A. "Determined Violence: Derrida's Structural Religion," *The Journal of Religion* 78.2 (April 1998) 197–212.

———. "How Religious Practices Matter: Peter Ochs' 'Alternative Nurturance' of Philosophy of Religion." *Modern Theology* 24 (2008) 469–78.

———. "Limited Inc/arnation: The Searle/Derrida Debate Revisited in Christian Context." In *Hermeneutics at the Crossroads: Interpretation in Christian Perspective*, edited by Kevin Vanhoozer, James K. A. Smith, and Bruce Ellis Benson, 112–29. Bloomington: Indiana University Press, 2006.

———. "Philosophy of Religion Takes Practice: Liturgy as Source and Method in Philosophy of Religion." In *Contemporary Method and Practice in the Philosophy of Religion*, edited by David Cheetham and Rolfe King, 133–47. London: Continuum, 2008.

———. "Re-Kanting Postmodernism?: Derrida's Religion Within the Limits of Reason Alone." *Faith and Philosophy* 17 (2000) 558–71.

———. "The Politics of Desire: Augustine's Political Phenomenology." In *Augustine and Postmodern Thought: A New Alliance against Modernity?*, edited by Lieven Boeve and Mathijs Lamberigts. Bibliotheca Ephemeridum Theologicarum Lovaniensium 219. Leuven: Peeters, forthcoming.

———. "The Spirit, Religions, and the World as Sacrament: A Response to Amos Yong's Pneumatological Assist." *Journal of Pentecostal Theology* 15 (2007) 251–61.

Yong, Amos. *Hospitality and the Other: Pentecost, Christian Practices, and the Neighbor*. Maryknoll, NY: Orbis, 2008.

www.ingramcontent.com/pod-product-compliance
Lightning Source LLC
Chambersburg PA
CBHW051053230426
43667CB00013B/2282